GW01552846

A Trumpe
the Housetops

*

The Selected Writings of
LIONEL FORMAN

A Trumpet from the Housetops

The Selected Writings of

LIONEL FORMAN

*

EDITED BY

Sadie Forman & André Odendaal

THE MAYIBUYE CENTRE
University of the Western Cape

Zed Books Ltd • London

Ohio University Press • Athens, Ohio

David Philip • Cape Town

UWC Mayibuye History Series No. 7

A Trumpet from the Housetops was first published in 1992 by:

Southern Africa
David Philip (Pty) Ltd.
217 Werdmuller Centre
Claremont 7700
South Africa

United Kingdom
Zed Books Ltd
57 Caledonian Rd
London N1 9BU
UK

United States of America and **Canada**
Ohio University Press
Scott Quadrangle
University of Ohio
Athens, Ohio 45701
USA

in association with
The Mayibuye Centre for History and Culture in South Africa

Copyright © The estate of Lionel Forman, 1992.
Editorial copyright © Sadie Forman and Andre Odendaal, 1992.
Preface copyright © Jack and Ray Simons, 1992.

Cover designed by Andrew Corbett.
Typeset by Rami Tzabar.
Printed and bound in the United Kingdom
by Biddles Ltd. Guildford and King's Lynn.

All rights reserved.

A catalogue record for this book is
available from the British Library.

UK
ISBN 1 85649 045 9 Hb
ISBN 1 85649 046 7 Pb

USA and **Canada**
ISBN 0 8214 1041 5 cloth
ISBN 0 8214 1042 3 paper

Southern Africa
ISBN 0 86486 228 8 Pb

The Mayibuye Centre for History and Culture in South Africa was recently established at the University of the Western Cape. Its plans include a museum on the apartheid era and an archive of the liberation struggle in South Africa. The UWC Mayibuye History Series is part of the Centre's publications programme, for which Dr Andre Odendaal is the series editor.

For our children, and their children

"But life is short; . . . It is with considerable pain that I give out this fragment. I am only comforted by the thought that perhaps, all sincere and earnest search after truth, even where it fails to reach it, yet, often comes so near to it, that other minds more happily situated may be led, by pointing out its very limitations and errors, to obtain a larger view."

Olive Schreiner

Contents

Acknowledgements	ix
Preface *Jack and Ray Simons*	xi
Introduction	xiii

Part One: A People's History   1

1. Colonialism and Land Dispossession   2

Tribal democracy	2
In the Days of van Riebeeck	3
A Robber Economy	9
British Occupation	14
The Struggle Within a Common Society	20

2. National Liberation and Socialist Movements, 1870-1914   25

The Working Class is Born	25
The First non-European Organisations	29
Indian Congress and APO	32
The Union of South Africa	35
The African National Congress	37
Enter the Socialists	42

3. The First World War and the Socialist movement in South Africa

War-on-War and the ISL	45
The ISL and "The Great and Fascinating Problem of the Native"	48
The First Contacts between the ISL and Africans	54
The ISL and the National Liberatory Struggle	57
The Industrial Workers of Africa	62
The Bucket Strike	66
Forerunner of the Treason Trial	69

4. The Communist Party and the ANC, 1921-50: Background to the National Question   72

5. The Congress Alliance and the Turn to Mass Action: The People's Reply   90

Part Two: The Treason Trial   99

6. "You Can Hang for Treason"   100

Public Support: The Origins of the Defence and Aid Fund	106

7. The Evidence Begins - Soup without Meat   108

The Secret Police	116

Part Three : "The Youngest and Proudest Cardholder": Action Years 1947-59   119

8. A Book for Karl   120

"Talking their Tongues Away"   120
"Young and Immature"   122
Students' Socialist Party   124
Nineteen Forty-Eight   126
A Visit to Caledon Square   129
Enemy of the State   130

9. Imperialism: "Commentator" on International Issues   133

How the Yanks were Dragged to Berlin   133
Sufficiency to Abundance   134
"Dit Lyk nie of Dulles dit Maklik Gaan He Nie"   139
Danger on the Eve of Geneva   144
Know the Facts on Vietnam   146
Angry Asia Also Abhors American Atomic Weapon   149
Power Through Violence   152

10. Keeping Alive Socialist Debate   154

Why do we Write and Argue so Little about Socialism?   154
Socialism not Treason   156
Revive Socialist Discussion!   158
Has May Day become the Forgotten Day?   158
Time for a Socialist Party?   162
Stalin and Dictatorship   163
Lessons from Hungary 1956   167

Part Four: The National Question   171

11. The Debate Fuelled   172

Don't Spread Malan's Lie   172
"Neither Duty nor Task of Editorial" *Yusuf Dadoo*   174
The Fog Under Which We Tend to Work   175
Discussion on South Africa's National Question   176
A Symposium on the National Question   179
Nationalisms in South Africa   180
Nationalisms in South Africa *Jack Simons*   184
Forman's response to Simons   188

12. The Debate Resumes   190

Forman to Potekhin, 18 January 1958   190
Reply from Potekhin, 17 March 1958   191
The Development of Nations in South Africa   192
Further Correspondence between Potekhin and Forman   198
On the Formation of Nations in South Africa *John McGrath*   202

Forman's Response to McGrath and Other Critics	208
Potekhin's Response to McGrath	211
Forman to Potekhin, 31 August 1959	214
Potekhin to Forman, 7 October 1959	215

Part Five: A Trumpet from the Housetops

217

13. "A Shining Sword"

218

Forman"s Last Letter	218
Tributes:	218
From Jack Simons at the Memorial Service	218
From the Treason Court	221
From the underground SACP	221
From Chief Luthuli	221
From Ruth First in *Fighting Talk*	221
From Douglas Maqina	222

Index   **224**

Acknowledgements

The editors express their thanks to Calder Publications Ltd., London for permission to use the chapters from the *South African Treason Trial*.

We are grateful to Aud Lise Norheim of the Norwegian Consulate for the generous grant to enable the Mayibuye Centre at the University of the Western Cape to co-sponsor this publication. Support from the university and colleagues in the History Department and the Institute for Historical Research, enabled Andre Odendaal to take the generous study leave which led to his involvement in the book. The Centre for Ethnic Relations at Warwick University and the Institute for Commonwealth Studies in London provided a home from home. The Ruth First Memorial Trust and the International Defence and Aid Fund for Southern Africa financed this microfilming of the Forman papers. And, at the last minute, Pauline Kahn and her and Sam's family and friends rallied and contributed financially to the needs of the project, for which much appreciation.

We thank Syd Shall for the practical help that got the book going. Christopher Saunders and Cirjal Rassool offered comments on Forman's history writing. Thanks also to Selma and Wilmette for reading, commenting and spending time on the national question, and to Amy, Ethel and Margie for their encouragement. Sara, Karl, Frank and Robin have been waiting long years for this work to be done. Thanks their patience and help. Margie, Eleanor, Wolfie, Gordon, Barry, Mike, Kate, Harbajan, John, Penny, Bill, Linda, Jeremy, Eliza, Yvonne, Essop, Bob, Bill, Kittie and the Brum Psychologists provided warm hospitality and friendship. Zohra Ebrahim offered up much of her time to help.

Throughout the years in exile Ray and Jack Simons unfailingly kept a persistent persuasion going to get Lionel's work published, which acted as a beacon of resolution. A meeting with Ronnie K. got the first synopsis off the typewriter. Liz Offen's expertise and effort with the computer and Cathy Connolly's disc conversion are thankfully acknowledged. On a visit to London Himie Bernadt reminded us of the song that Lionel's comrades had composed for him. On his return to Cape Town, Douglas Maqina, the ace *New Age* seller of the fifties, came to Himie's office and wrote out the song and its translation which ends this book. We thank them heartily. Our gratitude goes to John Daniel for his endless assistance in editing and tightening the text, for his time, energy and wisdom, without which this book could not have been. After John left for South Africa, Ralph Smith heroically took over the task of getting the book to its final print. Rami Tzabar typeset the manuscript and both he and Ralph were happily tolerant of the myriad corrections. To them and to all at Zed we offer our gratitude. Finally, thanks to Lizzie for her patience, strength and support, and to our families for carrying the load that our work has brought them.

Preface

In our foreword to *Class and Colour in South Africa 1850-1950*, we made a special point of our debt to Lionel. This was more than a gesture to a brave and talented colleague, whose early death deprived South Africa of an outstanding freedom fighter and man of many parts — youth leader, lawyer, editor, militant activist, historian and committed communist.

When reading Lionel's writings, before they appeared in print, we saw in him the quality of objective realism and openness that distinguished all his activities. He applied the concepts of historical materialism to his historical writings. We learnt from him the possibility and importance of historiography, of trying to understand not only what people did, but why, and the consequences of their actions for future generations. This approach led us to examine closely the policies and roles of outstanding labour leaders, pioneers of socialism, who founded the South African Labour Party, the Independent Socialist League and, on 30 July 1921, the Communist Party of South Africa (Section of the Communist International). We had in mind especially the three men who guided and shaped the growth of marxist influence: Bill (W.A.) Andrews, David Ivon Jones and S.P. Bunting. In the early stages of their careers in South Africa, they were deeply involved in white labour politics, and therefore isolated from the stirrings of African, Coloured and Indian nationalism.

Some colleagues objected to the approach taken by Lionel and ourselves. They thought it wrong to criticise our heroes for defending "on Marxist grounds" the "maintenance of the colour bar in industry". They argued that the pioneers of scientific socialism in South Africa were "bound by the inevitable limitations of their time, their background and the pressures that moulded them." To condemn them for doing what they had to do was "unhistorical" and unjust.[1]

Harmel and others like him overlooked the response of national liberation leaders who rightly condemned white supremacy in every shape. The gap between them and white labourites widened after the formation of the all-white, men-only parliament in 1910 which stimulated the formation of the African National Congress in 1912.

Its first big campaign was against the Native Land Act of 1913, a segregation measure approved by the Labour Party without exception. Its leader, Colonel Creswell, told Parliament during the debate on the Bill that his Party was the first to advocate complete territorial separation between black and white South Africans. The reserves, he argued, should be consolidated into a continuous tract "so that the natives might have their own institutions and develop along their own lines." Was it wrong of anti-apartheiders in later years to condemn such disgusting vote-catching tactics addressed to the white minority in support of a land policy that destroyed the basis of African village and family life, and

xii *Preface*

committedgenerations of men to the horrors of migratory labour and life in compounds, hostels and township slums?

The socialists who broke away from the Labour Party in 1914 acted in protest against the majority's decision to support such policies. Bill Andrews, Jones, Bunting and others began climbing a rough and tortuous road that enabled them to discover and develop their true selves. They found redemption in a multi-racial movement for liberation from the colonial past and for government by women and men of all races in a single parliament elected by voters under a constitution based on the principle of universal adult suffrage without distinction of sex, race, colour or creed.

Lionel Forman had the making of a great scholar in every sphere of activity in which he was involved — as a lawyer, editor, historian and most of all in his practical contribution to the revolutionary movement. Thirty-two years have passed since he died (at 31 years of age) yet his contribution continues to inspire new generations of radicals. There is no better testimony to his life and work than the tributes paid to him by radicals on every occasion when history is discussed.

We owe a great debt to Sadie for her persistence in bringing together Lionel's writings by which she has preserved for posterity the work of a great thinker and devoted revolutionary.

Notes

1. Michael Harmel writing under the pseudonym A. Lerumo in *Fifty Fighting Years: The South African Communist Party 1921-1971*. Inkhululeko Publications, London, 1971, p.vi.

Jack and Ray Simons.

Introduction

I

In December 1956, 156 leaders of the Congress Alliance were arrested in dawn swoops throughout South Africa and flown to Pretoria in military aircraft to face charges of treason.

The Treason Trial became a landmark in the history of the liberation struggle in South Africa. It dragged on for more than four years, generating considerable excitement at home and abroad. The basis of the state's charge was that the ANC and its allies, via policies enunciated in the newly adopted Freedom Charter, were part of a communist-inspired conspiracy to foment revolution in South Africa. Pointing out parallels with the Nazi-orchestrated *Reichstag* fire trial of the 1930s, the ANC in turn used the trial to attack the government's apartheid policies and to articulate an alternative vision for a non-racial, democratic South Africa. All those charged were eventually found not guilty and acquitted.

The marathon trial had the dual effect of both immobilising South Africa's resistance leaders and bringing them together in a kind of people's parliament — the "treason cage", a specially constructed wire mesh enclosure which served initially as the dock in a makeshift courtroom set up in the Johannesburg Drill Hall. The accused were seated on "row after row of chairs, as if they were delegates at a conference".[1] Eli Weinberg's famous photograph of the 156 trialists shows the rich mix of personality and political leadership assembled by the state. Near the back is the "Chief", Albert Lutuli, Nobel laureate and President of the ANC — his hand resting gently on the shoulder in front of him. In the centre of the first row, the President of the Congress of Democrats, Piet Beyleveld (later to turn state witness against his former comrades at the famous Rivonia and other trials) is sitting on the ground. Directly behind him sits Moses Kotane, a giant in the history of the liberation struggle. Among those seated in the same row are Ahmed Kathrada and Helen Joseph. In the next, Nelson Mandela's towering presence stands out. He is a dignified head higher than his colleagues next to him. Two rows behind Mandela one immediately notices the then Secretary-General of the ANC, Duma Nokwe. Joe Slovo, Ruth First, Gert Sibande, the so-called "Lion of the North", and Walter Sisulu looking serious are bunched together one back and to the left. This is truly a who's who of politics. There are also the lesser known faces . . . like the person standing behind Sisulu's right shoulder: accused No. 83, Lionel Forman. Forman is one of those backroom figures amongst the 156 whose achievements have become blurred by time. His face is one that would not be instantly recognised by the current generation of activists. Yet the story of this man, five from the right in row seven, his thumb up

xiv Introduction

in the *Afrika* salute, is one of the most remarkable of the whole turbulent decade of the fifties.

Lionel Forman confronted three big adversaries in his lifetime — apartheid, capitalism and illness. Dogged since childhood by a serious heart disease, resulting from a bout of rheumatic fever at the age of five, he grew up with a grossly enlarged heart caused by leaking valves and regular, almost weekly, attacks of auricular fibrillation — vibrations which sent his pulse rate soaring. To arrest these, the medical experts prescribed massive daily doses of quinidine and lesser ones of digitalis. By the time Lionel was 21, his doctor expected the worst: "The outlook for this young man is distinctly gloomy . . . I do not doubt that within a year or two he will have become more or less disabled." A year later, he warned that "The immediate prognosis for survival is extremely low."[2]

As a last resort, his doctors recommended that Forman go to London for "recently devised" heart surgery. The Harley Street specialists however, concluded that his condition was too serious for the surgery to be effective and that he did not have long to live. Although he had disregarded his illness as much as he could, Forman acknowledged that the "quacks know their business ... Every heartbeat is increasing my little leakage and the time must come when the floodgates break".

But Lionel Forman did not sit back and await the inevitable. He had too much to do. With stoic disregard for body-breaking disability and a pressing sense of urgency, he threw himself into the struggle against the apartheid system proceeding "like a fireworks display corruscating in all directions" to achieve prominence as a student leader, newspaper editor, lawyer, political activist, historian and Marxist theoretician.

Then, in 1959, he was offered the chance of new heart-lung bypass surgery devised by the then little-known surgeon, Dr. Christiaan Barnard. Barnard was an "old-friend . . . They had been at UCT together and Lionel trusted him to do a good job". He did not hesitate and had the operation on the morning of Monday October 19. Barnard repaired three faulty valves. The operation seemed to be going well. But, Barnard reported, "an assistant had clamped an artery and torn it — there was not the chance for the blood to flow back into his body when the machine was disconnected. At 4.31 p.m. Lionel Forman died".[3]

Sadie Forman had given birth to their daughter Sara five days earlier and was still in the nursing home. Anxious about the pending operation, she had been unable to sleep since the birth. At 1.15 p.m., told by her doctor that the operation had been a success, she went to sleep. A few hours later, she was woken by Dr Barnard with a group of friends.

The tributes streamed in by the hundreds. Chief Lutuli said, "His courageous stand in the freedom struggle will always inspire us". The writer, Lionel Abrahams, wrote that, "If any great number of men lived such lives the world's needed revolutions would be automatically accomplished".

Introduction xv

In his last waking moments, as the pre-operative drugs began to pull him towards sleep, Lionel wrote what was to be his final letter to Sadie:

If this doesn't come off you're not to mourn for me. I'm going without the slightest fear of death and if I die it will not hurt me at all, except in the thought that it will hurt you. . . If there is any meeting of friends, what I want said there clearly and unequivocally is. All his adult life he tried to be a good communist. . . Now I am legally safe as houses, I want it trumpeted from the housetops, Lionel Forman believed in communism for South Africa with a burning passion till the day he died, and in all his adult years that passion never once diminished. . . No, I'm sorry, I can't fight this confounded drug. I didn't want it, because I am as calm as can be but they insisted. My love to all. Tell the treason trial we'll achieve freedom in the lifetime of Karl and Frank and Sara — and you Sadie — whether they like it or not. Forward to the total abolition of the colour bar — forward to communism in South Africa . . . don't mourn and don't let the children mourn. Tell them they must have love for their fellowmen, they must exorcise all race prejudice and understand why it is abominable. . . (If anything is written they must say), he tried to be a good communist. Often he failed but he tried and his life was to bring . . . — no, it isn't the dope thats getting me, but they"ve come for me. All my love my loves. Lionel.

300 people attended the memorial service for Forman. Despite the presence of the Special Branch, those in attendance stood and sang the *Internationale* in public "with clenched fist held high" for the first time since the Communist Party's banning in 1950.

II

Lionel Forman was born in Johannesburg on Christmas Day, 1927. He was the second child of David and Sarah Forman. David was an immigrant from Lithuania. Like many other Jews who had fled the pogroms, poverty and anti-semitism of Eastern Europe, he went first to Aldgate in London's East End where he stayed for two years. Sarah Shribnick had been born in Bethnal Green, London, of poor parents who in the early 1920s decided to go to South Africa. Lionel's parents met on the boat taking them to the country whose streets they had been told "were paved with gold".

But the reality was very different. Lionel grew up in Rosettenville, a white working-class area. His parents rented a small shop and worked long hours — "from six o'clock in the morning to ten at night". The family lived in two rooms attached to the shop. Many of the white democrats who supported the Communist Party and Congress movement in the 1950s shared a similar background. A large proportion were Jewish with a history of persecution, strongly-felt anti-fascist ideas and a knowledge of revolutionary Marxism, which stemmed from their Eastern European origins.

xvi Introduction

Forman was politicised at an early age. He was still a child when he witnessed an assault on a black worker in the shop next door and became aware of the injustice of racial discrimination. He was influenced intellectually by the left-wing Jewish youth club, Hashomer Hatzair (HH), which he joined as a teenager. There was "much discussion of the works of Marx and Lenin" in HH, and this made an impact on Lionel. However, he soon became disillusioned with the organisation because of its "Israeli-oriented ethic". By the age of 15 he had switched to the Young Communist League (YCL). Forman read avidly the Marxist classics, played an active part in the YCL debating society and became a member of the YCL national committee. He started too a long friendship with Ruth First, his co-delegate to the first national YCL conference. On one occasion she saved him from possible expulsion from the YCL after he had made a provocative speech from a Party platform.

When Forman went to the University of Cape Town at the age of 17 he was admitted into the Communist Party, even though he had not yet reached the required age of 18. He described himself as "the youngest and proudest card-holder in the Party". He gained an M.Soc.Sci. at UCT, but politics took up most of his time. In 1947, he led a boycott of a racially exclusive mayoral reception during the NUSAS national conference, organising instead a successful "no colour-bar dance" (*Cape Argus* 3 July 1947). He was expelled from NUSAS for this but re-admitted when he threatened legal action unless he received a public apology. As secretary of the Students' Socialist Party, he campaigned against student groups which supported the National or United parties and against a conservative university administration which refused to allow free political expression on campus.

The headquarters of the Communist Party were in Cape Town in the 1940s and Forman was active organising, pamphleteering, electioneering, writing for *The Guardian*, the Party's unofficial newspaper, and speaking regularly at public meetings on the Parade. His writings tell us much about resistance politics at the time of the National Party's coming to power. Participating in the campaigns of the anti-segregationist Train Apartheid Resistance Committee, he learned an important political lesson: "talk and theory were useless without the courage to face the enemy". He was struck by the fact that although members of the Non-European Unity Movement involved in the campaign were "high-calibre intellectuals, they showed themselves to be "quite lacking in gut" and shied away from direct action.[4] Forman was by then convinced that the best way for South African socialists to make progress was for them to locate themselves in the broader national democratic struggle.

At the end of 1949 Forman returned to Johannesburg to study law at the University of the Witwatersrand. In Johannesburg he felt somewhat rebuffed by the local Party leadership and put this down to the tensions that existed between the Johannesburg and Cape Town branches in the late 1940s, as well as to his strong opposition to the Party's decision to dissolve

Introduction xvii

itself as a pre-emptive move in the face of the Suppression of Communism Act. In 1950, Forman took over the editorship of *Wits Student*, transforming it from a bland faculty broadsheet into a lively campus paper. With his friends Ruth First and Harold Wolpe, he was prominent in the left lobby at Wits. They tackled issues like creeping apartheid at the University and the inferior position of the black campuses in the National Union of South African Students (NUSAS).

Forman was also active in national student politics and in the same year was elected to the national executive of NUSAS as director of research. In the cold war climate of the early 1950s, student politics was characterised by a fierce battle between liberals and the left over NUSAS affiliation to the Prague-based International Union of Students (IUS). Forman was in the forefront of opposition to growing calls for disaffiliation. While abroad for treatment for his heart condition, he represented NUSAS at the IUS annual conference in Warsaw in August 1951. Western delegates argued for withdrawal from the IUS, but Forman helped persuade them to remain. He proposed that a unity meeting be held the following year to thrash out differences arising from the expulsion of the Yugoslav Students' Union after Tito's break with Moscow. Forman was delegated by NUSAS to stay on in Prague to work at IUS headquarters. *Wits Student*, now edited by Charles Bloomberg, described his appointment as "unparalleled in NUSAS international relations" (6 July 1952).

Forman spent two years in Prague. For him this was a special period. For the first time he experienced life in a non-capitalist society while broadening his intellectual horizons by living and working with students from all over the world. (One of his contemporaries in Prague was the controversial French lawyer, Jacques Verges.) Forman worked in the IUS press section producing *World Student News* while helping to organise the Unity Meeting he had initiated. Held in Bucharest in August 1952, the meeting failed to preserve international student unity in the face of steadily deteriorating East-West relations. The western student unions left the IUS and grouped themselves into a separate international student body, the Coordinating Secretariat (COSEC).

Lionel was joined in Prague by Sadie Kreel and they married in Prague's Old Town Hall in June 1952. Eleven months later their son Karl was born. Also during this period and contrary to the pessimistic predictions of his South African and British doctors, his health improved. This was a result of special treatment by Czech doctors which included weaning him from a dosage of about forty pills a day, to three. After the birth of their second son, Frank, in 1954, Forman wrote to his Czech doctors with this news and credited them with extending his life.

On the expiry of Lionel's term at the IUS (July 1953), on their way back to South Africa, the Formans stopped in England, where they rented a cottage at Seaford on the Sussex coast. Forman enrolled in a writing course at a correspondence college and wrote an autobiographical book for Karl whom, he feared, might never get to know his father. Four months

xviii   Introduction

later an SOS arrived from South Africa: Brian Bunting, editor of *Advance* (successor to the now banned *Guardian*), wanted to travel overseas and would Lionel return to South Africa to edit the newspaper in his absence? *Advance* was the most vociferous anti-apartheid newspaper in South Africa and the main mouthpiece of the Congress Alliance. Bunting had been invited to visit the Soviet Union and needed to do so before his passport expired, after which he knew he would be prevented from travelling abroad again.

Forman accepted enthusiatically. But first he wanted to finish his book. Working to a tight schedule, Forman had completed the book by mid-December, having written in only three months a 73,000 word volume. Though written in the third person, it was an autobiography in which Forman referred to himself as David. In its 48 chapters Forman shared with his son his feelings about life and politics. In addition to such topics as first love, marriage and religion, he wrote about racialism, nationalism, the YCL and student days, Comrade Bill Andrews, the 1948 election, the *Guardian* newspaper, the resistance against train apartheid in Cape Town, and his experiences in Europe, including a visit to Auschwitz.

With the manuscript sewn into Karl's mattress, the Formans arrived back in South Africa on New Year's Day 1954 on the Cape Town Castle. They were welcomed home by customs officials, agitated because Forman's passport had expired the previous year. They searched every inch of their luggage (but not the baby's mattress!). All their books and a wedding present of an engraved Czech book were confiscated. The Minister of Justice had warned in 1949, "We are not going to stand for any nonsense from the Communists in South Africa". The *rooi gevaar* bogey was still very much an issue. If Forman needed further proof, he was officially "listed" under the Suppression of Communism Act within months of his return.

Forman got straight back into the political fray. The Buntings sailed out on the Cape Town Castle's return journey and the next day Lionel started work on *Advance*. Editorially he consistently attacked what he regarded as the incipient fascism of the South African state and promoted the objectives of the broad Congress movement as well as the socialist, anti-colonialist and anti-imperialist aims of the Communist Party, which had been secretly reconstituted in 1953. Drawing on his own recent experiences abroad, Forman launched a weekly "Commentator" column on international affairs, an innovation which became a permanent feature in the newspaper. When Bunting resumed the editorship, he took over writing the column under the byline "Spectator".

Forman also seized the opportunity of his editorship to launch a debate on a topic about which he had been thinking for some time — the national question. In an editorial — "Don't Spread Malan's Lie" — Forman argued that the Congress movement should abandon use of the word "race" in favour of "national groups". By using the "false word race" to categorise people, the liberation movement was helping to spread "the philosophy [of

Introduction xix

the ruling classes] which keeps us in slavery". Moreover, the importance of language and culture needed greater recognition. The dependence of the urban-based liberation movement on the English language, Forman suggested, confined the struggle to a relatively small section of South Africans. It had to be taken "into every kraal, hessian shack and pondokkie in terms the people can understand". The best way to ensure this, he argued, was to encourage the many national groups in South Africa to develop fully their own languages and culture.

Presaged in Forman's vision were the *toyi-toyi* dances and the vibrant cultural expression of the struggles of the 1980s:

> Our Zulu poets must sing sagas of liberation in their mother tongue — the people must rock with laughter at Sotho satires on the Nats. Let our very folk dances exemplify a kick in the pants for Malan and our music the drumbeats of freedom.

He concluded by suggesting that the liberation movement needed to "study and understand fully the forces of progressive nationalism and utilise them in the struggle for freedom" or it would "stumble and falter". In Forman's view, people's nationalism was a healthy phenomenon, completely different from the exploitative "rich man's nationalism" of the "apartheiders".

The editorial evoked a considerable response. While some, like Joe Matthews of the ANC Youth League wrote welcoming it, a senior SACP official, Dr Dadoo, criticised Forman for using an editorial to raise issues of "theoretical controversy". He suggested they should take the form of "separate articles". So in the issue of 22 April 1954 Forman developed his ideas into a full-scale article entitled "Discussion of South Africa's National Question". In it he examined definitions of the term "nation" and "why it matters" but then went on to stress that it was also important that "the class struggle must not be blurred" which he felt was a danger if the emphasis was put on "race".

In response to this article, the Forum and South Africa Clubs, left discussion groups in Cape Town, convened a special debate on the issue. Forman participated together with Kenny Jordaan of the Non-European Unity Movement, the ANC's Thomas Ngwenya and the noted lecturer and marxist, Jack Simons. In terms of the debate within the Congress movement, the main lines of distinction were between Simons and Forman.

Reflecting the dominant position in the ANC and the SACP, Simons argued that, given the history of divide-and-rule through the vehicle of segregation and apartheid in South Africa, the liberation movement had to stress the unity and oneness of South Africa's people. Pointing out that South Africa was not a multi-national country but rather a nation in the making, Simons strongly attacked what he claimed was Forman's view that different national cultures in South Africa should enjoy the right to national self-determination. Unlike in Europe, Simons argued, the demand here was for equality within a common society and "it would be wrong to

xx Introduction

disturb or deflect this development by stressing tribal, racial or cultural differences". He accused Forman of advocating a neo-apartheid position.

Angered by what he saw as a misinterpretation and denying that he had called for self-determination for national groups, Forman stood by his argument. Accusing his critics of superficial thinking, he denied that "the guarantee of national autonomy in a people's democracy" bore the "slightest resemblance to apartheid". He was convinced that the best way to a single united South African nation (and eventually a single world culture) was to create conditions by which "the different national cultures in South Africa may first flower, and then merge". He acknowledged that it was not yet time to press for self-determination because, he believed, there were not yet any nations in South Africa, only pre-nations, but "the time will surely come when it will be a correct and popular demand".[5] He also conceded that his views were not necessarily definitive, stressing instead the urgent need for debate because of the lacuna that existed on the question of what constituted a nation in South Africa.

Forman's ideas on the national question were never accepted as policy by the Party or the Congress movement. But they did highlight the differing, often contradictory positions within the movement, and the need for theoretical clarification. Did South Africa consist of many nations, four nations (white, coloured, Indian and African), two nations (black and white, oppressor and oppressed) or one nation? Or could one not even talk of a nation? Over the years there has been some confusion on the issue. Raymond Suttner has pointed out, for example, that the word "national" is used in two ways in the Freedom Charter. In the important clause "all national groups shall have equal rights", the Charter appears to be referring to four distinct racial groups while elsewhere in the Charter the word "national" refers to all South Africans.[6]

Critics have declared that the former reference shows that the Congress movement envisages the creation of four nations in South Africa, or that it's struggle is based on the premise that there are four nations in South Africa.[7] Suttner, the current political education head of the ANC, however, contends that this four-nation theory never was Congress policy and that it survives "not in the Charter itself or amongst its supporters but mainly in polemical writings against it and the democratic movement as a whole".[8] The raw material in the chapters on the national question debate in this book should provide fertile ground for activists and academics concerned with the so-called "four nations" debate of the 1950s.

But at the time the debate did not develop, even though the two sponsoring clubs decided to set up a liaison committee "with the specific purpose of organising a nationwide discussion on the national question". The SACP stifled the debate when it took a policy decision not to discuss the question at this point. Nonetheless, the national question continued to be one of Forman's main pre-occupations. As Ray Alexander has commented, "the more he studied and wrote, the more convinced he became that the way to freedom lay through a recognition and glad acceptance of

Introduction xxi

South Africa's multi-national composition".[9] Four years were to pass before Forman could again develop his arguments in print. So let us return to Forman's unfolding career.

When Brian Bunting returned from his overseas trip in May 1954 to take over again as editor of *Advance*, Forman went to Johannesburg to complete his law studies at Wits which had been interrupted by his stay abroad. After completing his degree, he returned to Cape Town in November 1954 and set up in chambers in Parliament Street as an advocate. He was soon defending trade unionists and other victims of apartheid until "not a week went by when one or other of the political cases Lionel defended was not reported in the press". According to a former colleague he was brilliant in court and "extremely valuable to the movement" because he was one of only a few advocates at the time who would readily represent it in the Supreme Court.[10]

But earning a living was hard going because Forman did not charge his clients in political cases. When Albie Sachs returned to South Africa in 1990 after more than two decades in exile, acclaimed as a writer, thinker and internationally recognised legal expert, he acknowledged the influence Forman had had on him as a young lawyer in the 1950s; Forman taught him that it was the responsibility of the progressive lawyer to put himself at the disposal of the oppressed without expecting payment, Sachs told a welcoming audience in a moving first speech after his return. Right up to a fortnight before his death, when he was banned while defending Ronald Segal (editor of the *Africa South Journal*) in a highly publicised trial, Forman used the courts at every opportunity to fight apartheid.[11]

However, Forman did not confine himself to his legal practice after qualifying as an advocate. In fact he became better known as a journalist and political activist. From the start of his political life he had been involved as an occasional reporter and photographer on party journals, helping with political education, propaganda, publicity and sales. As Ben Turok has recalled, "You . . . joined the *Guardian* when you joined the movement . . . "[12] This was certainly the case with Forman. After his stint as editor of *Advance*, he continued to be closely involved with the paper. When it was banned in October of the same year, he wrote a letter to the *Rand Daily Mail* (29 October 1954) slamming the establishment press for its half-hearted defence of press freedom, and announcing the imminent appearance of a successor called *New Age*.

He became one of the core group running *New Age*. There are a number of references in the next few years to Forman being editor of the newspaper. But this did not mean that he was solely in charge. *New Age* was effectively run as a collective. We remain a moment with the newspaper which was in many respects unique. Started in 1937 as *The Guardian*, it appeared weekly for 25 years, becoming the longest running left-wing newspaper in the country. In a recent article, Don Pinnock describes this as something of a political and financial miracle:

xxii Introduction

> From week to week it teetered on the brink of closure, with pennies in the bank and policemen at the door. it was banned outright five times, sued, fire bombed, spied on and had its presses sealed. It was banned from news-stands and constantly raided by the police. Several Commissions of Enquiry investigated its activities. Its editors received personal banning orders, most of the staff were arrested and charged at one time or another, its street sellers were harassed and beaten up, and eight staff members went on trial for high treason.[13]

When it was banned for the first time, it became only the second paper to be closed for political reasons since Lord Charles Somerset halted the *Commercial Advertiser* in 1824. It kept bouncing back, changing its name after every banning: from the *Guardian* to the *Clarion*, the *People's World, Advance, New Age* and finally *Spark*.

The paper was important for a number of reasons. First, it provided the Communist Party with an effective mouthpiece. Party members denied that it was an official organ, but this public stance was tactical. It was controlled and run by party members, it consistently reflected party policy and its position on international matters was virtually indistinguishable from the foreign policy of the Soviet Union.

Secondly, the newspaper played an important role in building the Congress movement in the 1950s, laying thereby the basis for the present formal ANC/SACP alliance which was cemented in the 1960s. The dissolution of the CPSA in 1950, and the rapid growth of the ANC into a mass movement at the same time, encouraged communists to work much more closely with the national movement than they had in earlier decades. They started to give priority to the national struggle and threw their energies into it. This position was reflected in the pages of *Advance* and *New Age*. By the mid-1950s it had become the semi-official mouthpiece of the ANC, the "weekly heartbeat" of the liberation movement. According to Pinnock, the ANC relied heavily on the skills, finances and media of the Party and its members as it transformed itself from a "disparate organisation (geographically compartmentalised and without funds or a newspaper)" into the "single fighting force" it had become by the end of the 1950s. The newspaper served as a key mobilising and organisational tool for the ANC and, according to Brian Bunting, "The ANC/Communist Party alliance couldn't have happened without it".[14]

New Age was important, finally, because the small core group of journalists who worked for it exercised a significant influence on the anti-apartheid struggle, probably far greater than that of their equivalents in the commercial press in regard to government policies. A handful of key party people ran the paper. Brian and Sonia Bunting, Lionel Forman, Fred Carneson and Alex La Guma formed the backbone at headquarters in Cape Town. Then there was Govan Mbeki, regional editor for the Eastern Cape, M.P. Naicker who ran the Durban office, and Ruth First, Michael Harmel and Ivan Schermbrucker based in Johannesburg. Working as a tightly-knit

Introduction xxiii

team, these few individuals largely shaped the policy of the paper. Their world view and politics to a large extent became those of the liberation movement. What they wrote became "the way in which the liberation movement came to see itself".[15] The importance of *Advance* and *New Age* therefore went far beyond the outward signs of a struggling newspaper, battling to stay alive. And, though few in number, the influence of its journalists was enormous. It was here that Forman probably made his most lasting impact.

The state recognised this when they arrested him on charges of treason; along with seven other *New Age* staff members, he was among the 156 leaders of the Congress Alliance netted in countrywide swoops in December 1956 and taken to Pretoria to stand trial. His arrest unleashed a fresh burst of energy from Forman who relished the excitement, the spotlight and the political opportunities provided by the trial. Within days he had smuggled a defiant letter out of prison for publication in *New Age*. Refusing to use his ill-health as an excuse for any kind of exemption from the rigours of prison or the trial, he soon started covering the proceedings for *New Age* from the "treason cage". His weekly reports were provocative, levelling fun and political contempt at the state and its agents.

In March 1957 he accepted an invitation from the veteran trade unionist Solly Sachs to co-author a book on the trial, ignoring warnings that this might lay him open to further charges. An ex-Communist Party member and secretary of the Garment Workers Union for 25 years, Sachs was then living in England after being forced out of South Africa by state harassment. They agreed that "Sachs would work on the international dimensions of the trial and contribute an analysis of the South African state. Forman would provide the inside story from the Drill Hall and a brief outline of the rise of the ANC and other Congresses culminating in their common programme, the Freedom Charter".[16] Their book, *The South African Treason Trial*, was banned in South Africa, but it generated considerable publicity abroad. In a review in *Tribune* (20 December 1957), Fenner Brockway was moved to write, "This is courage not to be measured". "Has a prisoner under a death charge ever before written and published the story of his trial whilst it was still going on — written it challengingly, glorifying in his crime, pouring scorn on the prosecution, exposing to the world the depraved principles of the Government which holds him?"

As "Accused Number 83" wrote the story of the trial, he started delving back into history to look at the lessons of previous treason trials and to unravel the background and development of the Congress Alliance whose leaders were now facing charges. Soon he was engrossed with this historical work, doing research whenever he got a respite from a busy court routine. He buried himself in newspaper archives and within months he'd decided to write a "people's history" of the liberation struggle in South Africa. One unintended consequence of the landmark treason trial, therefore, was that it produced one of the most industrious historians of the 1950s.

xxiv Introduction

Not surprisingly, Forman's first history article was on "Treason Trials in South Africa." It appeared in the Congress journal, *Fighting Talk*, in February 1957. He then tackled the task of writing a 20,000-word overview of nearly 300 years of South African history. He had hoped to include this in the book with Sachs, but it was left out, probably for lack of space. Historical research and writing now became his overriding interest. He took the task seriously enough to register for a Ph.D on "The History of African Political Organisations, 1870-1948" at the University of Cape Town in 1958.[17]

By this time he was also writing regular historical articles for *New Age*. Between July and September 1958, the newspaper published his first substantial writings in the form of seven instalments on the "History of the Liberatory Movement". The articles were subsequently published — in revised form and with one chapter added — as a booklet by *New Age* in April 1959, and reprinted in October. Its title was *Chapters in the History of the March to Freedom*. Forman wrote that the basic conflict in a largely agrarian South African society up to 1870 was of "national entities" over land. In the 1870s, however, South Africa entered an "entirely new epoch" of capitalism following the diamond discoveries and the ensuing industrial revolution. The class struggle of "the working class (irrespective of nationality) against the bosses (irrespective of nationality)" started alongside the national struggle between "white and non- white". "The liberation movement, whose leaders are today charged with treason, is a fusion of [these] two streams into a mighty river", he wrote (3 July 1958). He then went on to deal with early working-class organisation, the first black political organisations and the formation of the modern day ANC in 1912.

His aim was to write a "systematic history of the liberatory movement" as a "useable" past for the ANC (and clandestine SACP). Having grown rapidly during the 1950s to mount for the first time a challenge to white minority rule, the ANC had a keen appreciation of the importance of history. Congress leaders regularly evoked history and Congress publications carried historical features. During the Treason Trial, for example, the Rev. J.C. Calata compiled a short history of the ANC. Joe Matthews, Tennyson Makiwane, Michael Harmel, Brian Bunting, Fatima Meer and R.V. Selope Thema were among others who wrote historical pieces, while ANC President Chief Lutuli, Z.K. Matthews and Selope Thema also wrote autobiographical memoirs which, however, remained unpublished in the 1950s.

A scholar, Luli Callinicos, writing 30 years later has noted that "Ultimately, popular history is located in the present . . . it starts from the need to understand and directly confront, not the past for it's own sake, but present day situations and problems".[18] Nowhere was this more true than in the case of Lionel Forman. His articles were topical and related directly to current events. On May Day 1958, for example, he wrote on the way that day of international working-class solidarity had been celebrated in

Introduction xxv

the past in South Africa (*New Age*, 1 May 1958). During the women's anti-pass struggles in late 1958 he recalled the earliest campaign in the Orange Free State 45 years before. That week happened to be the 75th anniversary of the first independent African newspaper, *Imvo Zabantsundu*, so he discussed it's history as well. Around "Dingaan's Day" (December 16), the holiest of Afrikaner nationalist holidays, celebrating the victory of the Voortrekkers over the Zulu, he explained why Dingane had killed the Voortrekker leader Retief. Launching straight into the ruling-class holy cow, he wrote, "On December 16 there will be the usual spate of nauseating claptrap from pulpits and platforms and press about how at Blood River . . . the forces of civilisation and of light, the messengers of God himself, destroyed the power of barbarism and darkness in the form of Dingane's Zulu. It may be a good idea to arm ourselves in advance against being submerged in the wave of emotion by taking a look at the facts"(*New Age* 11 December 1958). Having done so, he listed eight sources ranging from contemporary diaries to works by both "respectable" (McMillan) and radical (Mnguni) histories in an understandable act of caution.

A few months later on Van Riebeeck Day (April 6), another important white holiday commemorating the arrival of the first European colonists, Forman denigrated the "founding father" of white South Africa in an article headed, "Van Riebeeck was a robber" (*New Age* 2 April 1959).

Forman's *New Age* writing was history with a difference in the 1950s. It directly countered ruling-class versions of South African history used to justify the existing order. It also challenged, even if indirectly, the focus of an academic history establishment embedded firmly within the system of white domination, its interpretations and, in fact, the whole process of historical production in the universities at the time. Likewise, all school texts were based on a white and often racist perspective.[19]

As already noted, Forman's history was popular and usable, with no pretensions to academic objectivity. His interpretations challenged and deviated sharply from those of academic historians in important respects. His writing departed from the ethnocentric orthodoxy of the time. He elevated the history of black South Africans rather than that of the ruling minority; he referred to the indigenous peoples by the names they had themselves used (*Khoi Khoin*) instead of pejorative descriptions (Hottentot) adopted by the white rulers; he stressed the negative not the positive, or so-called "civilising", effects of European colonialism; in fact, the colonialists were robbers who had taken the land of the indigenous people from them by force.

Forman also rejected the notion that South African history was essentially about the clash between black and white as the established colonial, Afrikaner nationalist and liberal historians tended to emphasise. For him race and class went hand in hand. The advent of the industrial revolution was the central event in South African history, and not the long succession of dates which marked South Africa's constitutional development. Today, these revisionist and historical materialist ideas enjoy wide currency in

xxvi Introduction

South Africa, but at the time they were unusual, if not original. Forman was in fact developing a basic (still little known) Marxist analysis of South African history pioneered by activist intellectuals like Eddie Roux, Hosea Jaffe, Dora Taylor and Kenny Jordaan who were linked either to the Communist Party or the Non-European Unity Movement.

Finally, Forman emphasised a collective, "bottom up" approach to history writing. His focus and the process he followed bears striking resemblance to current experiments in "people's history". in South Africa. He sought "widescale participation in the preparation of the history". Readers of *New Age* (4 December 1958) were "not merely invited, but urged" to send in their comments and criticisms, and to help locate material. He wanted this to be "an experiment in collective participation in history writing". Ordinary people's experiences needed to be recorded "to fill gaps and make corrections". Many of Forman's political colleagues were drawn in to help as well. For example, in 1957, he accompanied Joe Slovo and others on a trip to Durban during a recess in the treason trial, and with the help of Jacqueline Arenstein, Forman got permission from the veteran ICU and ANC leader, A.W.G. Champion, to take his substantial collection of papers (stored in a leaking shed) to Cape Town.

These were later deposited at UCT, becoming an important source for scholars. Colleagues in the *New Age* office and the Natal Indian Congress such as M.P. Naicker collected material and did research for him. Even activists in London were roped in. S.R. "Mac" Maharaj, now on the national executive of the ANC, wrote to say he had tried without success to trace copies of the early ANC newspaper *Abantu Batho* in the British Museum and the British Public Library in London. Party veterans were consulted regarding facts and interpretations. Under the heading of Queries he wrote in his notebook, "Ask e.g. Moses [Kotane], Rebecca [Bunting], J.B. [Marks], Jimmy La Guma, Ray Harmel, Louis Joffe". Forman was particularly keen to correct what he regarded as the "distortions" created by Eddie Roux whose books *S.P. Bunting* and especially the classic *Time Longer Than Rope* were the most important (and then still virtually the only) full-length works on political resistance in South Africa. Roux's ex-Party colleagues regarded his work as "biased and malicious". Even worse, one of them wrote, "his indiscretions border on informing and have in fact been used against us (in the Kahn-Carneson select committee and elsewhere)".[20]

A pile of correspondence on Forman's *March to Freedom* booklet helps shed some light on the internal processes and debates which occurred within the Communist Party with regard to ideological work. Particular care was taken with party publications which were subjected to rigorous scrutiny and debate by a relatively small group of activists. Party members therefore involved themselves in finalising the text and preparing the booklet for publication. They included Michael Harmel and Ruth First in Johannesburg and in Cape Town Brian Bunting and, of course, Forman himself. These colleagues made a number of suggestions, some of which

Forman found useful but the process was a difficult one. Harmel initially opposed the re-publication of Forman's articles in the form of a booklet. He felt Forman was acting individualistically and that the booklet was unbalanced. He complained that it "gives the impression that the author considers the small and relatively insignificant socialist movement of the time to be of more importance than the national liberation movements . . ." In a letter to Bunting he wrote this was not only a "construction weakness": the extra articles "throw the whole thing off balance and give it a twist, a wrong slant which we shall have to answer politically if not in any other way . . . all sorts of things are going to be read in it . . ."[21]

These criticisms not only delayed publication, but also led to certain personal and political tensions. In a letter to Ruth First, Forman charged Harmel with "uncomradely" behaviour and "zeal to prevent the publication of ideas that may prove to be wrong" and he spelled out his own attitude towards debate within the party:

> . . . I think it is possible to become over-careful in one's zeal to prevent the publication of ideas which may prove to be wrong. The only way that one can achieve that safety is by publishing nothing at all that isn't completely run-of-the-mill. I think that our theoretical publications do tend to be so cautious that they are sometimes not as interesting and stimulating as they could be and this could have a harmful effect on the level of advancementof theory in our movement.

> It seems to me that particularly in discussing the early history of the movement there is no room for taking a little risk that something may be written by someone else much better. Where a movement is blessed with a Lenin it can expect to have its writing correct first time. But where, as in South Africa, we rely on ordinary folk, the process should be something like this: A work is published dealing with a worthwhile field of study. A major portion of it is directly useful and acceptable. Portions of it arouse controversy; there is discussion on the controversial points. They are cleared up. A big step forward is made. If for fear of controversy we refuse to print the work, the issues are never cleared up. No big step forward is made and we stagnate.[22]

Harmel's response, in which he lectured Forman on the importance of collective action, sheds further light on intra-party debates at the time:

> . . . This business of "zeal to prevent publication" sticks in my throat. We, the movement collectively, work very hard to establish, distribute and keep going publications which express and help our collective point of view, and therefore those whose extremely responsible task it is to write for these publications have a duty to express that collective point of view and not just ride our own individual hobby-horses . . .

xxviii Introduction

> . . . If you look at it like this, you'll see that I am not contesting
> your "right to say and print things which I believe to be wrong".
> I'm emphasising your duty to print things which you yourself can
> reasonably believe to be correct because they have been submitted
> to the only test which people like ourselves can recognise as valid:
> collective discussion — where possible (and here history is not like
> last week's news, as there is ample time for discussion) before
> publication.
>
> It's not a question of being afraid of controversy out in the open, but
> while some sorts of public controversy should not only be permitted
> but even welcomed and stimulated, there are obviously lines to be
> drawn.[23]

The matter was eventually settled with Forman accepting amendments,
largely proposed by First, which he agreed improved the work, and Harmel
acknowledged that his "first comments were rather bad tempered and
destructive".[24]

Part of Forman's difficulty with Harmel stemmed from the somewhat
maverick reputation he was acquiring within the Party. He was intellectually independent, and did not accept uncritically all the Party's positions.
For example, he was critical of the decision to dissolve the Party in 1950
and he alone, with only reserved support from Albie Sachs, expressed
opposition to the 1956 Soviet invasion of Hungary at a meeting of Party
members in Cape Town called to discuss the issue.[25]

Forman had also disturbed some in the Party hierarchy when he entered
the debate on the national question in *Advance* in 1954. As stated earlier,
Dr Dadoo had complained that the issue was unnecessarily theoretical for
a newspaper editorial and more suited to a discussion article. However,
when Forman tried to take it further in the Congress journal *Liberation*, the editorial board decided not to publish. "The prevalent
majority approach" in the Party was that " . . . in view of the fact
that the primary political issue here is unity of all the oppressed —
i.e. of all Non-Whites, irrespective of national differences — it is
incorrect even to discuss at this stage the national question".[26] Editor
Hilda Bernstein apologised to Forman for the "long delay" (in deciding whether or not to publish) and said she could not agree with "this
withholding of any comment, but to date that is our Board's majority
decision".[27]

He also consistently called for more public discussion on socialism and other theoretical issues, insisting that the draconian restrictions of the Suppression of Communism Act had legal loopholes and
that these should be exploited for public discussions and writing.
Consequently, and against the wishes of Party colleagues, he
and Sadie brought out a cyclostyled pamphlet in March 1958 called the
South African Socialist Review. In an opening statement Lionel asserted
that the *Review* did not "infringe even the lunatic provisions of the

Suppression of Communism Act" and he went on to reprint the Constitution of the banned Communist Party, using the loophole provided by a government Select Committee discussion. Though no other issues were produced, this edition was not banned. A year later in October 1959 — the month of Forman's death — the underground SACP launched its official journal, the *African Communist*.

Forman returned to the national question debate in 1958 after the publication in the Soviet Union of a book on South Africa which referred approvingly to his 1954 articles on the subject. The author was the doyen of Soviet Africanists, Professor I.I. Potekhin of the USSR Academy of Sciences, who later became the first director of the Africa Institute in Moscow. The study dealt with "The formation of the South African Bantu into a national community". SACP members in South Africa translated parts of it and when Forman read the translations, he contacted Potekhin via an intermediary (Vella Pillay) in London and started a regular exchange of letters. In October 1958, Potekhin published another piece on "The making of nations in Africa". It appeared in *Marxism Today* (October 1958), then the theoretical voice of the British Communist Party, initiating a long-running debate in the journal. Potekhin's article was also reprinted in the Congress discussion journal, *Liberation* (December 1958).

This intervention by Potekhin led to the reopening of the debate and Forman joined it enthusiastically with two pieces published in the April and August 1959 editions of *Marxism Today*. One of the articles was re-published in *Liberation* (July 1959) in a slightly revised form.

Potekhin, following Stalin, defined a nation as having four main characteristics — a common territory, a common language, a common culture and a common economy or national market. He then wanted to show how these concepts could be applied to Africa. Forman, in his two articles, examined these definitions and tried to measure their applicability in South Africa. In doing so he drew heavily on historical insights acquired from his recent research. For instance, he sought the roots of an African nation in South Africa in the first cross-tribal, proto-nationalist organisations such as the *Imbumba Yama Afrika* (or *Nyama*) formed in the early 1880s. Their emergence followed the mineral discoveries which "transformed South Africa from a collection of primitive pastoral and agricultural communities into a single economic unit and smashed the tribal system and sped on the process of the unification of the Africans". He concluded that there were "still no nations in South Africa" — it was more correct to talk of the various ethnic and language communities as "pre-nations" (or *narodnosts*, a category he borrowed from Potekhin). Adhering to his analytical departure point that South Africa is a multi-national country, Forman suggested that a possible answer lay in "some form of multi-national federation".[28] He also speculated that the Afrikaners, by incorporating the "Coloureds", could one day "obtain the opportunity" to develop into a nation, "being given the essential territorial basis for such development, as has happened in the USSR and China."[29]

xxx   Introduction

His ultimate projection was for a single South African nation: "A single African nation [in South Africa] is likely to develop before a single South African nation does. And similarly it seems likely that Zulu, Basotho and other nations will develop before they merge into a single African nation in South Africa."

While Forman's views accorded closely with those of Potekhin, his comrades in South Africa were once again strongly critical. Fellow *New Age* worker, Fred Carneson, writing under the pseudonym of John McGrath, fired a broadside at Forman's "quite erroneous" conclusions and accused him of "deserting reality" at some points: "He discusses [self-determination] in the abstract, as if we already had a single, socialist soviet state in South Africa. He forgets that the struggle has not yet been won, and that the course of the struggle might take a very different path to that he has mapped out."[30] Relishing the debate, Forman countered with a rejoinder to Carneson in the same issue of *Marxism Today*.

In a lengthy but unpublished article entitled "The Backround to the National Question in South Africa", Forman elaborated his ideas. The article, which originated as a letter to Potekhin, traced the relationship of the SACP to the national movement from its inception in 1921 to its dissolution in 1950. The work encapsulated his thinking, and Forman regarded it as his most important writing on the subject. He was critical of certain crucial policy decisions and actions of the CPSA from the 1920s onwards, particularly in their disregard for the importance of a growing African nationalism.

The (white) pioneers of South African communism had "stumbled often, did not always point out the best route and sometimes even had wearily to retrace their footsteps down alleys which they had not perceived to be dead-ends". Serious mistakes had been made because of a "shallow" understanding of Marxism-Leninism. The article underlined once again the fact that while Forman was committed as a Marxist to class analysis and class struggle, he believed that national rather than class slogans and the "development of a healthy people's nationalism" was the key to the advancement of the South African struggle. The national question had to be understood as a vehicle for the mobilisation of the rural peoples and, he believed, the revolutionary character of the national movement of all classes should not be underestimated.

Lionel found that he was getting distracted from other priorities. He wrote to M.P. Naicker that he'd got himself sidetracked on the national question. "Now I am going back to history. I wish the buggers would put me back in jail again so that I can spend all my time on it, without all these diversions". But his time had run out. He was to write no more. Just as he was reaching his prime, Lionel Forman died on 19 October 1959 at the untimely age of 31 years.

III

A Trumpet from the Housetops consists of a selection of Lionel Forman's writings. The editors have not attempted to provide a comprehensive analysis or overview of his work — this task awaits a formal biographer. The aim here is to let a relatively unknown voice from the 1950s speak, and to make accessible to present-day scholars and activists hitherto little-known or inaccessible material, on the politics of that decade. The vicious repression, bannings and censorship in the three decades after Sharpeville almost blanked out a rich history of struggle-located debate and intellectual work in South Africa. So strict were apartheid's censors, for example, that millions of people who regarded Nelson Mandela as their leader had no idea what he looked like for years. Ideas suffered the same fate. Now it is possible to start drawing back the veil over parts of our past. The purpose of this book, and the broader publications series and project to which it belongs, is to encourage this process.

The book is in five parts. Part One consists of Lionel Forman's history writing. In Part Two excerpts of Forman's inside account of the Treason Trial are reproduced. Parts Three and Four include selections from the *Book for Karl*, Forman's columns on international issues and other theoretical pieces which provide the reader with a more in-depth view of some of the perspectives, debates and activities within the Communist Party and the Congress movement in the 1950s. Part Five comprises Forman's last letter and a few of the many tributes to his life and work.

After Lionel Forman's death his wife, co-editor Sadie Forman, collated his papers and regularly prepared material for publication in *New Age* and elsewhere. She had worked closely with him and typed almost everything he wrote. Her edited booklets and articles of Lionel's writings usually appeared around the anniversaries of his death and birthdays. Colleagues continued to assist with editing and production.

But times were getting difficult. In the early 1960s open protest was becoming increasingly difficult and risky. Slivers of the lengthening shadows that loomed over individuals and the democratic movement as a whole slipped into Ruth First's correspondence with Sadie in May 1961. "PS Do keep copies of articles just in case . . . ", she wrote in one letter. And, in another, "Well — here we go. Arrests started this a.m. All fine so far." Not long afterwards, Ruth became a victim of the 90-day detention-without-trial legislation. By the end of 1963 progressive journals and newspapers like *Fighting Talk*, *New Age* and *Spark* and *Africa South* had all been forced to close. Huge numbers of activists were either banned, jailed or in exile.

It was difficult to publish anything, as printers were afraid to be associated with anyone on the left. After producing a home-made, cyclostyled booklet of Lionel's writings *Why Did Dingane Kill Retief?* with the help of some student friends, Sadie was banned in 1965. Four years later, not wanting either of their sons to be drafted into the army, she and the children

xxxii Introduction

sailed for the UK, having sent Lionel's collection of papers ahead in three large trunk-loads.

A Trumpet from the Housetops is an enduring tribute to a remarkable young South African. His last letter is a poignant declaration of freedom, reaffirming his belief in humanity. Combative to the end, he is looking beyond himself, even as he is overtaken by unconsciousness. It provides testimony to the enormous courage and political commitment of the man.

Forman was intellectually robust and independent. He relished debate and never shirked controversy. Thirty-two years after his death, Ahmed Kathrada, a member of the ANC's National Executive and a senior SACP figure, referring to "this time of turmoil in the socialist world and far-reaching developments in South Africa" recalls Forman's two outstanding characteristics: "his immense foresight and his readiness to express critical views on political matters which were not always consonant with mainstream thinking".[31]

His innovative writings therefore give some insight into the variety of thinking and the complexities of politics within the liberation movement at an important stage of its development. Forman was not one of the big political figures of the 1950s but as a leading journalist on *Advance* and *New Age* and as an advocate, party activist, historian and theoretician, he played an influential role in the politics of that decade.

A critical but dedicated member of the Communist Party, Forman's career moreover provides testimony to the role played by that organisation in the South African liberation struggle. Perhaps more than any other group, communists helped guide the ANC in the non-racial direction it took in the 1950s, a crucial decade in its history. Together with the Youth Leaguers, they played a central role in its transformation from a flabby pressure group into the militant mass movement which is now the challenger for the state power in South Africa. As the anti-Stalinist left historian, Jeremy Kriekler, has noted ". . . in the last analysis, this — not the shoddy, Moscow-induced politics in which they sometimes engaged — is their legacy."[32]

Notes

1. M. Benson, *Nelson Mandela*. Penguin, Harmondsworth, 1986, p. 71.

2. M.M. Suzman to Sarah Forman snr. 1 October 1949. The medical records quoted from here, indeed most of the sources used in this introduction, are drawn from a wide range of primary and secondary material in the Lionel and Sadie Forman papers (LSFP). For reasons of economy the editors have had to limit footnotes. Microfilmed copies of the Forman papers can be found in the archives of the Mayibuye Centre for History and Culture in South Africa at the University of the Western Cape.

3. S. Forman, "Lionel Forman — A Brief Life" (unpublished manuscript, n.d.) p. 15.

4. S. Forman, op. cit. p. 4.

5. The quotes from Simons and Forman are taken from their presentations to the Symposium on the National Question, organised by the Forum Club, May, 1954.

Introduction xxxiii

6. R. Suttner, "The Freedom Charter — The People's Charter in the 1980s", 26th T.B. Davie memorial lecture, University of Cape Town, 26 September 1984, p. 17.

7. See, for example, "No Sizwe" (N.Alexander) *One Azania One Nation; The National Question in South Africa*. Zed Books, London, 1979, pp. 96-100.

8. Suttner, op. cit. p. 17.

9. Ray Alexander, Foreword to L.Forman, *Black and White in South African History*. New Age pamphlet, Cape Town, 1960.

10. Interview with H.Bernadt, Cape Town, 4. August 1991.

11. "The Case of Lionel Forman" *Sunday Times*, 9 August 1959

12. D. Pinnock, "Keeping the Red Flag Flying". Paper presented to the conference on "A Century of the Resistance Press in South Africa", UWC Historical and Cultural Centre, June 1991, p.17. Pinnock's work has been heavily relied on in this discussion of the newspaper.

13. Pinnock, op. cit. p. 1.

14. Ibid. pp. 1, 5-6, 12-13, 19-20.

15. Ibid. pp. 6-7.

16. L. Forman to E.S. Sachs, 14 March 1957.

17. For a comprehensive overview of Forman's historical works see A. Odendaal, "Popular History in the Congress Movement in the 1950s and early 1960s; A Case Study of Lionel Forman's History Writings", Paper presented to the History Workshop, University of the Witwatersrand, February 1990.

18. L. Callinicos "The Peoples" Past; Towards Transforming the Present". *Critical Arts* vol. 4, no. 2, 1986.

19. See Odendaal, op. cit. pp. 9-10, 15-17.

20. See "Suggestions re History Series", filed with R. First to B. Bunting, 18 September 1958 and M. Harmel to B. Bunting, n.d.

21. M. Harmel to B. Bunting, 20 September 1958. See also R.First to B. Bunting, 18 September 1958.

22. L. Forman to R. First, 12 August 1950.

23. M. Harmel to L. Forman 16 September 1958.

24. Ibid., 26 October 1958.

25. Interview with Sadie Forman, 17 June 1989.

26. L. Forman to Secretary, Ethnological Institute, Academy of Sciences, USSR, 18 January 1958.

27. H. Bernstein to L. Forman, 30 July 1956

28. L. Forman, "The Development of Nations in South Africa", *Marxism Today*, April 1959, p. 116.

29. L. Forman, "Self-Determination in South Africa", *Liberation*, July 1959, p. 18.

30. J. McGrath (F.Carneson) "On the Formation of Nations in South Africa", *Marxism Today*, August 1959, p. 253.

31. Fax message from Ahmed Kathrada to the editors, 12 September 1991.

32. J. Kriekler, "Activists and Historians", *Southern African Review of Books*, vol. 3, nos. 3 & 4, 1990, p.31.

Cape Town Young Communist League Committee, c. 1946. Standing (left to right): Basil Jaffe, Ronnie Forgus, Myra Boskin, J. Ross, Lionel Forman; sitting (l to r): Ben Uranovsky, Teddy Myers, Jack Schedrin.

Conference of the International Union of Students, Budapest, 1952. Left to right: Lionel Forman, Nick Mortenson (Danish delegate), Ahmed Kathrada.

Interment of the ashes of Bill Andrews, 1949. Solly Sachs reads the address; among the mourners can be seen, *inter alia*, Dora Alexander, Morris Kagan, Beata Lipman, Percy Cohen, Alpheus Mabida, Sadie Kreel (Forman), Yusuf Dadoo, Abe Kreel, Hettie Macleod (September), J.B. Marks, Helen Joseph, Julius First, Rebecca Bunting, Jessie Macpherson, Benny Sachs, Minnie Goldsmith.

Treason Trial defendants entering the preparatory hearings. From left to right: Ike Horvitch, Jack Hodgson, Norman Levy, Piet Beylefeld, Ronnie Press, Ben Turok, Syd Shall (in front of van door), Lionel Forman (in front of Syd Shall), Sonia Bunting (almost obscured by policeman), Jackie Arenstein, Helen Joseph, Jan Hoogendijk, Yetta Barenblatt. The onlookers are members of either the police department or Special Branch.

Trade unionists defended by Lionel Forman, during their trial. Mildred Lesiah is in the centre, Nellie Jebeliza on her left, Vuyisile Mini behind Nellie Jebeliza, and Douglas Maqina on the extreme right.

THE ACCUSED, FROM LEFT TO RIGHT

Bottom Row: F. Adams, M. Asmal, Y. Barenblatt, H. Barsel, L. Bernstein, P. Beyleveld, I. Bokala, A. Chamile, S. Esakjee, B. Hlapane.

Second Row: A. Hutchinson, J. Hodgson, Helen Joseph, Paul Joseph, F. Keitsing, Moses Kotane, Jerry Kumalo, A. Kathrada, Leon Levy, Norman Levy, S. Lollan, F. Madiba.

Third Row: A. Mahlangu, V. Make, P. Mokgofe, Tennyson Makiwane, J. Makue, H. G. Makgothi, E. Malele, S. Malupe, Nelson Mandela, S. Masemola, L. Massina, July Mashaba, Bertha Mashaba, P. Mathole, J. Matlou, J. Mavuso.

Fourth Row: T. Musi, J. Modise, P. Molaoa, J. Molefi, M. Moolla, Dr H. M. Moosa, E. P. Moretsele, O. Motsabi.

Fifth Row: M. K. Mpho, S. Nathie, P. Nene, L. Ngoyi, B. Ngwendu, J. Nkadimeng, D. Nokwe, P. Nthite, A. E. Patel, J. Poo, R. Press.

Sixth Row: James Hadebe, M. Ranta, R. Resha, B. Seitshiro, N. Sejake, P. Selepe, S. Shall, M. Shope, Cleopas Sibande, Walter Sisulu, G. T. Sibande, Ruth Slovo, Joe Slovo.

Seventh Row: Oliver Tambo, S. Tyiki, R. Tunzi, M. Tshabalala, Rev. D. C. Thompson, Sonia Bunting, J. Busa, F. Carneson, A. Dawood, L. Forman, I. O. Horvitch, A. la Guma, C. Makhohliso, D. Mgugunyeka.

Eighth Row: J. Morolong, L. Morrison, J. Mpoza, J. Mtini, G. Ngotyana, G. Peake, A. Sibeko, R. September.

Ninth Row: A. Silinga, R. Turok, L. B. Lee-Warden, M.P., F. Baard, D. Fuyani, Rev. S. W. Gawe, J. Jack, C. Jasson, L. Kepe, P. Mashibini.

Tenth Row: J. Matthews, Prof. Z. K. Matthews, W. Mati, Florence Matomela, C. Mayekiso, W. Mini, E. Mfaxa, S. P. Mkalipi, W. Z. Mkwayi, B. Ndimba, J. Kampeni, B. Ntsangani.

Eleventh Row: B. Nogaya, T. Tshume, T. Tshunungwa, S. Vanqa, J. Arenstein, Dr C. Conco, S. Dhlamini, A. Gumede, J. Hoogendyk, G. Hurbans, Chief A. J. Luthuli, P. S. Manana, I. C. Meer, P. G. Mei, Bertha Mkize.

Twelfth Row: K. Moonsamy, Dr M. Motala, Dr G. M. Naicker, M. P. Naicker, N. T. Naicker, B. Nair, A. Ngcobo, D. Nyembe.

Thirteenth Row: E. Shanley, Dorothy Shanley, P. Simelane, M. B. Yengwa, G. Dichabe, Dr A. E. Letele.

Fourteenth Row: J. B. Mafora, Martha J. Motlhakoana, L. S. Monnanyana, A. Seochoareng.

Absent: L. Nkosi, S. M. Kumalo, Rev. A. J. Calata, Debi Singh, Stella Damons, T. Mqota, D. Seedat.

TREASON TRIAL

The ACCUSED

DECEMBER 1956

Aftermath of fire started by a bomb at New Age offices in Cape Town, c. 1958.

Cover of Forman's pioneering history booklet, published in 1959

I.I. Potekhin, USSR Academy of Sciences' leading Africanist.

Part One:
People's History

The chapters that comprise Part One include some of Forman's history writings on South Africa from the earliest times through to the 1950s, thus contextualising material in the rest of the book which relates to the struggles of that decade. In his introduction to the booklet *Chapters in the History of the March to Freedom*, he wrote, "although important pioneering work has been done by a number of writers, no systematic history of the liberatory movement has yet been written. Yet the story of the development of the movement is a fascinating, exciting and instructive one."

Chapter One, a reprint of a *Lionel Forman Anniversary booklet* entitled *Black and White in South African History*, was published in October 1960, a year after Lionel's death. It provides historical background dealing with South Africa's pre-colonial and colonial past up to the late 19th century.

At this point Forman's *March to Freedom* booklet starts. This forms a logical Chapter Two, and describes the beginnings of the class and national struggles in South Africa. The birth of the first black organisations, like *Imbumba Yama Afrika*, the APO, the Indian Congress and the ANC is linked to the advent of socialist ideas.

Chapter Three details the emergence of a revolutionary socialist movement in South Africa during the First World War. While the first two chapters reflect a popular newspaper-oriented style, this densely empirical chapter based mainly on research in the *International* (newspaper of the International Socialist League) gives the reader insight into the more substantive people's history of the liberation movement which he planned to have published. It is an example of hundreds of pages of rough work to be found in manuscript form in his papers.

Chapter Four is Forman's article on the history of the policy of the South African Communist Party on the national question, which he regarded as perhaps his most important work. This is the last major piece he wrote before his death and has remained unpublished. It should be read in conjunction with Part Four.

Chapter Five is reproduced from his book *The South African Treason Trial* and tells the story of the Congress of the People and the Freedom Charter.

1. Colonialism and Land Dispossession

Tribal Democracy

In tribal society the chief was, as a general rule, anything but a despot. On the contrary, the tribal system of government was democratic. Although the chief usually had an inner circle of advisers — relatives and influential sub-chiefs — all matters of tribal policy had to be taken to a great tribal council which was broadly representative of the whole tribe and included all sub-chiefs and headmen of local divisions of the tribe. In some cases his council was in effect the governing body of the tribe. The Basotho required, in addition, that important matters be taken before a general assembly of all the adult men. At these assemblies there was complete freedom of expression and speakers did not hesitate to contradict or criticise the chief. The chief could not act without the agreement of the people.

Tribal democracy extended to the village level as well, each district of the realm having its local headman, responsible to the chief, with his local council, from the decisions of which an appeal lay to the chief. The reason for the essentially democratic nature of the tribe was, of course, not that the chiefs were a particularly benevolent species of men but because it was only by leaving the power with the people that the chief was able to keep power. He had no standing or professional army to carry out his will. His armed force consisted of a people's militia, the tribal regiment, which consisted of the able-bodied men who were called up for military service when needed. He could only rule with their consent freely given.

Citizenship in a tribe was not determined by birth but by voluntary allegiance to the chief. If he ruled wisely and for the benefit of the whole tribe, his tribe, his power and his wealth would grow by the accession to him of dissatisfied members of neighbouring tribes less happily ruled. But if the chief ignored the wishes of his people he would stand helpless while his tribe diminished and split until at last someone ousted him from power and took over the chieftainship.

A sovereign can only enforce a law upon a majority which disapproves of that law if he has an effective apparatus of coercion, something in the nature of a police force. And the formation of a class of persons whose task is law enforcement is dependent on the development of an economy in which there is an advanced division of labour - an economy which has raised itself above the general subsistence level of African tribal society.

Thus it was that the sovereign was dependent for the maintenance of law on the people themselves. It was because the people themselves acted against those who offended against tribal custom that it was so difficult for Sir Jacob Dirk Barry to make Chief Cetwayo understand that there is a difference between a good law and law to which the whole nation agrees

— a principle obvious to Sir Jacob, who, as Judge-President of the Eastern Districts Court, headed a judicial system which spent much of its time enforcing "good laws" which were heartily detested by almost the entire black populace.

Thus, although there had evolved among the Africans a well developed system of political institutions, there were still no political organisations; that is, organisations formed by the subjects of a state with the purpose of influencing or compelling the making and unmaking of laws by exerting pressure on the lawmaker, or by overthrowing it and replacing it with a new apparatus of law making and law enforcement.

This was not because there were no political intrigues and conflicts within the tribe. Dynastic disputes, for example, were not infrequent. If the chief was unsatisfactory, a palace assassination might remove him to make way for a more acceptable relative. But no class of people with a lasting grievance against the state resulting from dissatisfaction with their lot in life could come into being because if such a group came into being and could not obtain redress, it could — and did — simply move across to another tribe, or move away and form its own tribelet.

No slave system

There was no fundamental clash of interests between different groups within the tribe. When the harvest was good, the whole tribe feasted. When it was bad, all were hungry. This situation would no doubt have changed in the course of time. The chief and his relatives and councillors were a privileged group within the tribe and as the wealth of the community grew with the development of new and better methods of production, they would — if they followed the course of economic transition taken by similar primitive communities in other countries at earlier times — have formed the nucleus of a new slave-owning class.

Such a development was, in fact, taking place among the Tswana of Bechuanaland who had enslaved the Masarwa and held them under a form of domestic slavery.

As it was, however, the Europeans disrupted the course of African development before any transition to a slave system could take place and the powerful machinery necessary for the maintenance of such a state did not yet exist.

In the Days of van Riebeeck

Holland is today a small nation of little world importance, but in the seventeenth century she was a major power. Through the Dutch East India Company, established in 1602, she came to dominate the extremely valuable trade with India. The sea route from Europe to India was via Southern Africa, and Dutch ships, like those of England and other trading nations, frequently stopped at the Cape to obtain water.

4 People's History

In March 1647, a Dutch ship, the Haarlem, was wrecked at the Cape and the survivors spent a year there. When they were rescued and returned to Holland, two of the officers of the Haarlem, Leendert Janssen and Nicolaas Proot, wrote a glowing report on the possibility of establishing a refreshment station there for the Company's ships, a half-way house breaking the murderously long journey from Amsterdam to the Dutch East Indies. Food was plentiful, the soil fertile, and the African tribes friendly.

Their year at the Cape had proved, they said, that any description of the natives of the Cape as "a brutal and cannibalistic people of whom nothing could be expected" was nothing more than idle "sailor's talk". It was true that Netherlanders had sometimes been killed by them but that was because the Europeans had taken their cattle by force.

The Company decided to set up a small refreshment station. But who were they to send? Who was going to take on the job of commander of a non-existent grocery five thousand miles from civilisation? Hopefully they offered the post to Proot. He turned it down with thanks.

Ex-thief van Riebeeck

Then they remembered a man called van Riebeeck. He was a company official in Japan who had been caught red-handed stealing his employers' goods and shipped home. He had got away with a fine and the sack, and for years he had been pestering the company with pleas for reinstatement.

It had been the convoy on which he was travelling home in disgrace which had stopped at the Cape to pick up the Haarlem survivors, so he had some qualifications. He had spent eighteen days in South Africa. The matter of embezzlement? Well, there wouldn't be very much for him to steal at the Cape!

Jan van Riebeeck was back in the service of the Company. He was given the Janssen and Proot Memorandum to read and he zealously drew up lengthy comments. He took issue at once with the Memorandum's estimate of the African Khoi-Khoin at the Cape. They were, he said flatly, "a brutal lot, living without conscience" almost as if he were grooming himself as the "Founder of White Civilisation" and putting those "liberalists" Janssen and Proot in their place.

The Company wrote out clear and explicit instructions. The Natives were to be treated with the utmost friendliness. Under no circumstances were they to be molested.

On 6 April 1652, van Riebeeck landed at the Cape with 200 others — including his two step-daughters and three or four other women.

Autshumao*, chief of a small Khoi-Khoin tribe, the Goringhaikonas, numbering fifty, came to greet van Riebeeck on his arrival. The tribe had long bartered peacefully with ships which pulled into the bay for fresh water and any food available, and Autshumao went down in peace to the ship, thinking that like all the others it would rest a while and go away.

*In early Dutch history texts Autshumao is usually referred to as Herry while English historians named him Harry the Hottentot.

He went in peace to greet van Riebeeck, and he did not know that van Riebeeck would stay, and he, Autshumao, would in time be thrown into chains and imprisoned on an island, and that his people would be driven from the Cape to disappear from the face of the earth. And not only physically destroyed, but the name by which they called themselves has been buried with them, and the nickname the Europeans gave them — Hottentot — is known throughout the world.

Fortunately for the Dutch, Proot's estimate of the tribesmen was proved correct, van Riebeeck's wrong. For when they were most vulnerable, the inhabitants made no attempt to harm them. Small groups of Dutchmen frequently wandered far from the Fort into the heart of the African country, and never suffered the slightest harm from the tribesmen - indeed, they were always assisted by them. Nor could this have been due to any fear of retribution because the tribesmen were highly mobile, moving in unlimited territory which was well known to them and unencumbered by the heavy guns without which the Dutch were helpless. And the Dutch were possessed of highly valued copper and other wealth which must have been a source of rich temptation to the tribesmen.

"Let's take their cattle"

At first Dutch and Khoi-Khoin lived at peace. But only eight short months after he landed, van Riebeeck wrote to the directors thus of his unsuspecting neighbours:

> Would it matter so much if one deprived them of some six or eight thousand cattle? For this there would be ample opportunity, as we have observed that they are not very strong - indeed they are extremely timorous. Often only two or three of them would drive a thousand cattle within range of our cannon, and it would therefore be quite easy to cut them off. We notice also that they trust us in everything and without any fear come close to the Fort to graze their cattle. We make them even more fearless by encouraging them still more and more with friendly faces and kindly treatment, firstly, to see whether in course of time anything good might be done with them in the shape of trade or something else for the benefit of the Honourable Company, and, secondly, through their confidence in us, to be in a better position easily and without a blow, to deprive them of their cattle and take these for the Honourable Company, should we at any time receive the order to do so. It is really too sad to see so great a number of cattle, to remain so much in need of them for the refreshment of the company's ships, and yet be unable to obtain anything worth while in return for merchandise and kind treatment.

6   *People's History*

"Let's have slaves"

The original plan was to send the captured Africans to India as slaves. Later van Riebeeck set his sights higher and suggested that they be kept at the Cape in slavery:

> We could get excellent service from these people on the islands in flaying seals etc., and with the meat of these could feed them sufficiently without giving them anything else. It will have to happen one day or we shall derive no benefit from them at all.

The directors of the Company rejected van Riebeeck's suggestion to enslave the Khoi-Khoin because they said a people could not be enslaved in their own country unless they were first totally subdued and the Company could not and would not embark on such a tremendous undertaking.

The Khoi-Khoin began to know of these plans too late. The Journal entry on 10 February 1655 says:

> Only last night it happened that about 50 of these Natives wanted to put up their huts close to the banks of the moat of our fortress, and when told in a friendly manner by our men to go a little further away, they declared boldly that they would place their huts wherever they chose. If we were not disposed to permit them to do so they would attack us with the aid of a large number of people from the interior and kill us, pointing out that the ramparts were badly constructed of earth and scum and could easily be surmounted by them; and that they also knew how to break down the palisades, etc.

And then the Dutch had their first experience of a form of passive resistance. It was very effective. None of the tribes near the settlement were willing to barter their cattle. Trade was practically at a standstill, and van Riebeeck was beginning to get desperate. To break the blockade, van Riebeeck sent, on that day, a party of seven men into the interior to try to establish trade with more distant tribes. Their trip is in itself remarkable evidence of the peaceful attitude of the Khoi-Khoin. For during the nineteen-day journey the party met several parties of Africans, one of them 70-80 strong, all of which received them in friendship. "They always laid their assegais and weapons aside and as good friends approached our men," reads the Journal.

A brisk trade in cattle commenced once more and the Dutch received a new lease of life.

White settlement and a slave economy

Five years after the arrival of van Riebeeck's little band, the Company for the first time allotted land to nine of its servants (its Dutch employees) and encouraged them to become permanent settlers.

And then came South Africa's next important immigration wave — the men and women whose labour created the basis of modern civilisation in South Africa — the slaves. In 1658 about 400 West African slaves were

Colonialism and Land Dispossession 7

brought to the Cape — the forerunners of thousands of miserable souls from India, Java, Ceylon, East and West Africa, Madagascar. Many of the slaves introduced from Asia were prisoners of war and political exiles who had been seized in the colonial wars fought by the Dutch against the Javanese.

We must pause and remember those slaves. And we must honour them as white historians have not. These immigrants contributed more, far more, than the Huguenots about whom there is no dearth of praise; they suffered more, so much more on their long and bitter journey than did anyone on the Great Trek. It was not unusual for a third of the men and women in the slave ships to die on the voyage, and for another third to die within three months of their arrival.

They were sold to the white settlers as farm labourers, herdsmen and domestic servants. Some were left as servants by Company officials and some were set to work on public amenities and Company buildings. From that time, right until 1834, the agricultural and pastoral industry, the only important industry of the colony, was to be based on slave labour.

At first the whites, being inexperienced, were inefficient slave-owners. The slaves managed to escape in large numbers. Those of them who came from Africa knew only that they were still in Africa and their homes were somewhere to the North. As soon as they regained their strength after the dreadful conditions of the sea journey they made for home. And the settlers had to go on paying their instalments on the human flesh without having its use. That made them very angry indeed, and they established a custom which became firmly entrenched as a very pillar of white civilisation for the centuries ahead. They blamed it on the Africans.

Had not the Khoi-Khoin women been seen surreptitiously passing food and drink to the slaves? Well, then!

The absurd conviction held by van Riebeeck that the primitive Khoi-Khoin were stealing the slaves is one of the best illustrations of the need to treat with the utmost caution the manifold accusations which were made against the Africans throughout his Journal.

When the farmers came to him, literally in tears, at the loss of the men and women they had bought, van Riebeeck decided that he was strong enough and had sufficient backing to risk the kind of action against the Africans which he had been itching to take almost since his arrival. He arrested two sons of Gogosoa, chief of the Goringhaigua, wealthiest of the Khoi-Khoin clans, who happened to be sitting, unconscious of any danger, in the yard of the Fort.

Then van Riebeeck arrested Khamy, one of the leading Goringhaikonas (the other neighbouring clan), although it was clear even to the Commander that they could have known nothing of the disappearance of the slaves.

An invitation was then sent to the Chora, chief of the other neighbouring tribe, to visit the Fort. This suspicious man did not respond, but fled from the neighbourhood with his whole tribe.

8 People's History

The arrests, of course, did not lead to the return of the slaves, because the tribesmen had had nothing to do with their disappearance. Two weeks after the chiefs had been locked up, van Riebeeck began to feel that the situation was getting critical. He called a meeting of his council.

"The point has now been reached," he wrote on 3 July 1658, "at which the seizure of Shacher (i.e. Osingkima, one of the arrested chiefs) had become widely known throughout the country. This caused the greatest possible sensation." Jan van Riebeeck now began to be fearful that the cattle trade, upon which he was still dependent, would stop once more. And, in case of attack, there were now only 97 white men at the Cape, of whom 20 were invalids left behind by a passing fleet of ships.

Autshumao betrayed

But the Khoi-Khoin did not attack. Instead the frightened chiefs, believing that their lives were at stake, turned traitor. They united in protesting that the Company's troubles were being caused not by them, but by Autshumao. Only let them go, and they would support van Riebeeck in any venture he might undertake against Autshumao.

The delighted Council resolved "to entice Herry into the Fort by means of fair words and then to seize him."

Where Chora, who had far less knowledge of the white man, had fled at the sound of fair words, Autshumao came without hesitation to the Fort — within the hour. He joined the other prisoners. Then a party of soldiers was sent to fetch Autshumao's cattle. And so Chief Autshumao, just six years and three months after he had hastened to the beach to welcome Jan van Riebeeck, found himself South Africa's first political prisoner on Robben Island. Many more were to follow.

And the slaves continued to run away. This was solved by a resolution requiring that all except infants and very old people were to be kept at all times in chains.

The two prisoners, Osingkima and Khamy, released from jail as a result of their betrayal of Autshumao, returned to their tribes. It was the time of year when they normally moved away from the Cape seeking fresh fields, so they were able to turn their backs on the Fort and there were soon no Khoi-Khoin to be seen.

Six months later, when the peninsula grass was rich and succulent once more, the tribes returned with their cattle. They found every inch of peninsula grassland closed to them. Those who had betrayed Autshumao were left with no alternative but to follow Autshumao's path. As he had done five years before, they seized a herd of cattle and killed its owner.

The Dutch at once declared a war of extermination. They decided to call in the services of the prisoner Autshumao to lead them to the tribesmen. After carefully placing on record that they had no intention of keeping their promise, they promised Autshumao freedom and great rewards if he would do their bidding, and a boat was sent to fetch him from his prison on Robben Island.

Under the threat of death, he was forced to lead the way to the camping places of his compatriots. All in vain. There were sentinels watching from every hill.

But the Dutch, reinforced by soldiers from passing fleets, ranged far and wide on horseback, killing every black person they found. Then there was peace once more.

Autshumao duly learned that the promises made to him of freedom and riches were worthless. He had the sea trip to Robben Island once more. A good sailor by now, he managed to launch a leaky boat from the Island and to make a courageous escape to the mainland.

Dutch power was consolidated. The tribesmen were further weakened by some European illness (smallpox) to which they had no resistance and an estimated twenty per cent of their number died.

In 1672 the Company made its occupation "legal" by paying two Khoi-Khoin chiefs about ten pounds' worth of brandy, tobacco and beads for the whole of the territory from the Cape Peninsula to Saldanha Bay.

Resistance ends

And then, 20 years after the first arrival of the Dutch, the Khoi-Khoin tribesmen launched their last and most determined campaign of resistance. The Cochoquas, a powerful tribe, led by Chief Gonnema came down to the peninsula and began the campaign in the same way as had their predecessors, by the seizure of isolated herds.

But now there was a garrison of 100 white men at the Fort, many of them mounted on ponies. Five of Gonnema's men were caught in a cattle raid and taken to the Fort. They were all flogged, three were branded and banished to Robben Island for fifteen years.

For three years Gonnema's men continued to harass the Dutch, with little real effect. Then Gonnema withdrew to the interior and cut off the trade routes to the Fort. Very soon the scarcity of meat in the Fort was once more felt. For four years the blockade was kept up, and the Dutch were completely powerless to break it.

But the Khoi-Khoin were not aware of the success their campaign was achieving. They knew only that they were forced to keep their own cattle in the mountains away from good pasturage. When they sent envoys they were eagerly received by the Dutch and a peace treaty was signed.

This was virtually the end of the Khoi-Khoin resistance to white expansion and conquest. Apart from a small group who made off into the interior, the tribesmen, deprived of their pasture, were forced to trek into the arid desert or to seek a livelihood as menials and labourers.

A large proportion were to die from the effects of smallpox, measles and other diseases introduced by the whites.

A Robber Economy

During the 18th century the Cape Colony was a slave economy. Slaves, equal in number to free colonists, did all the manual work and were the source of all value. The most profitable investment available was that in slaves and as in all slave societies, the abundance of human labour militated against investment in machinery and other capital equipment, and weakened the incentive and initiative of the whole population.

But the chattel slaves, working in relatively small groups on the farms, in a territory unknown to them, and subject to the utmost terror, were in no position during the period of Dutch rule to offer any direct challenge to the rule of slave owners.

The slave revolts were aimed not at overthrowing the slave system, but were revolts against individual owners. They were either attempts to escape or, where they were initially desperate uprisings against unbearable cruelty, they were followed immediately by flight.

The first 100 years of slavery at the Cape are bloody with such revolts. Within a year of the first introduction of slaves, van Riebeeck's own slaves attempted, without success, to rise and escape to the sea. In 1660, 15 slaves and 14 Company servants conspired to escape. There were similar escape-revolts in 1707, 1714, 1719 and 1765.

When it is remembered that the punishment for escaping or uniting to escape, was hanging, strangulation or being broken on the wheel, and that even if escape succeeded the chances of survival in the unknown interior, or out at sea, were infinitely small, it is readily appreciated how appalling the lives of the slaves must have been, and how cynical the comments of the historians that the slaves were well treated at the Cape.

The class struggle of slaves and colonists took the same form — instead of a direct challenge, which was impossible — an attempt to escape from exploitation.

But for the colonist a trek to the interior, so glorified by the textbooks, was a far easier matter than it was for the slaves. And while the whites moved to new pastures, the slaves moved to certain starvation unless they were lucky enough to fall in with a Khoi-Khoin clan which might take them in.

In the course of their spreading out over the interior, the Europeans killed the Batwa (Bushmen) and Khoi-Khoin in their path ruthlessly. The picture of savage slaughter is as gruesome as any the schoolbook historians paint of Tshaka's wars.

By the middle of the 18th century, the Europeans "finally succeeded in dispersing and almost exterminating the Bushmen", in the words of historian de Kock. Not only were these almost defenceless people wiped out — in one single big raid in 1774, 500 were killed and 239 taken prisoner for the loss of one of the aggressors. Prisoners were treated in a most barbarous fashion, either by their captors on the spot, or with the sanction of the authorities at Cape Town, where, at the Castle, they were hanged, broken on the wheel or had their ankle-sinews cut preparatory to being imprisoned for life.

Boer and Bantu meet

The Boers and the Bantu met in the middle of the 18th Century, but for a long time the advance parties of both Boer and Bantu lived in peace as neighbours.

In 1780 the Company proclaimed the Fish River, along its entire length, as the frontier, thus including within the colony the Zuurveld, the desirable cattle country between the Fish and Bushman Rivers which, on his visit to the frontier, van Plettenburg clearly recognised to be Xhosa territory.

In December 1779, matters came to a head as the result of the criminal activities of a family of Boer thieves, the Prinsloos, described by the local Landdrost (magistrate) as "harmful and unrest-causing inhabitants." Eight or nine Xhosas were killed. There were no Boer casualties.

Now, eager to seize the Xhosa lands, two Boer commandos took the field, killed many Xhosa and stole large herds of cattle. Boer appetites were whetted. Another large group of armed cattle thieves was called together in October 1780 under a Company-recognised commandant, Adriaan van Jaarsveld.

An earlier exploit of which van Jaarsveld boasted gives an illuminating insight into the qualities which made up a Boer hero of the period. On one occasion, out hunting the Batwa people, he had 12 hippopotami shot and left lying on the banks of the Zeekoe River. The hungry tribesmen found the meat and while they were feasting, van Jaarsveld's commando opened fire, killed 122 men, women and children and captured 21 others — only five people escaped.

Van Jaarsveld with his mixed commando of about 130 armed Boers and Khoi-Khoin used a similar trick against the Xhosas. He went among the Imidange people who received him in peace. Then he threw a quantity of tobacco on the ground, and as the men ran to pick it up, the Commando opened fire.

The school history books call this "The First Kaffir War". In fact, it was nothing else but a large-scale cattle robbery in which none of the white robbers died but very many of the innocent victims did.

The "war" had no lasting effect on the "frontier". More Xhosas than ever before crossed the river and made "frontier" homes on the Zuurveld. Economic contact between black and white revived and was intensified, though illegal.

Black-white trade

Xhosas went for the first time in considerable numbers to work for the Europeans, and to trade with them. Sometimes they were treated fairly and benefited from the contact. Very often they were cheated or robbed.

12   People's History

During the early 1780s the rains fell and there was an abundance of pasture for the cattle. As long as there was rain and bellies were full, there was peace — uneasy peace, but peace nevertheless.

In 1785, in an attempt to bring the frontier Boers under control, the Company created the Cape's fourth administrative district, Graaff-Reinet, made up of the Eastern portions of Stellenbosch and Swellendam, and with borders on the Fish River. It included in the North-East a new strip of Xhosa and Batwa territory, that between the Fish and the Tarka and Baviaans Rivers.

But underneath the peace, there were those who were preparing for the next big cattle grab. In 1788, a Graaff-Reinet official wrote to Cape Town: "Some of the inhabitants here have already for a long time wished to pick a quarrel with the Xhosas in order that, were it possible, they might make a good loot, since they are always casting covetous eyes on the cattle the Kaffirs possess."

The Boers kept up a steady complaint that the Xhosas were stealing their cattle — blaming any loss — whether straying, the attacks of wild animals, thefts by fellow Boers, or by hungry Khoi-Khoin herdsmen — on the Xhosas. Even so, the tabulation of their complaints from January 1790 to May 1793 compiled by Marais from the official records, shows a total loss of only 493 cattle and two sheep — a figure which pales into insignificance when compared with the 5,330 cattle stolen by the Boers from the Xhosas in 1781. There can be little doubt, too, that the number of Xhosa thefts in these years was at the very least equalled by Boer thefts from the Xhosas.

The Boers complained of Xhosa assaults and aggression but the Company's own records show that the Europeans were in no position to make indignant accusations. Hooligans among them shot, raped, locked up, thrashed and kidnapped Xhosas, without punishment by the authorities. One of the most notorious, Coenraad de Buys, "took such cattle as he fancied out of the Xhosa kraals, had them driven to his farm, and when the Kaffirs complained, he made them lie on the ground and beat them almost to death. He had ordered the Hottentots Plaatje and Piqueur to shoot among the Kaffirs, of whom the former killed five and the latter four."

Ndlambe

In 1793, Ndlambe, Paramount Chief of the Xhosas west of the Fish, was eager to attack the Xhosas living on the Zuurveld, the Isidange who, he considered, were fugitives from his rule. A group of Boers joined with Ndlambe to launch a war against the Xhosas, the blame for which Landdrost Maynier subsequently placed unequivocally on the shoulders of the Boers who had provoked, to use his own words, "a peaceable nation", a "peace- loving people."

They attacked some Zuurveld clans seizing 1,800 cattle in two days, killing a number of their owners and taking others including several

Colonialism and Land Dispossession **13**

children prisoner. Then the Boers took fright when they saw how great a force Ndlambe had, and they fled. And Ndlambe, having thus been deserted by his allies, went back to his home across the Fish.

The Boers, fleeing in panic without having been attacked, left the Zuurveld Xhosas in control of the territory. Some of them were able to settle old scores. The farm of the hated Coenraad Buys was burnt to the ground and all his cattle seized.

Africans fight for Boers

Landdrost Maynier tried to organise a commando but he could collect together only 80 Boers. The rest had all run away. He called an emergency meeting and asked van Jaarsveld to raise a second commando, but this hero made a host of weak excuses. Four other officers approached also refused. Their horses were sick, they said. Maynier had to lead the commando himself. Reinforcements arrived from the Western Cape and a combined commando of 200 wagons advanced against the Xhosas. Such a force was irresistible and many Xhosas were killed. No fewer than 10,000 cattle were seized and 160 women and children kidnapped.

The main burden of the fighting was carried not by the Boers, but by the Khoi-Khoin. At all stages in our history we see it. The Europeans did not conquer the African peoples. They managed affairs so that Africans did most of their fighting for them.

Khoi-Khoin far outnumbered Boers in most of the commandos. They were placed in the most dangerous situations, suffered far more casualties than the Boers did, and they did this for remarkably little reward. After the campaign, all they got was one or two cattle each — and Maynier had to justify himself to the Boers for giving the Khoi-Khoin anything at all.

Just as in the raid of 1780-81, the Boers did not lose a single man in action in this campaign. The only casualties on the "European" side were Khoi-Khoin, three reported killed, three wounded. Many hundreds — perhaps thousands — of Xhosas were killed, however, for the tribesmen were in the open country quite helpless against armed horsemen.

Boers complain

Now the Boers began to fight among themselves. They complained at the smallness of the cattle haul, complained about the way it was divided, complained because the Xhosas were still living on the Zuurveld. And so greedy and shortsighted were they that they even complained because a small share of the loot had been given to the Khoi-Khoin, who had borne the main danger of the fighting.

The frontier Boers carried on a continuous campaign for the resumption of hostilities, calling on the Company not only to drive out the Isidange, but also to attack the Boer ally, Ndlambe. Maynier had far more sense than to support such a foolish policy. But he painstakingly made it clear that this was not because of any considerations of morality. The sole reason was that the Boers were still too weak. "It is impossible to oppose the

14   *People's History*

Xhosas by force, with any hope of success — at least until Providence makes our hands somewhat more free and we find ourselves in a condition to attack them with force and to bring them to obedience. For as experience has alas, more than too well proved, we should run a much greater risk of making matters worse than of improving them. "

There was a striking difference between the vigour with which the frontier Boers called for the formation of commandos and that with which they responded when they were called upon to come and fight in a commando. Marais in his book *Maynier and the First Boer Republic* has produced evidence to show how difficult it was to get the frontier Boers together and keep them together in commandos. One example given is the call to commando in June 1790 to which only one Boer and ten Khoi-Khoin responded. The official responsible resigned in disgust, declaring: "I cannot do commando only with Hottentots but with human beings. "

British Occupation

Like Holland before her, Britain was interested in the Cape only as a military base and stopping place on the way to India, another country whose trade she had taken from Holland. A large armed force was kept at the Cape, new harbour works were built and the colonists benefited from the expenditure. For the Xhosas, a change in the rulers of the country across the Fish made no immediate difference at all.

Nor were the Boers much affected at first. The Graaff-Reinet "republicans" hopefully petitioned the newly arrived British General Craig to seize for them the land "unto the Konab, or it may be unto the Kat River", and surrendered without a fight in February 1797.

In May 1797, Ngqika (Gaika), the chief of the Xhosas, came of age and claimed the chieftainship from the Regent Ndlambe. Ndlambe resisted and was held prisoner, and his followers, including his brother Jabisa, crossed the Fish and made their home on the Zuurveld.

Divisions of tribes into two new tribes, outward expansion and the resulting wave of movement as each tribe was pushed into conflict with the next were frequent occurrences in our history.

In this case, it was the Europeans on the Zuurveld who were forced to flee in haste from the path of the Xhosas, who were fleeing from Gaika. Within a few days, Xhosas controlled the whole territory between the Fish and the Sunday Rivers. This did not prevent the Boers from moving back into the Zuurveld too. By September 1798, about one-third of the 148 Boer families who had lived in the Zuurveld at the time of the 1793 attack on the Xhosas were back in their homes, farming once again side by side with the Africans.

The British had taken over the policy of the Company, based on a frontier at the Fish River and the driving of all the Xhosas over that river. Now with their forces in the area, the British were ready for their first trial of strength with the Xhosas, and in April 1799, Brigadier General Van der Leur organised a commando to fight the Xhosas.

Khoi-Khoin and Xhosas unite

One of the most important things about this campaign was the fact that the event which Maynier had foreseen — the union of Khoi-Khoin and Xhosas — took place.

Numbers of Khoi-Khoin had taken advantage of the British action against the Graaff-Reinet rebels to organise independent hostilities against their Boer oppressors. One of the British units returning from the action against the rebel Boers disarmed a large group of these Khoi-Khoin, led by Klaas Stuurman, and recruited them to march together with the British.

But when the commandos prepared to march against the Xhosas, Stuurman decamped with 700 men, 300 horses and 150 guns, and joined Ndlambe. In a battle on 27 June 1799, a Boer commando was routed and for the first time two Boers were killed. Boer resistance ceased for some time. When this news spread, a number of Khoi-Khoin labourers left the white farms to join Stuurman. Their defection caused consternation among the Boers and Van de Leur's reports about their "panic-stricken" and dastardly conduct show that he had developed an utter contempt for their fighting qualities.

The British General Dundas himself had to lead an army to the rescue, and he had to be content with an armistice which amounted to a complete defeat. The Xhosas retained their positions and were stronger than ever on the Zuurveld.

Because of the new unity between Xhosa and Khoi-Khoin the first British-authorised attack on the Xhosas had been even a bigger failure than the previous attempts of the Boers.

The British now began a determined campaign to divide the Khoi-Khoin from the Xhosa and the Xhosa among themselves. They immediately offered negotiations with the Khoi-Khoin leaders and in October 1799, they agreed to conclude peace on condition that the government should protect them against the ill-treatment of the Boers in the most efficacious manner, and should ensure that when they served the Boers they should be well paid and well treated.

The method of implementing this promise to ensure fair treatment for the Khoi-Khoin farm labourers was to establish a labour register, in which the terms of the contract between farmer and worker were recorded. This was, as Marais remarks, "the beginning of Masters' and Servants' legislation in South Africa."

As a means of splitting the Khoi-Khoin from the Xhosas, it was an immense success; 700 Khoi-Khoin workers left Stuurman to come to work on the farms. Wages were six to twelve rix dollars per year or, more usually, six to twelve sheep, or one head of cattle. Contracts were almost always for a year.

16 People's History

At the same time, General Dundas imposed his own form of control of "wanderers." The Boers were given permission to shoot any individual Khoi-Khoin who "wandered about."

The old dreary story now repeated itself. The Boers began to agitate for a new attack on the Xhosas, and reacted with the utmost horror at attempts to enforce the obligations in the labour contracts, not only on the Khoi-Khoin, but also on the Boers.

The efforts of the missionary, van der Kemp, which were actually having the effect of breaking up the Xhosa-Khoi-Khoin alliance, also infuriated the Boers. In their short-sighted arrogance, they complained because the missionaries were teaching the Khoi-Khoin "reading, writing and religion and thereby putting them upon an equal footing with the Christians; especially that they were admitted to the church at Graaff-Reinet."

The Khoi-Khoin left the farms once again and prepared to resist another attack.

Another "war"

Diplomacy was abandoned once more. The British authorised the Boers to try to smash the Xhosa-Khoi-Khoin alliance by force. A commando attacked Stuurman's settlement in 1802 and another "war" was under way. Once again, fighting the Khoi-Khoin the Boers suffered casualties, the son of the Commandant being killed in the first raid. Having seized all the cattle they could make off with, the commando was returning to its camp when Stuurman's men, together with a number of Xhosas, fell upon them. The commando surrendered and handed over its loot, and the Africans, showing a great deal more mercy than was ever shown to them, allowed the Boers to proceed on their way.

A second commando therefore took the field. Composed of 568 Boers, 132 Khoi-Khoin marksmen and 102 wagons, it killed more than 200 people and captured a great number of cattle — 12,600 in one place. But a month after he had made this report, the leader of the commando, van der Walt, was killed in action and his death caused a panic. The commandos decided to divide up the cattle and go home.

These cattle thieves now withdrew leaving the remaining Boer families to face the anger of the entire African population which had been aroused by the raids. A mass white exodus followed.

At the end of 1802, yet another commando went into action without success, and on 26 December, the officials of the Batavian Republic (the Cape had reverted for a short time to Dutch rule), immediately on taking over from the British, ordered an end to hostilities.

When they occupied the Cape for the second time in 1806, the British sent Lieutenant Colonel Richard Collins to report on the border situation. In 1809 he recommended, in effect, the implementation of the demands of the Boers — the driving of Ndlambe and the Xhosas from the Zuurveld and the seizure of their land as far as the Koonap River.

Colonialism and Land Dispossession 17

On 18 October 1811, the British ordered Colonel Graham, the frontier Commandant, to implement this plan. And in March 1812, Walker reports matter-of-factly that "a large force of troops and burghers swept 20,000 Ndlambis and Gumakwebes beyond the Fish."(*A History of Southern Africa* by Eric A. Walker)

By any standard, this British action ranks high as a war atrocity. 20,000 people whose home had long been the Zuurveld were suddenly swept away by force, and thrown destitute among a people unwilling and economically unable to receive them — the Ngqika Xhosas.

Hintsa

The Paramount chief of the Xhosa was Hintsa, but the British, finding that the lesser chief Ngqika could be bought over to betray his people, dealt with him as if he were the supreme ruler, though Ngqika himself protested that he could not speak for other chiefs.

More and more Africans were now finding themselves forced to work on European farms. It is likely that most of these were for one reason or other outlaws from their own tribes. These people had to choose between existence as semi-slaves on the farms, or starvation. In addition, the farmers were keeping children seized in the wars as "apprentices", differing from slaves only in that their owners had no legal sanction and they were not bought and sold.

The British persisted with the futile attempt to prevent integration. More laws were passed ordering the farmers to dismiss their African servants. In 1812, an army was again mobilised to drive Ndlambe back over the Fish River. The British being far stronger than the Company had been, managed to enforce the separation more effectively than previously.

Backed by British military might, the farmers increased their demands. Previously they had asked only for the cattle and the land of the Africans and had demanded with the greatest vigour that every black man should be driven across the Fish River and beyond. Now, having experienced the value of African labour, they did not want the government to drive all the Africans away any more. Their servants should be allowed to remain.

The buying over of Ngqika was linked with the beginning of the reversal of the official policy of economic segregation.

Trade with Xhosas

Rapidly expanding British capitalism was eager to develop all markets for her wares, and in 1817 Governor Lord Charles Somerset established a half-yearly trade fair at Grahamstown with a view to a trade that had been carried on between Xhosas and Boers since the first days of contact.

But only special Xhosas were entitled to come and trade. This valuable privilege was reserved for those having a pass from Ngqika. The Chief was thus given a trade monopoly by which he enriched himself.

Somerset now came to an "agreement" with Ngqika for the application of the so-called "spoor law" which was a method of recovering stolen stock

18 People's History

known to several tribal systems. If the spoor of stolen cattle led directly to a particular clan, the owner was entitled to recover the cattle or recoup himself at the expense of the kraal.

Enforced by one clan against another, the spoor law was one thing. But enforced by mounted gunmen against tribesmen it was quite another. The missionary J. Brownlee described it this way:

> In addition there was no way of checking the farmers' statements of how many cattle they may have lost, and as we have seen, the farmers (Boers) exaggerated thefts shamelessly and used the law as a cloak for massive thefts of their own.

Ndlambe and his people having been forced back among Ngqika and his people, it was inevitable that there should be strife amongst the Xhosas. When the strife came in 1819, the British used it as an excuse to cross the Fish River. They attacked Ndlambe and seized a large number of cattle.

Divide and rule intensified

The British now began to put into operation the policy of divide and rule whose techniques they had perfected in India. They saw the Tembus as a useful potential ally against the Xhosas. They attacked the Xhosas on 6 February 1829. According to missionary reports, "The soldiers went from village to village with torch in hand, till the whole country was lit up with the flames of its own dwellings."

It was becoming crystal clear that the British, to use the words of H. Lawson, "brought calamities compared to which the cattle raids of the Boers had been mere flea bites. The British way was not composed of cowardly cattle thieves, but of ruthless and dehumanised mercenaries whose profession was destruction. Moreover, they appeared in their thousands where the Boers had mustered only a few hundred. When they attacked the African people, the damage they were able to inflict was tremendous."

An even more successful application of the divide and rule policy was the adoption of the advice of Maynier on the treatment of the Khoi-Khoin. The crude Boer policies which had driven these valuable fighters into alliance with the Xhosas were changed drastically. In 1828, all legal discrimination against the Khoi-Khoin was abolished. And the following year about 3,000 Khoi-Khoin together with some "loyal" Xhosas were given land at the Kat River Settlement which had just been seized from the Xhosas.

This policy killed three birds with one stroke. It served to quiet those in Britain who were disturbed by the treatment of the Xhosas; it won the Khoi-Khoin as loyal subjects of the British Empire, and it also gave them a vested economic interest in opposing any return of the Xhosas to their territory. Indeed, the Kat River Settlement fought the Xhosas in the next war.

The 50th Ordinance of 1828 and the emancipation of the slaves in 1834 mark the emergence of a new political entity in South Africa — the Coloured People, composed of that portion of the descendants of the unions between Europeans and non-Europeans who did not pass as white, together with the Khoi-Khoin and freed slaves. The Coloured People as the result of this master stroke of British diplomacy were for a very long time to remain allies of the Europeans

This was the desperate position of the Xhosas in the 1830s. On one side, where they had previously to contend only with a handful of Boer settlers, now their land was occupied by 5,000 British immigrants driving their herds far into Xhosa territory, hungry for more land, ready to fight and backed by a powerful army.

It is in this period that we are able for the first time to obtain a direct description of events by people not blinded by their enmity towards the Africans. Until now we have had to rely on facts gleaned from boastings of wickedness, or rationalisations of it, or from ugly facts which neither a flood of words nor even complete silence could hide. The sympathetic eye-witness accounts beginning in the 1830s are invaluable not only for the picture they give of the period, but also for the clues they give into past events.

In 1830, Dr. Philip described the way the British were, with complete callousness, harrying Paramount Chief Maqoma and others from one place to another, and this in time of "peace." "Several of the chiefs, with their people, are without any fixed residence," he reported. "They have no security that the place they were in today would be theirs tomorrow," one of Ngqika's sons complained to him.

Nor did Maqomo fail to point out to the British that the people whose land they were seizing were the people of Ngqika who had been faithful servants of the British, and the chief they were oppressing was the son of Ngqika. The missionary Ross summed it up: "We used Ngqika as long as he served us. When he failed to conquer Ndlambe, we did so ourselves and then took Ngqika's territory."

A missionary recorded at the end of 1833: "As the Xhosas are now thronged upon each other, their cattle will be in such great numbers that at the first drought they will find themselves poor and dying with hunger." When the drought did come in 1834, the Europeans made matters even worse by pushing across the "frontier" into the African lands to compete with the Xhosas in the quest for sustenance.

Emancipation

They were trekking, among other reasons, because slaves were to be emancipated at the end of the year, and they were fleeing the Colony with their slaves, some of them in chains.

There was drought and starvation piled upon despair as the Xhosas watched Europeans, Khoi-Khoin, Tembu and Fingo eating up the land.

20 People's History

Despair piled upon burning anger at the white cattle robbers who shed even the blood of the chiefs.

On 21 December 1834, Maqomo and Tiyali led 12,000 men in a desperate march into the colony. They laid waste everything in their path, including the newly-built Lovedale Mission Station. For the first time they killed a number of traders who, because many of them were blatant murderers, were a class they hated.

But — unlike many of the white warriors — they did not kill or rape or molest the women, nor did they kidnap or in any way harm children. The toll of white lives throughout the whole territory was less than that frequently exacted by a commando on a single kraal in the course of one campaign.

The schoolbook historians who roll out with relish the stock phrases about the "terrible ravages" of the "barbarians" are often less loquacious about European fighting methods. The Colonel Harry Smith whose name they revere was by his own confession a fighter as barbaric as any. "You gallop in," he said, "and half by force, half by stratagem, pounce upon them (the Africans) wherever you find them, frighten their wives, burn their homes, lift their cattle and then return home in triumph."

Hintsa murdered

By now the Xhosas had had experience of the folly of massed attack against the guns of the Europeans, and, using the rocks and the bush, they avoided a head-on clash with the armies sent against them. But there was no way they could save their homes and crops from being burnt or their cattle from being seized.

From far in the interior at the end of April 1835, the Paramount Chief Hintsa came voluntarily to negotiate a peace. The terms of surrender dictated on May 10 were not very merciful. The whole territory between the Keiskama and the Kei was to be taken from the Xhosas, and they were to pay 50,000 head of cattle and 1,000 horses. In breach of any law of war or peace, Hintsa was held prisoner as hostage for the payment of the cattle demanded.

The day after the dictation of the peace terms, Hintsa was killed. The British "explained" that he had "tried to escape." His body was mutilated. This the British did not explain.

But they did hold a formal inquiry. It honourably absolved all the officers immediately concerned.

The Struggle within a Common Society

After the adoption by the British in the 1850s of a policy of non-interference in the interior, the Cape Colony enjoyed a long period of peace on the Frontier. The knowledge that Britain would not send military aid was a great peacemaker.

Colonialism and Land Dispossession 21

But the opening of the diamond fields led to an immense increase in the need for African labour on road-making, harbour and railway projects.

Shortly after he became the Cape's first Prime Minister, John Charles Molteno visited King Williamstown and urged upon a deputation of chiefs "the importance of coming into the colony to see the railway works, and of earning money with which to purchase valuable property such as cattle, sheep and horses."

In 1877 Sir Bartle Frere was sent to the Cape as the new Governor and the Transvaal was annexed. Following a clash between 40,000 stray Gcaleka Xhosas, led by Chief Kreli and the vassal (slave) Fingoes, Frere summoned Kreli to his presence. Kreli, with more prudence than his father Hintsa, who had in 1835 obeyed a similar summons and been shot, refused. Frere thereupon "deposed" Kreli, announced that the Gcaleka country would be taken by the Europeans and sent in his troops to smash Kreli's army and seize their weapons.

In the course of the fighting, Frere deposed the fiercely independent Molteno government when it sought to establish the right of the Cape to control the troops in its own territory. Molteno was replaced by John Gordon Sprigg, "Sir Bartle Frere's dummy" as P.A. Molteno bitterly described him. "Responsible government was now replaced by personal rule, through a ministry selected and held in power by Sir Bartle Frere and willing to carry out his behests."

The Sprigg government immediately launched what it called "a vigorous Native Policy", aptly described by James Rose-Innes as "the pink forerunner of that red-blooded policy of oppression, which since Union has been so influentially and persistently advocated." The first Sprigg measure making for the ending of tribal differences — the consolidation of the Africans as a single political entity — was the singularly ill-named Peace Preservation Act (1878) introduced some six months after a letter from the new British Colonial Secretary, Hicks Beach, to Frere asking "Can anything be done to put a stop to the importation and sale of arms to Natives?"

With the hypocrisy characteristic of legislation affecting Africans, the Act did not say what its real purpose was — the total disarmament of all Africans without exception, and of the Africans only. It simply provided that all private citizens must hand their guns and ammunition in to the authorities, who would then return them to "proper persons." Those not in this category would lose their guns and receive monetary compensation.

The essential fact about the Disarmament Act was that it was no longer necessary to place so great an emphasis on the gaining of tribal allies in the game of divide and rule. The Xhosas as a result of British intervention were crushed, and it was no longer necessary to "pamper" the Fingoes. The Europeans, British-backed, were strong enough to reduce the Africans to a single level. The distinction between Fingo and "Kaffir" became increasingly fine until it disappeared altogether.

22   People's History

The government did not even pretend to distinguish between the Fingo and Tembu allies whose arms had played so great a part in destroying Kreli and Sandile. All were to be disarmed alike, including the sons of Britain's staunch African ally, Moshoeshoe of Basutoland.

The Africans of the Cape, for whom their guns, next to their cattle, were their dearest possession, had long been alert for any disarmament threat, and Cape officials had been at pains to dismiss these fears as groundless. When in 1876 the Orange Free State government had disarmed the Africans of the Witzieshoek Reserve, the rumour had spread to nearby Basutoland that this was part of a concerted plan and that the Cape (of which Basutoland was then a part) intended to pursue a similar course. "I was able", governor's agent Colonel Griffiths reported "to allay the fears of the Chief Letsie of the Basothos by treating the rumour with contempt and telling them how unlikely and absurd it would be of us first to grant permits and thus arm those we intended shortly to disarm." Two years later the Disarmament Bill was published.

There was nothing the frontier tribes could do about the new law. The Fingoes, completely dependent on the European authorities, handed in their guns, as did the broken remnants of the Xhosas.

Basotho victory

The Basotho were another matter altogether. First they sent a deputation to Britain to petition the Queen against the law, and then, when they found that it was the Queen's law, they took up their 18,000 rifles in defence of their right to retain them. In September 1880, the Cape police moved in. Neighbouring African tribes rallied to the support of the Basotho. By October, "every tribe, the Griquas included, were against the government", according to the missionary Brownlee, including even a section of the Fingoes.

In the face of determined resistance the government was unable to impose the law and in April 1881 fighting ended with the withdrawal of the Cape police, their mission unaccomplished.

It was therefore, the Basotho who won the first political victory of an African people against an oppressive law imposed upon them as subjects of a white government in South Africa, and they won their victory by armed revolt. The Basotho lives lost in repelling Sprigg's police were certainly not sacrificed in vain, as the present Constitution of Basutoland testifies. Ironically, the very success of the Basotho revolt made it of small importance in the history of African political organisations in South Africa for it was so complete that the Basotho of Basutoland were able to break from the mainstream of South African political development.

Pass laws

The Disarmament Law was only one aspect of the deliberate policy to put an end to the privileges enjoyed by the "satellite" tribes, and to reduce all the Africans to a single level. Pass and vagrancy laws operated in exactly the same way. The pass laws were themselves nothing new. The pass was originally in the nature of a passport. Until 1828 there had been a total prohibition upon the entry of Africans into the Colony, but an Ordinance of that year (Ord. 49, 1828) enabled the Africans beyond the colonial frontiers, who were all foreigners in terms of the Cape Law, to enter the Colony in order to obtain employment.

Africans who came into the Colony without a pass were liable to imprisonment. They could be arrested by any landowner and if their arrest could not be effected without killing them, the law specifically provided that such killing was justified.

In 1857, with the growth of the permanent African population within the colonial border, it had become necessary to legislate to prevent "Colonial Fingoes and certain other subjects of Her Majesty from being mistaken for Kaffirs, and thereby harassed or aggrieved." To this end, a system was evolved for the issue of "certificates of citizenship" to all Fingoes, "any Kaffir or other Native foreigner" who could prove that he had spent ten consecutive years in employment within the Colony. At least 99 per cent of the employment period had to be employment other than as a hard labour prisoner. Even certificates of citizenship, however, could not be altogether effective in preventing Fingoes and other black subjects of Her Majesty from being harassed or aggrieved, for there was still no way of distinguishing at sight between a Native foreigner and a native Native. As a result, it was necessary to carry the certificate of citizenship on any journey away from home.

The Vagrancy Act of 1879 supplemented the pass laws and effectively plugged any loopholes in them. It provided that any person found wandering abroad and having no lawful means of support "could be arrested and unless he could give a good and satisfactory account of himself" he was deemed to be an "idle and disorderly person" liable to imprisonment for up to six months, with hard labour, a spare diet and solitary confinement.

In the hands of the administrators of the "vigorous Native policy" and with white tempers still hot from the "war" of 1877-78, these laws became a source of great hardship to Africans irrespective of tribe. From about 1878, the authorities ignored the provisions of the Act favouring the holders of certificates of citizenship and every African who wished to travel from one place to another was required to take out a pass.

As a result, a man wanting to go to Kingwilliamstown had first to get a pass from his magistrate, which would take up one day. Then he must have it endorsed at Komgha, where he lost another day. In Kingwilliamstown he must report his arrival and departure and on his way back report again at Komgha. Finally he had to return the pass to the magistrate. In addition, Africans who went out in an emergency or without their papers found themselves liable to arrest and detention, in which case they might once again be taken into custody.

In a letter to G. Rose Innes, Under-Secretary for Native Affairs, the Resident Magistrate at Kingwilliamstown wrote in July 1881 that the

24 People's History

withdrawal of the rights previously associated with the certificates of citizenship was "one of the sore grievances which the Fingoes have against us . . . " He added that "there is a very bitter feeling on the part of both Kaffirs and Fingoes against the Government. There is now a warm sympathy between them, which never before existed . . . the Fingoes and loyal Kaffirs say that for their loyalty they have simply been punished, and made the laughing-stock of those who have fought and rebelled . . . and that their attachment to the Government is now a thing of the past . . . They have at present no faith in our honesty, truth or justice and they openly state that they have been driven to this by our harsh treatment of them."

In October 1889, the *Christian Express*, which only eight years before had painted so joyous a picture of the new life opening for the Africans, etched out the new scene:

> The Natives of this country are at the present time more desponding, hopeless and untractable than they have been for a generation previously. The loyal are puzzled, bewildered and irritated; and those who are disloyal are exasperated and becoming almost dangerous. This is aggravated by want, which is now beginning to make itself felt in numberless villages. The last three or four years have witnessed a great change for the worse in the relations of the two races. There are four Acts — all of which press heavily on the Natives . . . . The Disarmament Act, Vagrant Act and Branding Act and the Pass Act. Three of these are new and the fourth has been resuscitated. They are the chief legislative landmarks of the last few years. The Native people had no real voice in their enactment, and no means of opposing their becoming law. But they have taken up an attitude of resistance — and they fight where they can, and they say they will rather go to prison than obey some of the mildest of them — the Branding Act.

The Branding Act was a measure requiring that all cattle be branded with a distinctive mark. Its purpose was probably to assist in tracing thefts, but was seen by the people as an introductory step either to the confiscation of their cattle or to the imposition of new taxes. The suspicions were strengthened by the fact that in practice the law was applied to Africans only.

The combined effect of these four laws was to speed up the political unification of the Africans by withdrawing the "privileges" which were the main source of friction between the Fingoes (and their satellite tribes) and the Xhosas.

The resulting consciousness that all Africans — irrespective of tribe and irrespective of anything they might do to ingratiate themselves with the state — had a common political destiny was the essential prerequisite for an all-embracing African nationalism.

2. National Liberation and Socialist Movements, 1870-1914

The Working Class is Born

In the great South African democratic movement of today, made up of people of all races and classes, with an immense diversity of political and philosophical beliefs, two forces work together in the firmest alliance against oppression and for freedom:

   i) The organisations of the oppressed people of all classes, led by the African National Congress, against national oppression by the dominant whites and for the full political equality of all South Africans;

   ii) The organisations of the working class of all national groups against the exploitation of their labour by the dominant capitalist class.

The history of the liberatory movement in South Africa is the history of the development of these forces and their interrelationship.

The purely national struggle has its source deep in the earliest history of modern South Africa beginning with the first futile battle in 1659 of the Khoi-Khoin led by Chief Autshumao, against the seizure by van Riebeeck of the best pasture lands in their Cape Peninsula.

Until 1870 the basic conflict in South African society was this conflict between different national entities. And the root of that conflict was the struggle for control of the land. Some of the names which stand out as landmarks in this struggle are Makana and Moshoeshoe, Dingane and Moselekatze, who fought back at the head of their people.

The whites, whenever they were strong enough to do so, seized all the good land. The Africans who had been there before were killed, driven away, or allowed to remain as servants or serf-like squatters. Only areas which could not be seized or which were not worth seizing remained for the Africans. These later became the reserves.

By the third quarter of the 19th century, this process of land seizure by the whites was almost complete. At the time South Africa comprised a collection of poor farming communities, and the country was of interest to the outside world only as a stopping place for merchant and military ships.

In the 1870s the discovery of diamonds at Kimberley led to the transformation of the entire economy. Money and machinery poured into the country. Great railway and road projects began. While it is not correct to say that South African history only started in 1870 — for the nature of the national oppression of modern times was greatly influenced by the 200 years of struggle that had gone before — it is certainly correct to say that

26 People's History

an entirely new epoch in our history began; that there was a qualitative change from one form of society to another; that there was an economic revolution.

Capitalism

Until then almost everyone had made a living through work connected with farming and marketing farm produce. Now the industrial revolution began. Farming ceased to be the basis of the country's livelihood. Mining became that basis. A capitalist economy came into being. With capitalism, a new class was born — the proletariat, that body of men who possess no way of earning their food except by selling their power to work in return for wages.

An embryonic form of capitalism and an embryo proletariat had already become discernible in the Cape Colony in the late 1830s after the freeing of the slaves. Diamonds turned the embryos into lusty, bawling infants.

Kimberley in the 1870s was the source, beginning as a tiny trickle, of a second stream of struggle, running beside that of the struggle between the non-white and the white — the struggle of the working-class (irrespective of nationality) against the bosses (irrespective of nationality). The mines needed men to dig and build and carry; the railways needed men, the ports needed men. The cry went out for black labour.

African proletariat

At Kimberley, the African proletariat was born. It was a most difficult birth. As if aware of the misery of the future, the infant fought against those who would wrest him forth. Previously it had been the struggle for land which had determined state policy, and African land now became secondary. The alienation of the Africans' land was no longer an end in itself but a means of driving the African out to work on mines, railways, docks and farms.

As long as the African was able to eke out an existence from his soil, he saw no reason to go out and be the white man's labourer. He may well have argued that there was as much reason for the white man to come and work as his herdboy as there was for him to go and work as the white man's herdboy.

The life of the cheap black labourer was not very attractive, and the wage rates were not sufficient to bring in the steady flow of labour required. It was necessary to drive the African out to work — to create an African proletariat. By definition, a proletarian is a man who owns nothing but his power to work. The need of the rulers of South Africa then was to strip the African of all but his labour power, to take from him all rights to the land from which he could gain food or graze cattle.

This was done principally by ruinous taxation laws against squatters; the introduction of individual tenure of land in the place of tribal tenure, and the abolition of freehold tenure. Measures such as these could not easily be enforced by the relatively weak government of the Boer republics

National Liberation and Socialist Movements, 1870-1914   27

and of Natal in the face of the African resistance. Because of this, the Natal whites had to import cheap Indian labour from thousands of miles across the seas and the Rand mine magnates had to bring workers from China.

This was obviously an economic absurdity. A strong state machine was required to drive out African labour. This was one of the main reasons for the move towards the merger of the separate South African states into the Union — one of whose first acts was the Land Act, which, at the expense of immense suffering, deprived the African of all rights to the land and turned the reserves into labour reservoirs.

The rulers of South Africa battled to drive the Africans out to become the labourers in industry. Such is the drama of history — the ruling class struggled so hard precisely in order to create the African working class, the class which would inevitably one day challenge and take over from its creators.

Ironically, while the white owners of the mines and industries were so eager to welcome African workers, who were potentially their greatest class foes, the white workers — who were brother proletarians — came to regard them with fear and hostility.

The diamond rush had led to a huge immigration of white workers from Europe, hopeful of making a quick fortune. These immigrants, with their education and training, became a skilled labour force in the mines. Large numbers of Africans were recruited but they were, at first, merely fetchers and carriers for the white men. They were men who walked straight from a primitive tribal society into the industrial age. Illiterate, they had no comprehension at all of machinery, nor any tradition of industrial discipline. In tribal society, the tasks of the men had been milking cows, erecting and defending the kraals, and sometimes hunting. Women had done all the farming and it was only at about this time, when the plough was replacing the hoe, that the African division of labour changed and the men became active farmers.

But it is remarkable how soon these men were using the universal weapon of the working class — the strike. In December 1882, before there is any record of a strike by white workers in South Africa, 100 Africans on a Kimberley mine stopped work for two days and brought the mine to a halt when wages were reduced. The strike was broken, however, and the workers returned on the bosses' terms. By 1884, there were at Kimberley no fewer than four different Non-European Benefit Societies, the predecessors of a trade union movement.

White workers — imbued with their strong British trade union tradition — had begun to form themselves into unions almost as soon as they settled into their jobs. A branch of England's Amalgamated Society of Carpenters and Joiners was established in Cape Town in 1882.

In the beginning, at Kimberley, there were thousands of independent diggers — including a sprinkling of Coloured men. Each staked his claim,

28 People's History

and sometimes on a plot as small as seven square yards each was a mine owner and employer of African labour.

As the surface scratching gave way to deeper digging, the need for machinery and capital grew. Syndicates were set up to buy out and squeeze out the individual diggers, and the bigger syndicates squeezed out, swallowed and destroyed the smaller ones in a ruthless drive towards monopoly.

By 1884, almost a whole capitalist cycle had been completed. The thousands of small white employers of labour had been pushed out of the capitalist class into the class which owned nothing but its power to work. The white proletariat had been born, and economically it was the brother of the black proletariat which it, in its small way, had exploited before.

If economics were a mechanical determiner of destinies, white and black worker would have stood together in class solidarity against the mine owner. But it is not.

White worker vs. black

The white worker saw — and saw correctly — that, as far as he was concerned, the biggest potential danger was that the bosses would reduce him to the position of the black man. The black man received a pittance, and if he would do the white man's work for a pittance, the boss would surely employ black labour. And while that would certainly benefit the black man it would equally certainly bring down the wages received by the white man. It was the white workers' view that anybody who talked to them about the solidarity of all labour should have his head examined. For the short-term interests of white and black workers were sharply opposed, although their long-term interests were, and are, identical.

Most people concern themselves with their immediate interests and leave the distant future to look after itself. White workers were no exception. They were willing to listen to the voice of those who, speaking of the solidarity of all workers, meant by that all white workers, and meant by it too, solidarity against anything which would strengthen the opportunity of the black worker to compete with the white and thus improve his lot.

The pattern was set for the hostility towards African advancement which has been the hallmark of the majority of white trade unionists — against which stand out like beacons the names of many advanced white workers' leaders who have fought hard against all odds for the recognition of the fact that white and black workers are brothers.

Symbolically, the very first strike noted in white trade union history was a strike by white workers against the very first attempt by employers to reduce them to the level of the Africans.

After each shift, the mine owners required black workers to strip naked and submit to a search for stolen diamonds. When, in October 1883, the mine owners announced their intention to extend this system to include European and Coloured diggers as well, the white men went on strike. After a year of sporadic labour stoppages, riots, and, on one occasion, a bloody affray in which eight workers were shot dead and forty others wounded by mine police guards, the owners finally abandoned the proposal.

The First non-European Organisations

The Africans in what is now South Africa enjoyed a measure of democracy long before the whites did, for rule by the chiefs-in-council was essentially democratic. Democratic government for whites began in 1853. Until then, neither whites nor blacks had had any say in the Cape government. The British governor had dictatorial powers. Agitation against this dictatorship had begun as early as 1827 when 1,600 Cape citizens signed a petition asking for the vote. In this agitation, Coloureds participated side by side with whites.

When Britain granted the Cape its first constitution in 1853, it did so on the condition that there was to be no colour bar, and non-Europeans in fact participated in voting for the election of the commission which, in 1848, drafted the constitution.

Non-Europeans could vote for, and had the right to be elected to, the Cape government. No one, however, could vote unless he possessed land worth £25 or earned £50 per year, and this at first effectively excluded all but a handful of non-Europeans.

Until the discovery of diamonds, Britain had been interested in South Africa only as a refreshment station for her ships and as a military base. Unlike India, South Africa was an expense, not a source of wealth and the interior of the country was of no importance. When the Boers trekked inland from 1836, the British made no serious attempt to establish authority over them or over the African tribes in the interior, adopting a policy of non-interference. Diamonds, however, changed British policy completely and she moved to establish control over the whole of southern Africa. She was motivated not only by the diamond wealth and rumours of gold but also by the pressure of new world economic developments. The era of imperialism was just commencing. The nations of Europe were beginning their cut-throat scramble to carve up Africa and Asia.

In 1874, Britain set out to unify South Africa in a single British confederation. She sought to smash African resistance once and for all, to extend British control over the Transvaal and Free State, and to limit the rights embodied in the newly won Cape constitution. In 1878, the British Governor unconstitutionally dismissed the first Cape Prime Minister, Molteno, replaced him with a puppet, Gordon Sprigg, and launched a policy of terror against the Africans. Their right to own arms was withdrawn, the pass and vagrancy laws were operated with a new vigour, as was a discriminatory cattle branding law.

With imperialist domination, came its antithesis — national liberatory movements. In the short period between 1882 and 1884, a number of very significant new political developments took place: the first African political

30   People's History

organisation, *Imbumba Yama Afrika*, seed of the African National Congress, was formed in the Eastern Cape; Afrikaners united into the *Afrikaner Bond* — forerunner of the Nationalist Party; Coloureds united for the first time as a distinct community to fight confederation; the first independent African church was established, and the first African political newspaper was published. Formed at about the same time as *Imbumba* was the Native Education Association, to the presidency of which Rev. Elijah Makiwane was voted in 1884. The Association did not confine itself to educational matters, as is shown by a resolution adopted on 20 June 1884 protesting against the pass laws.

In 1884 the Tembu Church, the first African-controlled church in South Africa was founded by Nehemiah Tile, a former Wesleyan Methodist Minister. Tile's breakaway from white *baasskap* in the church, and the powerful Ethiopian religious movement which subsequently developed, is of great significance as the first real manifestion of African nationalism. That Tile was a turbulent priest is illustrated by the fact that he was jailed in 1885 for urging the chiefs not to pay their taxes. Commented a newspaper, *The Journal*, "Advice and warning have been repeatedly proffered him by his friends but to no avail, his only reply is that neither the fear of imprisonment, nor banishment, nor death shall deter him from doing what he believes to be his duty to his chief and people."

The non-European electorate was growing steadily as wealth flowed into the colony as a result of the diamond discoveries. Coloured diggers on the diamond fields were already facing discrimination, in spite of the absence of race legislation, and they were among the first to organise as voters. An "Africander League (Coloured)" was formed at Kimberley in December 1883. Its rules declared "that the object of the League shall be to promote our own general interests and those of our class in Griqualand West."

At about the time of the 1884 general election, a Native Electoral Association was formed in the Kingwilliamstown constituency, which had the largest concentration of African votes. It was in this election that a division began to appear in Parliament between those who, like the modern Nationalists, believe that white supremacy is best maintained by naked force, and those who, like many modern white liberals, believe it is best maintained by benevolent fatherliness.

To the Kingwilliamstown constituency with its African voters came the liberal James Rose Innes, and the Native Electoral Association agreed to back him. There were seven candidates for the constituency's two seats and Innes was the only liberal. In order to ensure his return, the Association decided to advise the 90 registered African voters to vote for him and to waste their second vote rather than give it to any of his competitors. "This they did with a consistency which created a sensation in the opposing camps," Innes wrote. The result was that he headed the poll.

Later that year John Tengo Jabavu founded the first African political newspaper, *Imvo Zabantsundu*, with the financial backing of a group of white liberals. Their aim was to foster the African middle class, and to win over the intellectuals to support for the ruling class as allies against the African masses. Jabavu was a man of unusual intellect. He was made an editor of the missionary paper *Isigidimi* when he was only 21, became one of the first two African matriculants at 23 and the editor of *Imvo* at 24.

In 1884, too, early signs of a Coloured class-cum-national consciousness came from Port Elizabeth. In December of that year there was a move by the Coloureds to commemorate the jubilee of slave emancipation. A meeting called for "a more general and closer union among the Coloured classes, who have hitherto been separated by unimportant distinctions" and urged that the establishment of a newspaper "suited specially to the Coloured classes" be considered. It was to be in Dutch (the language of the Coloured people) and English.

Imvo's comment was perceptive: "In the progress of the Coloured classes. . . may be seen an instance of a people who have been, ever since the emancipation, endeavouring to force their way into the pale of European society, but the circumstances. . . have rendered the attempt futile; and we hail this harking back upon lines which alone can make them a not unimportant factor in this country, viz to build up . . . a society conscious of its independence and vitality."

Attack on the vote

In 1887, the Cape government launched the first attack on the voting rights of Africans. Until then the non-European vote had been negligible, the earnings and ownership requirements being sufficient to keep most of them off the rolls. But as the economy developed and land values rose, more and more Africans were qualifying. In the five Eastern Province constituencies of Kingwilliamstown, Queenstown, Victoria East, Aliwal North and Wodehouse, the non-European (predominantly African) vote had risen from 14 per cent in 1882 to 47 per cent in 1886 and in the latter two constituencies the non-Europeans were actually in a majority.

The government looked for a formula which would disenfranchise Africans, while at the same time giving the liberals and the British government an excuse for silence — which would be impossible for them if any actual colour discrimination was introduced. The formula found was a clause providing that a man's share in tribally owned land was not to be counted as part of his property qualification. Its effect was to strike about 30,000 Africans off the voter's rolls, reducing the African vote to negligible proportions.

This Bill had the effect of giving a sharp impetus to the growth of African political organisations, and meetings of Africans were held all over the Eastern Province to protest and draw up a petition against the disenfranchisement.

32 People's History

Jabavu's sedition

Jabavu threw himself wholeheartedly into the campaign, of which *Imvo* and he became the centre, playing a dynamic and progressive role. The government reacted exactly as every South African government has since. Prime Minister Sprigg attacked Jabavu in Parliament on 2 June 1887 calling him a "highly educated Native who publishes a newspaper in which he sets forth seditious articles. . . I am not sufficiently acquainted with the Kafir tongue to read the articles myself, but I am informed that they are most libellous and seditious." This was sheer falsehood and *Imvo* replied indignantly: "Loyalty to the Queen is one of the talismanic words engraven on the tablets of our heart."

When the Bill was passed by an overwhelming majority, a meeting of Africans at Port Elizabeth decided to ask the British Governor to refuse to sign, and then when he, of course, ignored this, a decision was taken to send a deputation to England to ask for a veto. A lengthy 20-clause petition to the Queen, drawn up by a lawyer and set out in almost incomprehensible legal style, was distributed and signed by Africans all over the Colony.

On 6 October 1887, a conference was held at Kingwilliamstown to choose the delegates. It marks an important landmark in South African history. All the African centres of any importance in the Cape were represented by the 100 or so delegates or observers who came from far and wide — Cala, Engcobo, Fort Peddie, Queenstown, East London, Herschel, Stockenstrom, Victoria East, Fort Beaufort, Grahamstown, Kingwilliamstown and Stutterheim. The Stockenstrom delegation included Coloured people and every African political leader of any consequence was there, or sent a message, including Elijah Makiwane, S[amuel] Sigenu, James.Pelem, D[aniel] Dwanya, [James] Dwane and Jabavu.

"The people have been moved less by actual disfranchisement," said an *Imvo* editorial, "than by the deprecating and ignoring of their rights to land. . . They are aware too that the object of (the government) is, by means of disfranchisement, to pave the way to doing what it likes with the rights and privileges of Natives, especially with rights to land. It is this agrarian question that has so much agitated the Native people and afforded life to the agitation. To show that it is quite possible for good to come of evil, the conference resolved that if the present be the first it should not be the last occasion when men representing the various Native races from various places should assemble to look into questions vitally affecting their rights as British subjects."

The Indian Congress and the APO

When the first Indians landed in Natal on 15 October 1860, Durban welcomed them with the greatest enthusiasm. A handful of Europeans were in occupation of huge tracts of fertile land. But it is not only land which gives wealth — it is labour. The problem for the Europeans was that the

National Liberation and Socialist Movements, 1870-1914 33

Zulus too had fertile land and the whites were still far too weak to seize it and give Africans the choice of starvation or semi-slavery.

That is why the Indians were so warmly greeted. Driven by the starvation British plundering had brought to India, these men came and worked for ten shillings (one Rand) a month and food and lodgings. They built the Natal economy and the fortunes of the white sugar planters. By 1886, there were 30,000 Indians in Natal, producing wealth for the whites and receiving subsistence wages in return.

Natal's constitution of 1856, like that of the Cape, had no colour bar. But within a year of the grant of responsible government in 1893, the Natal government set about disenfranchising the Indians. Again, just as in the Cape, it was necessary to word the Act so that it could be argued in Britain that there was no actual race discrimination. This was done by excluding from the vote any person (irrespective of colour) who was a native of a country which did not itself enjoy parliamentary institutions. The only people affected were, of course, the Indians.

In 1894, the Natal Parliament unanimously passed this law.

The attack on the Indians coincided with the arrival in Natal from India of Mohandas Karamchand Gandhi, a young advocate recently qualified in Britain, sent to South Africa to appear in a civil trial. The great Mahatma was quite unknown. It says much for the perspicacity of the Natal Indians that they at once saw in him the qualities of natural leadership which were to make his name a household word.

Just as had happened in the Cape, the attack on the vote was the stimulus to political activity. Until then, non-European political action of a non-military nature had been confined to the Cape. Now Natal joined in. In 1894, the Natal Indian Congress was formed with Gandhi as its leader.

If the earliest African national struggle was dominated by the desire of chiefs, intellectuals and the petit-bourgeoisie to break into the ranks of the ruling capitalist class, this was even more markedly the case with the Indian Congress.

Bambata

In 1905, the Natal government decided to impose, for the first time, a poll tax on the Zulus. It wanted both to raise money and to force them out to the mines and farms.

Chief Dinizulu "set the example" by paying his tax, but the impoverished people were in no mood to follow this example. They refused to pay. Police were sent to arrest one group of defiers and two policemen were killed. The government now launched unbridled terror against Africans. Twelve were sentenced to death for the killing of the policemen. Throughout Natal men were arrested on the smallest pretext, jailed and given up to twenty lashes for "sedition."

Matters came to a head when the government tried to depose a minor chief, Bambata, and with great courage he took to the bushes with his men and defied the authorities. The government now went in with machine-

34 People's History

guns. Four thousand Africans, including Bambata were killed. Government losses were 25 Europeans and six Africans.

Gandhi and the NIC supported the authorities, and supplied an Indian ambulance unit. Gandhi explained many years later: "I bore no grudge against the Zulus, they had harmed no Indian. . . But I then believed that the British Empire existed for the welfare of the world. . . At any rate my heart was with the Zulus, and I was delighted to hear that our main work was to be the nursing of the wounded Zulus." Gandhi's ambulance men were still in the field during the massacre of Bambata's followers when the Indians were given a sharp indication that their place should be side by side with the African — where they stand today in unbreakable alliance.

In 1906, the Transvaal government attempted to force the Indians to carry passes and Gandhi launched the first passive resistance campaign, a form of struggle which was to become the symbol of Gandhism, and was to shake the British government in India and greatly to influence the character of the South African liberatory movement. The heroism and sacrifice of the Indian and Chinese passive resisters led by Gandhi make a whole noble chapter in our history.

But passive resistance is a form of struggle which has serious limitations and Gandhism as a principle (instead of as merely one form of struggle among many) can be a serious barrier in the way of militant action. Gandhi wrote in 1909: "Some publicists have condemned passive resistance in a land filled with illiterate natives. I think it is best for them to let the illiterate men learn that if they feel a grievance, they are not to break other people's heads, but their own, in order to have it redressed."

The African Political Organisation

It is to the Coloured people that the credit must go for the creation of the first political organisation of non-Europeans from all over South Africa.

Britain's seizure of the Transvaal in the Anglo-Boer war had brought the whole of South Africa under British rule, and the formation of some form of South African union was now only a matter of time. Coloureds had, with good cause, always been alarmed by any talk of union with the northern states where Coloured people enjoyed no rights and in 1902 the African Political Organisation (APO) was formed in Cape Town.

Branches quickly sprang up all over the Western Cape. In 1903, Matt. J. Fredericks became secretary. His name is the first to stand out as a Coloured political leader of importance, though he has been all but forgotten today. In 1905, Dr. Abdurahman, one of the giants in the early history of the liberatory movement, became APO President. Though in later years Dr. Abdurahman lost his militancy, his name is overshadowed only by that of Gandhi in this period of our history.

The APO was very much influenced by the Indian passive resistance campaign and time and again it pointed to the campaign of the Indians as an example for the Coloureds. The outlook of the APO differed from that of the African and Indian organisations in one most important respect.

National Liberation and Socialist Movements, 1870-1914 35

Among Coloureds, there was a large and influential artisan class — men with a tradition of industrial labour — and this explains why the APO was, ideologically, considerably more advanced than the Africans or Indians.

Although predominantly Coloured, it was not racially exclusive and included many African members. One of its active Kimberley members was Sol Plaatje who was later to be one of the founders of the ANC. An extract from an APO editorial of 1909 shows an understanding of the nature of the struggle which cannot be found anywhere in the writings of the African and Indian leaders or the white socialists of that period:

Our political destiny is in our own hands; and we must be prepared to face the fight with grim determination to succeed . . . How are we to set about it? In our opinion there is but one way and that is the economic method. Undoubtedly the Coloured and Native races of South Africa hold the strongest weapon ever placed in the hands of any class. The very stability, the prosperity, even the continuance for but a few days of the economic existence of South Africa depends on the labour market; and we are the labour market. It may ere long come about that the necessity will be imposed on us, not in any isolated sphere of labour or in any particular district but in every sphere and throughout the whole sub-continent, to refuse to bolster up the economic fabric of the people who refuse us political freedom. That would bring the selfish white politicians to their knees. It would even go far to show the white manual workers the value of combination which is the only weapon whereby they will free themselves from the shackles of that cursed wage system, which is sapping the independence of the people, weakening the national love of honour, and increasing the severity and extent of poverty for the production of a few sordid millionaires.

An equally striking example of the APO's advanced political consciousness was this statement by its Johannesburg correspondent in 1909:

The fight must begin somewhere and it seems to us that the Pass Regulations is a good battleground for the first struggle. When once it has begun, consolidation of native forces will be the result. Success must not be looked for immediately, but the Coloured people must remember that the fight for freedom, national, political, social or economic, "though baffled oft, is ever won".

The Union of South Africa

With the discovery of gold in the 1880s, the economic centre of gravity shifted from Kimberley to the Rand. Almost immediately the infant Transvaal mining industry was howling urgently for black labour. In 1890, the Chamber of Mines wrote to Kruger's Transvaal Volksraad asking them to

36 People's History

do something about it. The Volksraad politely acknowledged receipt of the letter and put it into a pigeon hole.

In 1891, the Chamber threatened that it would close down the mines "if the Volksraad and government do nothing to assist them". The Volksraad and government still did nothing. Two years later, the Chamber proposed, among other things, "that the hut tax should be increased as an incentive to the Natives to work". And still nothing was done.

Was this because the Volksraad did not want to help the Chamber? Certainly not. The reason was mainly that the Boers did not have the military strength to make any effective attempt to carry out the Chamber's wishes. For the Boers had never "conquered" the Africans in the Transvaal or Free State. They had won some battles, lost others. But for the most part they simply coexisted in the territory with the still independent African tribes. Neither the whites nor the blacks were sovereign.

This was a state of affairs often found before (but impossible after) the coming of full-scale capitalism. Even after Britain had seized the Transvaal on behalf of the Chamber of Mines in the Anglo-Boer War, it seemed a safer and cheaper proposition to bring to the country indentured Chinese labourers than to enforce the Squatters Acts aimed at driving the Africans off the land. The Transvaal government's caution was seen to be justified in the light of Natal's attempts to impose a poll tax on the Africans there and the widespread resistance led by Bambata.

White union

One of the most powerful motives behind the formation of the Union of South Africa was precisely the need of the capitalist class for a single state machine powerful enough to subdue the resistance of the African people to the ruthless process of converting them into landless labourers forced to work at low wages for the profit of others. Union corresponded to the desires of the Afrikaner people, rising again to claim a greater measure of independence and self-government after the Boer War, as well as to the pressures of the mine owners and other capitalist elements for a stronger, more centralised and efficient administration which would implement their wishes. This combination of forces was symbolised by the first Union government under Smuts and Botha.

As a step towards Union, a National Convention of representatives of the governments of each of the colonies was called in 1908. Non-Europeans were neither consulted nor represented at the Convention. When the draft constitution was published the following year, it revealed that the Cape "liberals" had sold out and that the colour bar had been extended to the Cape and Natal Parliaments.

Non-European political organisations, which had placed great faith in the promises of the Cape liberals and had done little to make their own opinions felt at the Convention, were shocked into life. "Since 1852, nothing in the political life of South Africa has so disturbed the mind of the Coloured people as the draft South Africa Act", said Dr. Abdurahman at the APO's Annual Conference on 13 April 1909.

"At three Coloured and Native Conventions — the most representative ever held in South Africa — these clauses were denounced in language which showed unmistakeably the intensity and unanimity of the feelings of the people. The draft is the foulest work that South African statesmen ever attached their names to".

Black union

As Union was revealed to be a union of white South Africans against the blacks, the Africans in turn began the slow and painful process of black union against white domination.

Small African political bodies had recently developed in the Transvaal, Natal and the Free State. The Natal Native Congress was already causing the Europeans some worry. R. Plant, Inspector of Native Education in Natal, told the South African Native Affairs Commission in April 1904 that he saw "danger in the thing for want of control, it perhaps being an endeavour to try and get things that it would not be wise to accord them".

The Transvaal Mining Industry Commission, before which Transvaal Native Congress secretary, S.M. Makgatho, gave evidence in 1907, described the organisation as "an association which has generally brought the complaints of the Natives before the government. The members are educated Natives — some of them chiefs. Its objects are for the education of the Natives and the amelioration of their conditions."

The forerunner of the African National Congress, The Native Convention met at Bloemfontein in 1909 to discuss the effect on Africans of the impending Union. This was the first occasion on which African political leaders had come together from all over South Africa to take decisions affecting their interests in common.

It was not for its direct achievements that the Convention was important. Its main decision was to send a delegation to England to appeal to the British Parliament not to pass the colour bar "blot on the Constitution." The petition to Britain was, of course, futile. But the seeds were planted for the growth, with Union, of a single political organisation of Africans pursuing a national policy independent of the Europeans.

The African National Congress

With Union, organisations of all types which had existed separately in each colony commenced to amalgamate on a country-wide scale. The Africans were no exception.

All the Colonial Congresses, Vigilance Associations and the like, were summoned to a meeting called by P. Ka Isaka Seme at Bloemfontein. The South African Native National Congress was formed there on 8 January 1912. A list of 21 "objects" was drawn up, including the following:

38 People's History

To encourage mutual understanding and to bring together into common action as one political people all tribes and clans of various tribes or races and by means of combined effort and united political organisation to defend their freedom, rights and privileges;

To educate Parliament and Provincial Councils, Municipalities, other bodies and the public generally regarding the requirements and aspirations of the Native people and to enlist the sympathy and support of Europeans;

To educate Bantu people on their rights, duties and obligations to the state and to themselves and to promote mutual help;

To record all grievances and wants of the Native people and to seek by constitutional means the redress thereof. . .

To agitate and advocate by just means for the removal of the "Colour Bar" in political, educational and industrial fields and for equitable representation of Natives in Parliament or in those bodies that are vested with legislative powers or in those charged with the duty of administering matters affecting the Coloured races;

To be the medium of representative opinion and to formulate a standard policy on Native Affairs for the benefit and guidance of the Union Government and Parliament;

To discourage and contend against racialism and tribal feuds or to secure the elimination of racialism and tribal feuds, jealousy and petty quarrels by economic combination, education, goodwill and by other means;

To establish or to assist the establishment of National Colleges or Public Institutions free from denominationalism or state control;

To encourage inculcation and practices of habits of industry, thrift and cleanliness among the people and to propagate the gospel of the dignity of labour.

Although the Congress in its early days did not yet boldly advance the central demand for equality which has become the hallmark of the movement now, it was a long step forward in the conditions of the time.

At the time when Congress was formed its leaders did not and could not have in mind the modern type of liberation movement, based upon a mass membership of workers and peasants, organised in a network of local branches which ceaselessly lead the people into political action, around their immediate needs and interests, as they do today.

Political and national consciousness had hardly penetrated to the mass of the people. The urban African population was relatively small, unsettled and transient. Tribal life and institutions were far more of a reality and an influence than they are today, after half a century of swift capitalist development in the Union.

Role of chiefs

In fact, Congress could not have come into being at that time without the support and blessing of the chiefs. The chiefs played a large part in the ANC in its early years. In fact, Seme, who was himself a protege of the Swazi Queen Regent Labotsabeni, credits the chiefs with having been the real initiators of Congress. "Although I have the honour to have been the convenor of the Conference," he wrote, "yet it was the Chiefs, Maama, Seiso, Molema, Sekukuni and others who came to the nations, call to Bloemfontein that day who really dedicated this Congress." (Seme and other Congress leaders of this period frequently spoke of the tribes as "nations".)

The dream which Moshoeshoe had cherished 50 years before of a great alliance of African peoples to resist their separate conquest was at last coming into being. But though the chiefs supported Congress in the hope of furthering their own class aims, they were not and could not have been the initiators and moving spirits. Already the vitality and social function of the tribal system was beginning to crumble. The chiefs were becoming less and less the independent leaders and democratic spokesmen of their peoples; the government was gradually moving towards making them its obedient agents and civil servants, liable to instant dismissal for disobedience. Hence it was that the dream of Moshoeshoe was furthered not by chiefs, as independent rulers, but by a new class — the class of intellectual leaders and professional men who everywhere in the world have played such a vital part in the early stages of national liberation movements.

John L. Dube, leader of the Natal Native Congress, was elected President and Sol T. Plaatje the first General Secretary. The Vice-Presidents were Dr. W.B. Rubusana, Meshach Pelem, A. Mangena and S.M. Makgatho, leader of the Transvaal Native Congress. Who were these men?

Seme: A lawyer who, like Gandhi and Abdurahman, was a graduate of a British university. Born in Natal, he began his legal practice in Johannesburg in 1910. He was legal adviser to the Swazi people;

Plaatje: Born at Boshof and educated at a mission school, he became a court interpreter and newspaper editor. He was also an author of several books, the best known of which was *Native Life in South Africa,* the first of the very, very few political histories by black South Africans. He also wrote literary and poetical works.

Dube: Founder of Ilange Lase Natal in 1906, he was a Methodist parson;

Rubusana: Later to be the first and only African ever elected to a South African legislative body (the Cape Provincial Council), an Honorary Ph.D. of McKinley University and the first moderator to be appointed by the Congregational Union of South Africa;

Pelem: A teacher, later an interpreter, and then a recruiter of African labour for the railways;

Makgatho: Son of a chief, he was educated in England and became a teacher at Kilnerton. A large landowner, he was President of the

40 People's History

Transvaal African Union from 1906 and later of the Transvaal Native Congress;

Mangena: The first African to qualify as an advocate, he practised as an attorney in Johannesburg.

The structure of Congress at the beginning reflected this alliance between middle-class intellectuals and chiefs. The Constitution was modelled to a considerable extent on American, and especially on British, parliamentary institutions and procedures. Congress was divided into a Lower and an Upper House. Paramount Chief Letsie II of Basutoland was unanimously elected Governor of the Upper House, the House of Chiefs. There was a speaker, a sergeant-at-arms, and a chaplain.

Congress statements were full of eulogies to the British king and pledges of loyalty and devotion. They stressed that it was the chiefs and their loyal African subjects who were the true servants of imperialism, while the Boers, in whom so much faith was placed by the Crown, were potential traitors.

Nor did Congress have any of the class consciousness manifested so clearly in the APO. One of the very first ANC-sponsored conferences — in Kimberley in July 1913 — the time of a particularly bloody strike by white miners — adopted a resolution "that the Natives dissociated themselves entirely from the industrial struggles on the Witwatersrand and elsewhere and preferred to seek redress for their grievances through constitutional rather than by violent means."

Can this be read as a criticism of the Congress of that period? Of course not. For Congress in its early years was a creature of its environment and it was similar to other early national movements born under comparable conditions.

The early policy statements, for example, of the leaders of the Indian National Congress in India were in many cases almost identical word for word with those of the ANC. Said R.C. Dutt, Indian Congress President in 1901: "The people of India are not fond of sudden changes and revolutions. They desire to strengthen the present government, and to bring it more in touch with the people." And an earlier President had declared: "The educated classes are the friends and not the foes of England — the natural and necessary allies in the great work that lies before her."

Similarly too, early government policy both in India and South Africa was not to discourage the Congresses but to treat them as a safety valve and to patronise them.

Does this mean that the ANC was, in its early years, a reactionary force? On the contrary, the ANC represented the most progressive politically organised force among the African people and its nature was determined by the fact that the African working class was still comparatively small and completely unorganised.

In later years, as the power of the chiefs declined and that of the lawyers, doctors, traders, priests, and clerks grew, Congress became militant, developing into a typical example of a "bourgeois-national' organisation, its

National Liberation and Socialist Movements, 1870-1914 41

attention being focused on the struggle to establish a place for the African small businessman in the economy.

These words of Seme's, before an ANC Annual Conference, put the Congress philosophy of that period in a nutshell: "Most of the failures which the Africans have met in business so far have been largely due to the fact that Native businessmen do not and cannot count upon any steady support from our own people. . . Through this Congress we can and should create our own markets and enough employment for our sons and daughters. . . Let us through this Congress come together and ask the government to give us land wherein we may develop ourselves."

Step forward

Jabavu played no part in the foundation conference of the ANC, and he and *Imvo* fulminated on the "Northern Native extremists" who endangered "the political freedom we have long enjoyed" in the Cape.

The purpose of Union, as we have seen, was partly in order to enable the state to drive the Africans off their land into the cities, and the means of doing this — the Land Act of 1913 — was announced almost immediately after Union. The fight against the Land Act was the ANC's first fight. It decided to send a deputation to Britain to plead against the Act. Futile as the deputation itself was, the collection of money at mass meetings all over the country and its intensive propaganda, served to arouse the political consciousness of the people.

The reactionaries did everything possible to hamper the campaign. Sneered Jabavu's *Imvo*: "A 'Native Congress' of busybodies in other people's affairs. . . talk such twaddle. . . they must take the Imperial Government for a pack of simpletons to grant interviews on such supremely laughable errands." The government banned a number of ANC meetings called to discuss the appeal to Britain.

APO and ANC

The APO had welcomed the formation of the ANC with the greatest warmth, and the two organisations were firm allies. An attack by Jabavu on Abdurahman in 1913 drew from Saul Msane, one of the most militant Congress leaders of the period, this scathing reply: "In your career of political sycophancy and legerdemain you have at length involved yourself in such a position that you do not dare to come out openly and stoutly in defence of your own countrymen. . . Unlike Dr. Abdurahman you evidently fear to be called a red-tied agitator. We want no contemptible cowards in this crisis."

The ANC deputation against the Land Act duly set sail for Britain, and was rebuffed.

South Africa, like the rest of the British Empire, immediately joined Britain in World War 1; Botha and Smuts invaded South West Africa, then a German colony, and South African troops were sent to fight in Europe. The ANC, like the APO and the Indian Congress, unhesitatingly decided

42   People's History

to support the war effort, in the hope that Britain would recognise their loyalty and take steps to improve the position of their people. These hopes were bitterly disappointed. All that happened was that the Congress organisations ceased their agitation and lost ground during the war years. It was a setback from which the APO, in particular, never recovered.

But the war served as the impetus for the development of a new force in South African politics — the International Socialist League, later to become the Communist Party of South Africa, which was to break with the sterile colour-bar policies of the Labour Party and to make an invaluable contribution to the national liberation movement of the oppressed people of the country.

Enter the Socialists

Militant working-class ideas, and rudimentary socialist ones, had already begun to make their appearance in South Africa in the 1890s, but many years were to pass before any names were to stand out bold for their contribution to the liberation movement. The reason for this is obvious. Conditions in South Africa were such that no indigenous socialist movement was yet conceivable, and the early socialist movements were not made up of South African socialists but of men who were already socialists when they came to South Africa and whose political understanding had been formed in a society completely different from that here. In addition, the workers who emigrated from Britain to South Africa did not as a rule come from the settled workers, the most advanced of the the trade unionists, but from the adventurous spirits and fierce individualists who hoped to make their fortunes abroad.

It was in Cape Town, immediately after the Anglo-Boer war, that the socialist movement began to emerge. In May 1904, from the foot of the van Riebeeck statue in Adderley Street, Cape Town, Wilfred Harrison (later to be a founder member of the Communist Party) announced to the world the aims of South Africa's first significant socialist body, the Social Democratic Federation (SDF): "The abolition of Capitalism and Landlordism, the socialisation of all means of production, distribution and exchange, that is, the ownership and control of all the means by the people for the people."

Cape socialists

A little later, the SDF established its headquarters on the second floor of Chames Buildings, 6 Barrack Street, Cape Town. South Africa's first socialist newspaper, the *Cape Socialist*, was issued in 1904 (from the same offices as *New Age*).

A terrible depression had followed the Anglo-Boer War, and the militant policies of the SDF were gaining support. The Federation staged a number of unemployment demonstrations in 1906. A photograph of a 13-man SDF

National Liberation and Socialist Movements, 1870-1914 **43**

and trade union deputation to Parliament shows that one of its members
was a Coloured, John Tobin, who later became a shameless renegade.

It was at the height of this campaign in 1906 that, for the first time,
South African socialists found themselves jailed for their beliefs. *Cape
Socialist* editor, A. Needham, and N.B. Levinson, a Committee member,
were charged with incitement and held without bail. Defence funds were
set up in Durban and Johannesburg where, the SDF minutes record con-
descendingly, "there were a good number of socialists, but no aggressive
public propaganda work was being done." Even the Mayor of Cape Town
contributed to the Defence Fund and with the triumphant acquittal of the
accused, the SDF found popularity greater than ever. A steady flow of
recruits was drawn in.

By 1906, the socialists were holding meetings using no fewer than four
languages — "Dutch, Malay, Kaffir and English" — and Coloured socialists were taking part in committee discussion. The APO and the socialists
were on the friendliest terms, not only in Cape Town but also in Kimberley,
where the Labour leader Trembath had been supported by the APO in the
municipal elections. The crucial 1909 conference of the APO, at which
the Draft Act of Union was discussed, was held in the Socialist Hall in
Buitenkant Street, Cape Town.

When the socialist leader Tom Mann visited South Africa in 1910, the
APO backed his

> vigorous appeal to all wage-earners to organise and present a united
> front to the power of capitalism which ever sought to enslave the
> wage-earner. We are pleased to see indications here and there
> throughout the Coloured world of the superlative need of organisa-
> tion being gradually recognised by wage-earners; but in South Africa
> there is little evidence of any such desirable lesson being learnt.
> Instead of that, we notice increasing tokens of division, distinct
> sectional hatred and antagonism. Added to all the ignorance that
> prevails amongst even skilled white artisans as to the necessity for
> integrating all their unions, there is a strong prejudice against their
> Coloured co-workers. . . It is time that the white labour leaders told
> their rank and file that the driving of white and Coloured people into
> separate kraals will play into the hands of their enslavers.

Who was South Africa's first prominent non-European socialist? Almost
certainly Dr. Abdurahman.

In October 1911, a white socialist, Arthur Noon, addressed an APO
meeting on "Socialism and the Native Question" and the APO reports Dr.
Abdurahman's contribution to the discussion as follows:

> As a public man he could not help being Socialist, for all men who
> read and thought and endeavoured to improve the position of the
> lower classes of society were inevitably driven to Socialism. The
> condition of the working man today seemed to him to be worse than

44 People's History

that of a slave, for the Coloured workman was not only virtually a slave of the capitalist, but had in addition to look after himself, whereas the health and condition of the slave was always a matter of serious concern to the master. Yet the workmen had in their hands the best possible weapon for bettering their condition, viz: co-operation. With co-operation the Native and Coloured labourers of South Africa could bring the white capitalists to their knees within 48 hours.

But although the conditions existed for the establishment at this early stage of close links between the national movement and the most militant white socialists, the white socialists failed badly.

From the white Labour Party in the Transvaal came a blast of the most vile racialism in no way distinguishable from modern Nationalist Party propaganda. Instead of turning from this in disgust and seeing that no party whose spokesman utilised the crudest racialism could have anything in common with socialism, those who were opposed to racialism decided to remain loyal to the Labour Party.

The close relations developing between white socialists and the non-European liberatory organisations disappeared overnight with the decision of white Labour throughout the new Union to follow the leadership of Transvaal Labour and accept its colour bar policies in the first general election of 1910. Labour won no Cape seats in the election and Maginess, the President of the Cape Labour Party, complained bitterly at an APO meeting the following year: "It was largely due to their President (Dr. Abdurahman) that the Labour Party of that Province was unrepresented in the Union Parliament."

This APO meeting revealed that there were those present who had a far deeper understanding than Maginess. The Coloured workers mocked Maginess' praise for Smuts with whom Labour was in alliance, and explained to him that Smuts was by nature a capitalist. Dr. Abdurahman summed up his feelings in the words "the whole Labour Party and the white workers on the Rand are about the most selfish lot I have heard of."

3. The First World War and the Socialist Movement in South Africa

The war of 1914-18 gave white socialists the necessary stimulus to new ways of thought. The Second Socialist International, to which the South African Labour Party affiliated in 1913, had at its Basle Conference the previous year adopted an Anti-War Manifesto, in the drafting of which Lenin and Rosa Luxembourg had been dominant figures. The South African Labour Party had endorsed the anti-war resolution without reservations.

In 1914 the great powers went to war and the leaders of socialist parties everywhere turned their backs on the Basle resolution. All over the world, the Marxist minorities in the socialist movement adhered to the International's resolution and split from, or were driven out of, their political homes. The splinter groups formed their own parties, and these in turn formed the base of the new Communist Parties.

That was the exact pattern followed in South Africa. On 2 August, after the fighting between Germany and France had begun, but before Britain had declared war, the South African Labour Party's Administrative Council, of which Bill Andrews was chairman, adopted a resolution in which it condemned "a war which can only benefit the international arms manufacturers' ring and other enemies of the working class, and appeals to the workers of the world to organise and refrain from participating in this unjust war."

Similar resolutions were adopted by the SA Industrial Federation, the Social Democratic Federation and the Social Democratic Party in Durban. But Wyburgh, editor of the Labour Party's *The Worker* defied this decision and used the newspaper as a vehicle of enthusiastic pro-war propaganda. He was backed to the hilt by Party leader Creswell.

Just as was the case all over the world, the great majority of the workers responded to the war hysteria and flocked to the colours, ready to die in battle against the workers of other countries in a cause which was in no way their own. Within two months the Industrial Federation had rescinded its anti-war resolution, and branch after branch of the Labour Party had rejected the Administrative Council's stand.

War-on-War and the ISL

The advance-guard of the Labour Party, however, fought hard. In September, they launched the War-on-War League. Colin Wade was Chairman, P.R. Roux Secretary, and S.P. Bunting Treasurer. A foundation member was David Ivon Jones, the Labour Party's Secretary. The first issue of the League's paper — the *War on War Gazette* — a printed four-page weekly,

46 People's History

appeared on 19 September 1914. Condemning the Labour patriots who had succumbed to the press propaganda that election victory would go only to the "flaggy-waggiest", and who were supporting the war purely for election purposes, S.P. Bunting wrote in the first issue of the *Gazette* that even on this basis the pro-war stand would fail. "We are all impressed with the decisive value of the Dutch vote. The Dutch are, naturally, not British chauvinists; many of you think you are going to win them by flaunting the Union Jack. Will you not rather alienate them? And you know what that means to the future hope of the Party."

Labour's pro-war stand probably did more than anything else to ensure that the Party would never again be a force, even among the white workers in South Africa. It amounted to an abandonment to the Nationalists of the Afrikaner workers who were gradually entering the labour market and who were very soon to dominate it.

Bill Andrews was not among the League's sponsors. It was one of Andrews' characteristics to hesitate long and ponder very deeply before associating himself with any stand which would be unpopular in the trade union movement. His biographer, R.K. Cope, wrote in *Comrade Bill* that "he was opposed to the war, and yet he knew that to stand out and fight against the current working-class opinion would shatter the great movement he had shared so largely in building. The whole weight of tradition and upbringing as a skilled British artisan were against him, while there was added his responsibility to the electorate as a Member of Parliament. Strongest of all was his lifelong training in the working-class movement to work with the team, the union or the party, even when disagreeing with decisions. Such weighty considerations were in the scales on the one hand, while on the other was only the distant light of international socialism. In the whole of the British Empire, but a handful of Labour leaders had chosen the latter course."

At the special parliamentary session in September, Andrews voted with the Labour Party and the government for war. Only one Labour MP, W.B. Madeley, abstained, but he too later swung into line in full support of the war. Shortly afterwards Andrews admitted his mistake, made no excuses for it, and took his place among the anti-war advance guard. The League's constitution was essentially pacifist. The sole requirement for membership was that applicants must pledge themselves to oppose this or any other war at all times and costs.

In actual fact, however, the League's statements on the war were based squarely on an understanding of socialist internationalism and were Marxist in approach. The *Gazette* was censored out of existence on 28 November 1914, but not before it had played its part in mobilising an anti-war majority at the Annual Conference of the Labour Party at the end of December that year. The majority, according to Cope, "in the interests of unity", decided not to impose their will on the Conference but to put forward a resolution allowing everyone "freedom of conscience" in his stand on the war. They were influenced by their strong doubt that the

The First World War and the Socialist Movement in South Africa   47

majority opinion was an accurate reflection of the views of the rank and file. The resolution was adopted unanimously and Andrews and Jones were re-elected Chairman and Secretary of the Party.

With their new awareness of international working-class solidarity, the War-on-War-ites organised that year — for the first time in South Africa — the celebration of May Day with "a picturesque but attenuated procession through Johannesburg, ending with a meeting in the rain on Market Square, enlivened by a small band. In the evening there was a social at the Grand National Hotel" (*International*, 6 May 1921).

The sacrifice of principles to preserve unity rarely pays dividends. With the approach of the general elections and the certainty that in the war fervour of the time an anti-war policy would lose votes, Creswell and other right-wing leaders swung into action against the left. The daily press, which had hitherto completely ignored the War-on-War League, began to launch violent attacks on it, and Creswell himself issued a manifesto condemning the anti-war leaders for "refusing to do their duty to the country". The need "to see the war through was imperative by the necessities of the Empire."

In reply Bill Andrews, Bunting, Jones, Gideon Botha, Forrester Brown, George Mason and 13 other Labour Party members issued a leaflet called "The Labour Party's Duty in the War". Labour's duty, they said, was "not at all hazards to win the next elections, but to stand firm to the principle of peace and to the identity of interests of the international working class in war and in peace."

At a special conference in August 1915, with the general election looming large in the minds of the delegates, Creswell's policy won by 82 votes to 30. The right-wing leaders did not worry their heads about unity. They pushed through a resolution "to support the Imperial Government wholeheartedly in the prosecution of the war" and in a very short time all the leftists had been expelled or had resigned rather than sign the pledge to support this policy insisted upon by the Creswell supporters. As a result, the Labour Party lost its three leading officials and seven other members of its executive. According to Cope, "a remarkable array of businessmen, stockbrokers and office-seekers from other parties found their way onto the Executive. Unity, principles and championship of the working class were sacrificed for the sake of the elections." The left wing was driven out as a splinter group and had to begin the painful process of building an organisation from scratch.

At first they believed that they could continue their fight from within the Labour Party, and, though resigning from its executive, formed themselves into an International League within the Party and launched, on 10 September 1915, the first issue of their own weekly newspaper, the *International*, under the editorship of David Ivon Jones.

Bill Andrews resigned from Parliament and announced his intention of fighting a bye-election, and another of the League's founders, J.A. Clark, similarly resigned his provincial council seat.

48   People's History

The League, at the proposal of Bunting, sent a letter drafted by him to the ISL's British counterparts proposing the formation of a new international organisation. The letter was headlined in the *International* (17 May 1915), perhaps just a little brashly, "The League's Message to Europe — A World Party." South African socialists were therefore among the first to call for the formation of the Third International. In actual fact, unknown to the ISL because of the war censorship, a conference similar to that proposed in the ISL letter had already been held at Zimmerwald in Switzerland, early in September.

On 22 September, the League decided by an overwhelming majority to sever all connection with the Labour Party, and the International Socialist League (ISL), direct forerunner of the Communist Party, was born. Andrews was elected Chairman, Jones Secretary. Bunting was one of the members of the management committee. Eight branches of the Labour Party came over to the League.

The ISL and "The Great and Fascinating Problem of the Native"

Towards the end of 1915, the most advanced white socialists, led by David Ivon Jones and S.P. Bunting, began to urge upon the International Socialist League that it pay attention to the needs of the Africans.

The third issue of the *International* (24 July 1915) — the one in which the formation of the ISL was announced — was the first to mention the non-white population. The paper recorded, on its back page, that as the result of the refusal of the Labour Party conference to adopt a resolution permitting the enrolment of non-European members, the *Cape Times* had been able to make anti-Labour election propaganda in the Cape where the Coloured vote was a very important factor; thereafter the Cape Town Labour Party candidates had given a special pledge "to agitate for the extension of the franchise to all civilised men, white or Coloured, throughout South Africa."

This, the *International* noted, was "directly contrary to the Party Constitution" and it wondered whether the Cape members would be treated as strictly as those in the Transvaal who had refused to go along with the Party's pro-war policy. But, on the merits of the Cape action, the *International* was still non-committal. It satisfied itself with the remark that "there is no doubt that a radical re-investigation of the Coloured problem is necessary. The Labour Party's Coloured programme is fast becoming antiquated."

In the same column there is revealed a similar lack of certainty in the approach to the Afrikaner workers. Commenting on the decision of two English-speaking Labourites, Nield and Connolly, to join the Nationalists, the paper says: "When Messrs. Nield and Connolly, and perhaps Postma, get fed up with the Nationalists, as they assuredly will if they recover their socialism, let them not come out without a decent following of Africanders.

Perhaps, after all, the only way to socialise the Africander people is by the growth of a native Africander Socialist Party."

Though the *International* was crystal clear, despite the utmost jingoist propaganda-spewing hatred of the Germans, that on the world scene all workers were brothers, German, British, French and Italian alike, and should be bound together in a single world workers' party, the need demonstrable by the identical arguments for a single South African workers' party of Briton, Afrikaner, African, Coloured, Indian was something which even the most advanced of the white socialists had to discover and lay bare with an immense effort.

Bunting wrote of the international situation: "many of us are only just discovering that socialism, to be effective, must be international. We knew it, and had forgotten it, before. The limpid philosophy of the *Communist Manifesto* had been muddled away by state education and a commonplace press, both emphasising the history of the ruling class only, both idolising the Nation" (24 September 1915).

He might well have used identical words to describe the rediscovery which was just beginning that within South Africa too, socialism, to be effective, must be international.

How far even an enlightened man like Bunting still had to go before the rediscovery would be complete was illustrated by a later passage in the same article when, condemning all nationalism, he commented that "our natives prefer continued submission to their own exploiters in the sacred cause of a Black and White crusade, rather than co-operate with white philanthropists who would better the conditions of their labour."

But the rediscovery process was underway. On 1 October 1915, there appeared in the *International* an editorial which marked the first bold step towards a truly socialist policy. Though unsigned, the editorial bears the clear stamp of the style of David Ivon Jones.

"We have glorious tasks to perform for South Africa and socialism during the coming years. The nature of these tasks will happily prevent our being spoilt by overmuch public applause. A dilettante and exclusive internationalism will however have to be guarded against. The International Socialist League will have the more significance the more it tends to pull the working class of South Africa with it. This involves a corresponding interest in industrial organisation with a view to giving it an international outlook.

"Moreover, an internationalism which does not concede the fullest rights which the native working class is capable of claiming will be a sham. One of the justifications for our withdrawal from the Labour Party is that it gives us untrammelled freedom to deal, regardless of political fortunes, with the great and fascinating problem of the native. If the League deal resolutely in consonance with socialist principles with the native question, it will succeed in shaking South African capitalism to its foundations. Then and not till then, shall we be able to talk about the South African proletariat

50 People's History

in our international relations, not till we free the native can we hope to free the white."

In a news round-up on the back page, Jones drove home his point. A feature of the League's Sunday afternoon meetings on the Market Square, he reported, "is the little knot of interested natives and Coloured men always there. Some buy the *International*. Let who will sneer, nothing convinces us of the universality of our appeal so much as this. We shall never be on bedrock until we can command the attention of the dark-skinned proletariat of South Africa."

It is true that implicit in the editorial was a notion which bedevilled many white socialists right up to the beginning of the present decade — that the whites would win socialism for the blacks. Years were to pass before South African socialists — including, of course the black socialists whose number grew steadily over the years — began to understand that the very opposite was true. It was the Africans who would bring socialism and freedom to the whites. Nevertheless, Ivon Jones' editorial marked an important milestone, and in every subsequent issue of the *International* he stressed this new-sung theme, strongly supported by Bunting and cautiously, almost painfully, by Andrews too.

Obstacles to a progressive policy

The chief obstacle the progressives had to overcome was the fear of most Transvaal socialists that any recognition of the African as an equal would doom the ISL to stagnation as a small "debating society" without influence among white workers. In the Transvaal, where white socialists had identified themselves with Labour's colour-bar policies, they had become a power in the trade union movement. And their policies seemed to be justified by the fact that white workers had engaged in a series of militant struggles against the bosses. On the other hand, where, as in Cape Town and Durban, the socialists had refused to go along with the white-labour policy, they had shrunk into small and uninfluential bodies. To turn against the colour bar appeared to result in the loss of all influence with the white workers, and this, in the eyes of most white socialists, was to cut oneself off from the entire labour movement.

The African proletariat was still relatively very weak and it was most difficult for a white trade unionist to visualise a labour movement based on the Africans. In a few years' time, with the meteoric rise of Clement Kadalie's great Industrial and Commercial Workers' Union, Africans were to demonstrate how great a force they were, but, until they saw it happening, there were few white trade union leaders who believed it possible.

An advanced socialist — one who knew something of dialectical materialism and of political economy — would have understood the inevitability of the rapid growth of the African proletariat. But it must be clearly understood that most of those in the new War-on-War League and then the ISL were not advanced marxists. They were socialists of many hues — Fabians, co-operators, syndicalists, anarchists and a host of others includ-

The First World War and the Socialist Movement in South Africa 51

ing pacifists and conscientious objectors. They were outside the mainstream of socialist theoretical ferment then taking place in Europe, and being in the main new immigrants, were not sufficiently inside the mainstream of South African life to enable them to make any fundamental theoretical contributions as South African socialists.

On the war issue, however, every man who was a sincere socialist — no matter what brand of socialism it was — stood united. And as a result, the very thing which militants had so feared came to pass. The anti-war socialists were stripped of all power in the white labour movement. They became a small, isolated group. White workers broke up their public meetings, tore up their newspapers and reviled them.

In South Africa's second general election in October 1915 the ISL stood two candidates: Bill Andrews contested Georgetown (Germiston), the seat he had won for Labour three years before, and A. Clark, Langlaagte. They lost their deposits resoundingly, with 82 and 58 votes respectively. But the Labour Party, in spite of its pro-war policy was, in the words of the *International* (22 October 1915), "discovered by the electorate in its swindle." Of its 44 candidates, only three were returned. Creswell, who stood, as was possible at that time, for two seats, lost both.

The ISL was not slow in pointing out the moral. "We trust that this lesson will not be lost on these faithful Labour voters that Labour can never compete with the Unionists in jingoism . . . if the Labour Party is not international socialist, it has no right to exist. This is the verdict of the people. . . Had the Party suffered the same defeat on the policy which above all others it is in the world to consumate — international socialism — what is now a disaster would have been but a step forward on the straight road of working class emancipation" (*International* 22 October 1915).

The old ways died hard: The 1916 conference

Even though the only people who would listen to socialist speakers were African and Coloured workers, the old ways died hard.

At the end of October 1915, P.L.C. Clark of the Durban Social Democratic Party wrote to the *International* (12 November 1915) commenting on a Johannesburg proposal that Durban and Cape Town socialists should link up with the ISL. An obstacle in the way of this, as far as Durban was concerned, he said, was the fact that the ISL had expressed

> no clear attitude as regards what is known as the "white labour policy". If that policy is part of the socialism which the League is to conserve, it is not in accordance, I think, with international principles and policy of the Durban Socialist Party, and would be a very great barrier in linking up. The Socialist International Party knows and should know, neither race, colour, nor creed. In its reply the following week, the *International* (19 November 1915), rather surprisingly, avoided the issues. The ISL would "come to clear declarations on these matters that agitate our (Durban and Cape Town) comrades, not through academic studies and debating so-

52 People's History

cieties, but by emerging from actual grips with capitalism and militarism, emerging with mandates from the struggle rather than from the study.

This was an excellent statement of the interrelationship of theory and practice, but it must have left the Durban and Cape Town comrades pondering on the type of "mandate from the struggle" the ISL would require before arriving at the theory that socialists should know neither race, colour, nor creed.

In December, indignant at the promise made by the trade union leaders to Smuts that they would assist to the utmost in the war effort, Jones saw that the source of this betrayal of the workers lay in the colour bar system. In the *International* (3 December 1915) he wrote:

> Slaves to a higher oligarchy, the white workers of South Africa themselves in turn batten on a lower slave class, the native races. Himself kicked by his capitalist masters, the "correct" and accepted attitude towards the "nigger" is to kick him, to teach him his place, and to stand no impudence (meaning "independence"). Gingerly attempts to show him that in the extension of freedom for the native lies the only salvation of the white worker invariably aroused storms of execration. And thus has the South African Labour movement grown up, more intolerant towards the native slave than any working class in the world, and consequently more parasitical than any other. To such a movement, talk of the international unity of the working class could never arouse sincere response among a rank and file so placed.

He foresaw a new movement which "will break the bounds of craft and race and sex. It will be founded on the rock of the meanest proletarian who toils for a master. It will be wide as humanity. It will recognise no bounds of craft, no exclusions of colour. The old order and the old leaders have been tested and found wanting. The capitalists are demolishing them to make room for the finer movement that is to come."

In January 1916 the League held its first conference. In a pre-conference statement in the *International* (10 December 1915), it announced that conference "will not enter into the laborious work, and perhaps superfluous work, of drawing up detailed planks of a party platform in the old style. The war may brush all these into the limbo of quack remedies. Indeed, at the present abnormal rate of development, both in the methods of capital and the education of the working class, it would be unwise to enter into the details of a policy."

One can infer from this remarkable paragraph an acute reluctance to come out with a clear statement of policy on the issue of the colour bar. Men of firm principle, the ISL leaders must have known that when they took a stand it would be the stand already urged by Jones and Bunting, for there was no reply to their argument. They were reluctant, not because

The First World War and the Socialist Movement in South Africa   53

they feared to take an unpopular stand — their staunch opposition to the war in the midst of the war hysteria is sufficient proof of this.

As yet no-one had even raised the possibility of their turning to the African worker as the basis of their socialist strength. A stand against the colour bar seemed to doom them to becoming the sort of small "debating society" which the ISL trade union leaders so openly scorned. There must indeed have been a sigh of relief when one of the ISLers came forward with a draft proposal that it was not necessary to draw up "detailed planks of a party platform", and that it was "unwise to enter into the details of a policy."

But although it prudently sidestepped the key question raised in Clark's letter — support of opposition to the white labour policy — the pre-conference statement did come out boldly, and infinitely far ahead of any other European body, in a round condemnation of the oppression of the Africans and a call for their organisation as workers. It declared: "The workers must be told to cease from tyranny. They must, if they would be free, cease from the enslavement of their coloured and native fellow workers. Organisations of the workers must start from the lowest fool of a poor Kaffir who works for a baas, and has to crawl to his master more or less like any member of the Amalgamated Society of Engineers. The first demand of the movement must be for freedom for the Kaffir. Abolition of the indentured and compound system, and the gradual but systematic abolition of the Pass."

The Management Committee put forward a proposal "that we encourage the organisation of the workers on industrial or class lines, irrespective of race, colour or creed, as the most effective means of providing the necessary force for the emancipation of the workers." This proposal was greeted by the International as "the great revolutionary fruit of an otherwise pointless agitation. This will be the permanent advance made in the outlook of the Labour Movement. It will attempt a change not only in our attitude towards the slave races of South Africa, enlisting their co-operation in the emancipation of Labour, but will shift its adherence from political to industrial organisation as the primary method of wresting power from capitalism."

At the Conference itself, attended by 32 delegates, Bunting, never one for diplomacy, took the bull by the horns and put forward a resolution ("Petition of Rights for the Native"): "That this League affirm that the emancipation of the working class requires the abolition of all forms of native indenture, compound and passport systems; and the lifting of the native worker to the political and industrial status of the white."

A delegate quickly moved that the matter be referred to a committee for a report on "the proper socialist policy on native affairs" and Colin Wade put forward "biological evidence" on the inferiority of the Africans. When this proposal to delay the decision was defeated, Wade moved the addition of a clause that the ISL would, until the Africans' status had been so lifted, endeavour "to prevent the increase of the native wage workers,

54 People's History

and to assist the existing native wage workers to free themselves from the wage system."

The resolution as amended — Bunting and Jones appear to have accepted the amendment — was carried by "an overwhelming majority", and socialist theory, after a momentary grab at the sun, fell back into Alice-in-Wonderland.

The First Contacts Between the ISL and Africans

A week before the first ISL Conference, 3,000 Africans at the Van Ryn mines went on strike. According to the *International* (14 January 1916), they "did well for their race, but did better for the working class. The spectacle of the white workers being backed out by their black slave is an unparalleled phenomenon."

The ISL resolution to try to lock out black workers from industry "until they are lifted to the status of the whites" was unfortunately a paralleled phenomenon. It was paralleled by the numerous occasions on which progressives, over-anxious for unity with the Colin Wades, permitted them to turn clear common sense into arrant nonsense.

Nevertheless, the conference resolution discussed above was a go-ahead signal for those who were trying to turn white socialist attention towards Africans. The Johannesburg Central Branch began to make a feature of "native affairs" in its lecture syllabus, and February 1916 saw a landmark in the history of the liberatory movement — the first coming together in the Transvaal of white socialists and the African National Congress.

The occasion was a socialist meeting on the Land Act addressed by one of Father Huddleston's predecessors of the Community of the Resurrection, Father Francis Hill. He, correctly, described the Act as being aimed at driving Africans out to work for whites. Present at the meeting was Saul Msane, a leading figure in the ANC and one of the delegates sent by them in 1913 to protest against the Act, and several other ANC leaders. Msane told the meeting that so strictly was the ANC observing its pledge not to criticise the government for the duration of the war that he did not feel that he should say anything about the Act.

This meeting, coming within weeks of the ISL resolution to "prevent the increase of the Native wage workers" served to reveal dramatically to the more advanced socialists the nonsense of their resolution. The Land Act had killed any illusions anyone might have about keeping the working class white. The contact was showing that white socialists had at least as much to learn from black congressmen as the ANC had to learn from them.

In an article prompted by Father Hill's lecture, Bunting expressed the view that "this unjust law aroused such indignation among the natives of the Union that we were in danger of a South African, if not a Pan-African, war between natives and whites had not the European war intervened and

The First World War and the Socialist Movement in South Africa   55

been judiciously used by the Union and Home governments to extort a temporary acquiesence" (*International*, 18 February 1916).

So remote was even a man of Bunting's calibre from the realities of the non-European organisations that he too thought in the conventional terms of a sudden black-white conflagration involving the whole continent. But Bunting, like Father Hill, saw clearly the purpose of the Land Act — to drive the African "cheap, helpless, and unorganised, into the labour market" — and the importance of the Act in killing stone dead the idea of keeping the African out of the white economy. The African was coming into the labour market and this was a fact which could not be ignored.

Bunting introduced the article by quoting the recent ISL resolution on the need to endeavour to prevent the increase of the African workers. It did not appear to be a criticism of the resolution, but the long concluding sentence is one of the best examples of the beautiful clarity of insight and expression which occasionally broke through the complex and rambling style which was Bunting's — a mass of classical allusions, Latin and obscure poetry which sometimes made the divining of his meaning a job for a quiz kid.

"Perhaps if Marx had lived today in Johannesburg he would have founded his International Association of Working Men, not on the well paid craft unionists who themselves fatten on native labour and form the "Federation", but rather on such class-conscious elements as he could find among the black workers, who groan under a hundred special and serious disabilities of their own, in addition to those attaching to all workers — disabilities which naturally hinder them from joining up with the white, and hinder the white from linking with them, who form the bulk of the South African Proletariat" (*International*, 18 February 1916).

Now the role of the African worker became a regular editorial theme in the *International* and as the matter was argued, the nonsense of the amendment to the original Bunting resolution became apparent and its principle was clearly exposed.

On social relations, however, the white socialists had not yet broken free. An *International* (5 May 1916) article spoke of "an ethnological tendency. . . which makes for the natural apartness of white and black." Capitalism had "tampered" with this and brought them together. Socialists, by destroying capitalism, would allow natural apartness to reassert itself. "The way to healthy social segregation is through industrial co-operation."

In June 1916, an African addressed a Johannesburg socialist meeting for the first time. ANC leader Robert Grendon, editor of the Congress organ *Abantu-Batho*, spoke to the ISL on "The link between black and white," with a large number of Africans present. They startled the ISL stalwarts by proposing that the meeting begin with a motion of condolence at the recent death of one of the Allied field marshals. Jones, who was in the chair, turned the proposal down. Saul Msane, in his contribution to the discussion, said that the important thing was to educate white workers.

56 People's History

"The trade unions had been formed to fight the Natives. Let them remove restrictions and the Natives would join the unions."

The Grendon meeting was roundly condemned in the daily papers. One Labour Party MP called for the deportation of the socialists for telling the Africans to organise. Now, as socialists and African liberatory leaders began to meet, it became all the clearer that each had something to contribute to the other. When, in June 1916, a number of Europeans were murdered by African gangsters in Florida and white passions were aroused. The ISL issued a statement condemning the lynch hysteria in forthright terms.

In the following month, the ISL chalked up another first — the first article by an African in a socialist publication in South Africa. Herbert Msane contributed four paragraphs to the *International* (21 July 1916) on the origin of the Ethiopian Movement and how it split from the white Wesleyans. By then, the policy of the ISL as expressed through the *International* was firmly established as one of solidarity with Africans as fellow-workers in a common struggle, although a beginning had not yet been made to the finding of effective means of putting the policy into effect.

From then on, most of the hedging and indecision disappeared and the socialist principle was reiterated time and again in such clear terms as this: "The job is to create among workers the feeling of unity with all those who labour for wages, irrespective of what pigment may have been injected by nature into the labourer's skin, or what tools he may or may not have learnt to use. That is the only unity" (*International*, 22 October 1916).

Not all opposition to this view had yet disappeared from the League. Colin Wade was still arguing at public meetings that "too much equality might throw back the movement. The 'biological' factor had to be considered. The native had a long history to go through to deserve equality. Besides he was too contented, and from the contented no movement could be built. To bring down barriers would bring down wages" (*International*, 25 August 1916). But, although Wade's amendment making nonsense of Bunting's resolution had been carried all but unanimously only seven months before, his views had now clearly become minority ones in the League.

In August 1916, on the second anniversary of the declaration of war, the League issued a call for peace written by Bunting [entitled in his characteristic style: "Let Saints on Earth in Concert Sing."] A week later, the police raided the *International*'s office, arrested Jones and seized the few remaining copies of the leaflet. Bunting, the paper's lawyer, was phoned for help, but as soon as he arrived, he too was arrested. The charge was the distribution of "matter calculated to excite public feeling."

In the Transvaal municipal elections of October 1916, the ISL issued an election manifesto which, for the first time, included a call to white workers "to stretch out the hand of industrial unity to the native workers."

The fight for the admission of Africans into white trade unions was by no means a futile one. Meeting in October 1916, delegates of the various trade unions in the building industry who came together to discuss the formation of a single industrial union favoured the admission of Coloured men into the union. The Engineers already had such a clause, although it was not put into effect.

The goal at which the ISL began to aim was the putting of these theoretical provisions into practice.

The ISL and the National Liberatory Struggle

Abantu-Batho, the ANC journal, never notable for its militancy, was, during the war years, particularly docile. But, in November 1916, there appeared an article "Native Drudgery" which revealed that the awakening of white socialists was being paralleled by that of African nationalists. There is no room for doubt that this was no coincidence, but was the direct result of the first contacts between them which 1916 had witnessed: "The unskilled labour and all kinds of drudgery both at the mines and in the urban areas, are done by the native people. . . They form the major population of the country and they belong to the working class. They are the mainstay of the country's industries and the backbone of the land's prosperity. . . and they are the most worked and the least paid."

After describing the lot of the African ("a European thinks more of his dog than he does of the black man who does all the work for his comfort"), the long hours of heavy work, the low pay, the editorial concluded very lamely: "We would ask the Transvaal Native Council to inquire into the question of how natives are employed especially in big towns, with a view to approaching the Native Affairs Department on the matter. In the absence of organised Labour Unions among the natives, it is suggested that the inquiry should be directed to hours of work, rate of pay, general treatment, particularly of women and girls."

This article turned the attention of the ISL for the first time to the question of the national liberatory struggle as distinct from the class struggle.

Jones was away ill and the editorial on this topic which appeared on 1 December 1916 was probably written by Bunting. He thought that, for a time at least, the Africans would be "overdistracted with political struggles for status, franchise, parliamentary representation, capitalist state education, and the like — under the leadership of intellectuals prone to batten on the movement." But he predicted that the time would come when, having become more predominantly concerned with the economic struggle in industry, the African movement would take on "the clear revolutionary socialist character, and at the same time become self-led, class conscious enough to dispense with the middleman, and powerfully enough organised to defy the inevitable attempts at repression and reaction by a government alarmed too late."

This is a prediction which could have been made true by now had the socialists, in the years ahead, not failed at crucial times to reach the heights

58 People's History

of clarity and understanding demanded of them in their relations with the Congress movement.

In this first article on the subject, Bunting dismissed *Abantu-Batho* — "as the Johannesburg native paper, edited (consciously or unconsciously) under the aegis of the Native Affairs Department and capitalist class." This was not the way to win friends and influence people. But it is a tribute to Bunting that his blunt words were due to natural bluntness and not to a failure to see the potential importance of the national movement.

"The increasing understanding among white workers that natives are their fellow workers. . . coupled with the opening of the native eye as foreshadowed in the article quoted, is big with promise for the future of the Labour movement in South Africa. We invite the white Labour union and the Transvaal Native Council to seize every opportunity of conferring together on this common movement of theirs."

The awakening was proceeding apace. At the end of 1916, the government increased its endeavours to recruit Africans for heavy work — non-combatant — in the army with an appeal "what will you say after the war when your Father, King George, shall want to know what you have done to assist him in the war?"

An African, B.G. Phooko, wrote an open letter in reply in the *International* (15 December 1916) attacking the government's lack of concern for the welfare of the Africans: "You ought to know that the financial prosperity of South Africa is due to the Native labourer. . . Again you ought to know that if the natives of the land would (to use labour language) down tools for one day, the whole superstructure of beautiful white South Africa would come down in a terrible crash."

By the time of the second ISL Conference in January 1917, Bunting had reached out towards a realisation of the idea which came hardest to white socialists — that they would not bring socialism to blacks, that indeed there would not even merely be black allies in the movement to socialism — but that Africans would inevitably dominate the entire movement.

The Conference decided to fight Creswell in a parliamentary by-election then due in Troyeville and Colin Wade was nominated as candidate. His election manifesto was mainly devoted to the demand for peace, but it included a call to the workers to unite irrespective of colour or creed, and an attack on the Labour Party's white labour policy because "willy nilly, the native workers are here to stay." Thus, Wade's election manifesto quietly rescinded the decision of the first ISL Conference on this point.

He got 32 votes. Creswell won with 800 odd. The socialists had hit rock bottom with the white electorate — a position they were to maintain with equanimity throughout the years ahead.

But the ISL had no regrets. Jones commented in the *International* (2 February 1917) that the "ISL must find its economic basis in the growing mass of propertyless industrial proletariat. But this great mass of the proletariat. . . happens in South Africa to be Black and therefore disfran-

The First World War and the Socialist Movement in South Africa 59

chised and socially outcast. . . whether it be 32 votes or 2 votes, this must increasingly become the political issue for us: Freedom to combine and political rights for the native worker."

Soon after the by-election, the Native Administration Bill was introduced to place Africans at the mercy of the Native Affairs Department, without recourse to the courts. The Governor-General was given powers, by proclamation, to make laws affecting almost every aspect of the life of Africans. The ISL called a protest meeting in March in the Trades Hall, a historic meeting for it was the first political action taken by the socialists on a matter not directly linked with white workers — a political protest against a law affecting Africans.

The League was beginning its struggle to win the Africans to its ranks, and press advertisements inviting all "irrespective of race, colour or creed" to come to the meeting resulted in a packed hall. The crowd was, however, mainly white, with a sprinkling of Africans. Jones was chairman and Saul Msane was the main speaker, followed by Bunting and Horatio Mbelle. "I hail you as conquerors of race prejudice", said Msane in his opening words. A motion condemning the Act in the strongest terms was carried unanimously.

In their May Day celebrations that year, the ISL made sure that there was, for the first time, an African billed to speak on the City Hall steps — Horatio Mbelle. But a large crowd of soldiers and civilians turned out to prevent the meeting and thronged the City Hall steps menacingly, long before it was due to begin. Prudently the ISL called the rally off. Bunting and Jones were later manhandled by a group of soldiers and rescued by an officer, and several other ISLers were also assaulted. The evening social, held in the Masonic Hall, was similarly broken up. The mob violence was not directed against Mbelle's inclusion among the speakers, but by the mounting pro-war enthusiasm of the time.

As a response to the challenge of the May Day mobs, the ISL decided to nominate Andrews and Bunting for the Provincial Council elections. Andrews stood for Benoni, which had the reputation of being the reddest and most militant centre on the Rand; Bunting for Commissioner Street, Johannesburg, where there was a high proportion of Jewish immigrants in the electorate.

The issue of the *International* (18 May 1917) which announced this also declared: "The most acute form the class war can take in South Africa today is the preparing of the minds of the people to the inevitable coming of the power of the native proletariat, and making its coming beneficent to all. And 'the people' includes the native workers." But the League's lengthy election manifesto, nevertheless made no mention of the black worker or the colour bar. It dealt only with the war issue and had as its slogan "Down with War and Militarism! Up with the Social Revolution!"

Bunting, in fact, tried to make the Provincial Council election in Commissioner Street as a vote of confidence in the Russian workers in the historic period between the February and October Revolutions. "We have," he wrote in *International* (8 June 1917) "the glorious opportunity, by voting Socialist, of associating ourselves unmistakably with the magnificent lead of the Workmen's and Soldiers Committees (the Soviets). Shall we let it slip?. . . Think of the day when your children will ask 'Daddy what did you do in the great Revolution?'" This was an allusion to the current recruiting poster: "What did you do in the great war, Daddy?" Three hundred and fifty-five would be able to reply: "Son, I voted for Andrews in Benoni." Seventy-one voted for Bunting.

The tactic of not mentioning the thorny issue of the colour bar in the manifesto did not succeed in keeping it out of the election discussions. The Labour Party used the ISL's "native policy" as its trump card in its anti-ISL argument. "The Labour Party is entirely against equal rights for white and black . . . vote for Andrews and you vote for the downfall of the workers and the blanket or kaffir vote."

With its lack of white support emphasised once again, the ISL was still making little headway among Africans. The ISL meetings were not drawing white working-class audiences, "while, as for native workers," the *International* (29 June 1917) commented, "notwithstanding repeated advertisements welcoming 'all irrespective of colour,' they are still too shy and suspicious of the whites to attend except on rare occasions."

At the meeting on Market Square the following week, to mark the anniversary of the killing of the workers in the strike of July 1913, however, the *International* (13 July 1917) found it "most gratifying to see a number of natives, men and women, in the hall, a feature which, when it develops will inevitably widen our speakers' outlook and make real our professed repudiation of race or colour distinctions. Let each of our speakers ask himself: 'Did my address interest or appeal to those natives in the audience? If not, is it their fault, or is it my fault for dealing with purely white man's affairs, pitching my key to an audience of shopkeepers instead of proletarians?'"

After the Benoni election, Andrews set down, for the first time, his thoughts on "the position of the native and coloured workers." He had found it certain, he said, that as soon as one opened the subject he would be met with the parrot cry "Do you want your sister or daughter to marry a nigger?" Whether socialists liked it or not, white workers wanted answers to such questions as: "Are we prepared to give them the same educational facilities as the rest of the community?"

Andrews in the *International* (20 July 1917) submitted for discussion these points:

- Firstly, Africans must be considered, without reservation, as part of the proletariat, not as "passive creatures waiting for their white brothers to emancipate them. They will have to be considered in all matters of interest to them." They must organise industrially — "whether in the white unions in the initial stages or in parallel organisations is a matter of tactics which native and white worker must mutually agree upon."

The First World War and the Socialist Movement in South Africa   61

- Secondly, the special laws affecting Africans must be fought and he must obtain civil equality. "Possibly, as other workers have done, they will have to begin organising outside the law and having become articulate, force the repeal of laws barring their further progress."
- Thirdly, in regard to political power. "This need not be worried about. The capitalist will give large masses of their native and coloured workers votes long before they are class conscious and class-organised sufficiently to be a danger. At the present stage of native education, such as do exercise the vote are largely found supporting reactionary institutions and organisations."
- Finally, intermarriage. This was an entirely individual matter and did not in the least depend on civil or political equality.

By mid-1917, then, the socialist movement in South Africa had undergone a qualitative change, and, ironically enough, it was Wade who carried the banner of racial equality into the election campaign which signposted the change.

But now the ISL was a small thing indeed. It had lost the support of the privileged white trade unionists upon whom it had formerly been based and it had not yet even drawn a single solitary recruit or potential recruit from the great propertyless African proletariat which it proposed to lead to socialism.

Theoretical errors

Most of the ISL leaders at this time were already attempting to base their thoughts on marxist principles, and it was the very fact that they had a deeper understanding of the economic forces at work in South Africa which led them into an important error in predicting the future development of the country.

Just as they believed that once the Afrikaner entered industry and became a proletarian, he would turn his back on nationalism and the Nationalist Party, so also they believed that capitalism would destroy the colour bar. They saw clearly that the mineowners would inevitably attack the relatively high wage standards of white workers and that they would seek to employ the cheaper African labour in the jobs occupied by whites. This was the logical course capitalism must follow in South Africa and they believed the workers would require the same strength needed to destroy capitalism itself, in order to keep the African worker out of skilled work.

Already in March 1916, Jones had written in the *International* (3 March 1916):

The dilution of labour is coming on the Rand. The vanity of craft unionists blinds them to the process which is levelling all, skilled and unskilled, before the great lord of machinery. Into this white kaffir standard, all workers will be continually drawn as by a maelstrom. From all quarters we learn of the increasing control of

62 *People's History*

mine drilling and machinery taken by the kaffir worker, the aspiring kaffir-worker, a thirst for new knowledge with that spirit of 'awakening' constantly dulled in the white workers by whippets, bioscopes, religiosity and catch-penny press which a shrewd capitalism knows so well how to provide. He is content to let his control over the tools of production become more and more nominal and supervisory. Capitalism is the great leveller. The salvation of the workers depends on how soon they recognise what their masters have long ago recognised, that all workers are equal before the great God Capital.

A year later in the *International* (27 February 1917) the same idea was expressed this way:

The struggle for and against the Coloured worker is very similar to the struggle that took place between the capitalists and workers on the introduction of machinery to take the place of the hand workers. The blind resistance of the workers against machinery was futile. They were beaten in that struggle and the forces of evolution triumphed. So today the evolutionary forces will win. You cannot keep back the Coloured workers. They are here to stay. The capitalist class want cheap labour, and the supply is here ready to meet their demand. The white workers will have to divest themselves of their race prejudices. They will have to look at the problem from an economic standpoint, and not from the social or sentimental point of view. Their only hope is to organise these Coloured workers with themselves in a strong industrial union. By doing so they will be able to control the condition of their labour and raise the standard of living of these Coloured workers to their own level, failing this the white workers must inevitably fall to the Coloured standard of living.

But unfortunately white workers knew nothing of the laws of capitalist development and when, in 1922, the mineowners tried to drive in the thin edge of the wedge with which to destroy the industrial colour bar, the white workers came out fighting — and stopped them. They had not the strength to smash capitalism or even very seriously to imperil it — but they did have the strength to force capitalism to mould itself unnaturally around the colour bar industry. And capitalism moulded itself very comfortably indeed!

The Industrial Workers of Africa

In July 1917 South Africa's first black working-class organisation, the Industrial Workers of Africa, was formed in Johannesburg by ISL members. Jones and Bunting hoped to build the IWA into a large, all-in organisation of workers of all trades on the model of the American IWA which flourished until the First World War.

Its slogan was "*Si funa zonke*" ("We want everything"). This is what those who attended the first series of ISL meetings of Africans, in early

The First World War and the Socialist Movement in South Africa   63

August, to study the working-class movement, had replied when asked what they wanted.

The IWA met weekly at the ISL headquarters at 54 Fox Street. The government took an immense interest in the IWA and at least five of its early members were police agents. One of them, Wilfred Njali, was elected secretary, and another was a member of the IWA committee. When at one IWA meeting a member said that there were spies present, Bunting responded that there was "nothing to fear from the police." Within a short time he was to be proved wrong.

In December 1917, a conference was called to discuss non-European trade union unity. The first of its kind, it was attended by representatives of the ANC (Transvaal), the APO and the IWA. IWA members made up the majority of the audience, taking up one whole side of the hall. On the other side sat the members of the ANC, described by a newspaper as being "more sedate and middle-class looking," the Coloured workers, two or three members of the ISL, and more IWA delegates. All these organisations were represented on the platform.

Talbot Williams, APO Secretary, was the dominant figure at the conference. After being scheduled to speak at the SA Trade Union Congress held the same week, Williams had been told by its Secretary, Archie Crawford, that most of the unions had decided in caucus not to hear a non-European speaker. At this conference, Williams was able to have his say.

In spite of the temptation that there must have been for delegates to adopt a hostile attitude to the workers, the speeches kept the principle of the class struggle — irrespective of colour — in clear perspective. The conference appointed a multi-racial committee of workers to draw up a scheme for future co-operation.

At its third conference in January 1918, the ISL was able to note with satisfaction that its influence was far greater than its numbers might indicate. "During the year the outlook of the League has more and more clarified in the direction of our responsibility towards the native worker, and the solidarity of labour irrespective of colour has eclipsed the War-on-War principle in importance. It has become the revolutionary touch-stone, the magic word from which all reformist goblins flee, and the key to the capitalist fortress as well," Jones wrote in *International* (4 January 1918).

"We should so direct our activities," said the report of the Management Committee to the conference, "that the day when the native proletariat openly flings its challenge at capitalism, will find the majority of white workers ready to co-operate and stand shoulder-to-shoulder, so that the class struggle may not degenerate into a bloody race struggle of white versus black."

There was a non-European present at the conference for the first time — B.L.E. Sigamoney of the Durban Indian Workers' Union.

64   People's History

The October revolution from which the Soviet Union was born was still hot news when the delegates gathered, and one of their main resolutions was to place on record that "the ISL rejoices beyond measure at the triumph of the Russian revolutionary proletariat under the banner of the Bolshevik wing of the Social Democratic Party, and pledges on behalf of the advanced proletariat of South Africa its growing support to stand by the Russian workmen against the capitalist governments of the whole world, that of South Africa included." It was also resolved to keep the principles of the Russian revolution before the South African workers in the year ahead.

In February 1918 the ISL decided to distribute its first leaflet written by a non-European, a report of an excellent address by Talbot Williams on the need for the unity of the workers of all races. It also decided to undertake the most thorough distribution of this leaflet that it had yet done, and to distribute it at a number of different centres, for Williams was then on a tour of the whole country.

"The movement of labour in South Africa is beginning to find its centre of gravity, its home among the real proletariat," the *International* (8 February 1918) exulted. "But we have a lot to do. The revolution is knocking at the door, and the native and coloured workers must be told to wake up, and the white worker must be enlisted for the job of waking them up." This burst of enthusiasm was a little premature. The ISL never got round to the actual issue of the leaflet.

The Africans were waking up without being told to do so. That same month the African miners on the East Rand launched a boycott of all the mine concession stores. Prices had doubled during the war years, while wages remained unaltered, and the workers directed their protest against the storekeepers and their rising prices. The result was a solid boycott of the stores by the 30-40,000 Africans on whom they depended for custom. Attempts to break the boycott by fomenting inter-tribal fighting failed, and the boycotters remained solid.

After the ISL Management Committee gave its approval, the IWA and ISL joined in issuing 10,000 leaflets in Zulu and Sesotho to the boycotters. The leaflet began:

> Workers of the Bantu race! Why do you live in slavery? Why are you not free as other men are free? Why are you kicked and spat upon by your masters? Why must you carry a pass before you can move anywhere? And if you are found without one why are you thrown into prison? Why do you toil hard for little money? And again thrown into prison if you refuse to work. Why do they herd you like cattle into compounds, why?

> Because you are the toilers of the earth. Because the masters want you to labour for their profit. Because they pay the government and the police to keep you as slaves to toil for them. If it were not for the money that they make from your labour, you would not be oppressed.

The First World War and the Socialist Movement in South Africa 65

But mark! You are the mainstay of the country. You do all the work, you are the means of their living. That is why you are robbed of the fruits of your labour and robbed of your liberty as well.

There is only one way of deliverance for you, Bantu workers. Unite as workers, unite! Forget the things that divide you. Let there be no longer any talk of Basuto, Zulu or Shangaan. You are all labourers. Let Labour be your common bond.

Wake up! And open your ears. The sun has arisen, the day is breaking. For a long time you were asleep when the great mill of the rich man was grinding and breaking the sweat from your work for nothing. You are strongly urged to come to the meeting of the workers and fight for your rights. Come and listen to the good news and deliver yourselves from the chains of the capitalist. Unity is strength. The fight is great against the many pass laws that persecute you, and the low wages and the misery of existence.

And then the famous final words of Marx's *Communist Manifesto* rang out for the first time in Zulu and Sesutho: "Workers of all lands unite. You have nothing to lose but your chains. You have a world to win."

The authorities, then as now, believed that the communists were the cause of the boycott. The *Rand Daily Mail* (14 February 1918) called for the imprisonment of these "ill-balanced and fanatical socialists of the baser sort." It was before the days when Moscow was blamed for everything, so the *Natal Mercury* (February 1918) saw "the sinister influence of the Industrial Workers of the World notoriously financed by Germany. Once they permeate the natives with the pernicious doctrine that they are slaves, and so on, there will be trouble. . . In a crisis like the present, the British principles of fair play and justice should not be stretched too far. . . No one wishes their suppression more than the Labour Party of South Africa. . . there is the difference of the poles between the methods of the Labour Party and the Bolshevik actions."

In actual fact, the socialists had not known anything about the boycott until it was on, and although they gave it their support, they took the view that it was misdirected — it was not the concession stores who were the enemy so much as the Chamber of Mines.

The ISL socialists turned their attention in that year's May Day celebrations to the non-European workers instead of to the whites. This was due not to any alteration in theoretical outlook but to the experiences of the year before when a white mob had smashed the ISL demonstration. A meeting was held outside the Pilkington Hall in Ferreirastown where the Coloureds usually met — outside, because the owners would not let the hall itself to the ISL. The audience was 100-200, mainly Coloured workers. Talbot Williams, William Thebedi and five white socialists spoke (Hanscombe, Tinker, Barendregt, Israelstam, Kesler). This was the first time a May Day celebration had been directed to non-European workers and

66 People's History

the *International*'s (3 May 1918) verdict was that it was "a May Day demonstration with more in it than ever before."

The ISL's new orientation had its teething problems. At a successful social to celebrate May Day and the Marx centenary, there was a dance in which the colour bar was ignored. "It is worth considering," wrote the *International* (Bunting was editing at the time) "whether instead of courting social awkwardness the conquest of which, without the corresponding economic victory, is of little intrinsic value, the League should not specialise in promoting gatherings at which all workers can meet irrespective of colour or grade without incurring such difficulties, even if no halls are available."

The Bucket Strike

The concession store boycott failed to achieve its purpose, but the workers were now ready for action and this was sparked off by one of Johannesburg's first African strikes. Towards the middle of 1918 about 150 key white workers at the Johannesburg power station went on strike, and, faced with the paralysis of the city, the municipal council quickly conceded a wage increase.

A month later, 150 African sewage workers, responsible for the daily collection of the city's lavatory buckets — before the days of water-borne sewerage — came out on strike for an extra 6d a day. But they got very different treatment. Though faced with consequences quite as terrifying as those which would have resulted from the power station walk-out, the municipality did not for one moment consider the speedy granting of the workers' demands. Instead it had every one of them arrested, and a sad-faced African police force was roped in to do the nightly bucket collections.

These men could not cope with the situation and the city began to stink. The authorities adopted a course that had been adopted before and would be again. Chief Magistrate McFie sentenced the strikers to two months hard labour, it being a criminal offence for Africans to break their service contracts. The hard labour consisted of emptying lavatory buckets. McFie sent the workers back to work under police escort. He told them: "If you attempt to escape and it is necessary you will be shot down. If you refuse to obey orders you will receive lashes."

Even the European press was shocked; an indication of how strong public feeling was was shown when the *International* (14 June 1918) committed the most blatant contempt by describing McFie as "a bear on the bench" and "a capitalist jackal", and no action was taken against it.

The ANC called several protest meetings at the vicious sentence on the strikers. The ANC leaders still tended to be behind the rank and file in the strength of their sentiments, however. At one meeting, the ANC Secretary proposed the adoption of a petition to the Governor-General asking for remission of the sentence passed on the "misguided strikers,"

The First World War and the Socialist Movement in South Africa 67

but the meeting would not agree — and in fact adopted a resolution favouring a general strike. A detective taking notes was ejected from the meeting.

At the meeting there was a clear working-class consciousness — a call for a strike, a reference to a policeman as a fellow worker. The *International* commented: "The remark has been heard that the white socialists have failed to act as saviours of the oppressed scavengers at this juncture. The answer is that this habit of looking for salvation from 'above' or 'outside' is essentially vicious, and that nothing can save the proletariat except itself, enlightened and thoroughly industrially organised irrespective of colour."

The protests were not limited to socialists and congressmen. Both the *Cape Times* and the *Star* were moved to mild criticism, and the Bishop of Pretoria strongly condemned the sentence. The *SA Review* (14 June 1918), a Cape Town paper, even declared "McFie must go!" Only the white trade unions remained silent, absolutely and completely silent.

While it recorded European protests, the daily press gave no account of the large gatherings of Africans being held.

On 19 June, the Transvaal ANC packed a hall meeting of 1,500 to 2,000 Africans, a handful of Europeans — "parsons, missionaries and members of the ISL" and a large number of white and black police. The proceedings opened with the singing of "Nkosi Sikelele". The chairman announced that the Mayor, the Native Affairs Department and Magistrate McFie had all declined to send representatives to explain their attitude to the sentences, but McFie had said that he was willing to meet a deputation at the court — where he had passed sentence. The meeting rejected the proposal.

Speakers described the government as being "as oppressive as the German government" and called the Native Affairs Department "a detective agency." They said that the Africans could, if they chose, destroy Johannesburg in a day and close the mines in an hour but stressed that they chose not to. They said that if the government persecution continued, there would be bloodshed.

The ANC President, Ka Isaka Seme, warned the workers against the danger of striking and condemned the socialists on the grounds that they were all white men and would therefore join in shooting Africans down, just as they had passed a resolution against whites working alongside blacks.

The President of the Women's Section of Congress also spoke. A resolution demanded an all-round pay increase of one shilling a day to meet the rising cost of living, and the meeting seemed ready to declare a strike in support of that demand. Tinker of the ISL spoke, mentioning that there were not only white, but also black and yellow socialists in the world; he warned that passing resolutions was not enough, and thorough organisation by industries was necessary before a strike could succeed and that no excuse should be given to the enemy to employ violence.

68 People's History

A policeman making notes recorded Tinker as saying: "If the natives knew their force, they could destroy Johannesburg in a day or stop the mines in an hour; but to do that they would have to organise and all come out on strike, for which 20,000 men were necessary. Let them go home and organise, and tell the other boys to come out; if they meant to come out on Saturday the 29th, they must be quick. The strike was not for one shilling a day, but for Africa which they deserved" (*International,* 21 June 1918).

At the strike call, the government rattled its sabres. Soldiers were mobilised and marched through Johannesburg. The white trade unions acted true to form. They invited MacFie to a meeting of the Federation. He appealed to the Federation to organise white workers into a defence force to protect their women-folk against "a possible Native rising." He said that the African's wage demands would not have been dreamt of but for the "sinister encouragement of certain whites."

So alarmed were the white trade unions that, shortly after MacFie's address to them, the Federation sent two of its leaders, Crawford and Forrester Brown, to see the Minister of Defence to offer to raise special labour battalions to meet the "danger" of an African rising.

Nevertheless, moved by the strength of the national protest — and the representations of Wallers, President of the Chamber of Mines, and Taberer of the Mines Native Recruiting Corporation, who were extremely fearful of the possible effect of the dissatisfaction on their recruiting of African labour — the Minister of Justice indicated that he did not support the sentence and the workers were released. This was a tremendous victory for the national movement.

As a result of the release of the bucket strikers, the ANC called the strike off, but at certain mines the workers either did not know this or disregarded it, and came out as planned on 28 June 1918. By afternoon their strike had been defeated by massive police and military intervention. The effect of the Rand strike was felt throughout the country. In Durban, African dock workers put forward wage claims for the first time, though they did not succeed in winning any concessions.

A press campaign against the ISL as inciters of blacks reached a new peak, the main allegation being that the German government had placed £10,000 at the disposal of the League for the purpose of causing disaffection among blacks (in later years Moscow gold was substituted for German gold in these allegations). The *International* (5 July 1918) promptly published the true facts — and they showed how little the ISL had really done in furtherance of what it had for nearly two years described as one of its main tasks — assisting in awakening African workers. The only leaflet addressed to Africans with which it had been connected was issued by the IWA during the concession store boycott. Five pounds had been advanced for that purpose to the IWA which was patronisingly described in the same issue of the *International* as "a little body of native students of socialism which has from time to time, at its own request, been addressed by members of the League on the elementary principles of the working-class movement." In addition, the League had decided to issue APO leader Talbot Williams' speech, mentioned earlier, as a pamphlet but not enough money had been raised.

Again in the same issue, a call by the ANC for a protest strike was vigorously opposed. The ANC invited the ISL Management Committee to protest meetings and some went, and ridiculed the idea of attempting a strike when they were unorganised. ". . . whenever any of our speakers attended any of the numerous native indignation meetings that followed, they pointed out the unripeness of the native workers of the Reef for a strike, seeing that they were still absorbed with racialism and that it would mean much patient education and organisation before they could success-fully exercise their strength as a class."

This somewhat apologetic article added, however, "of course we are not apologising. A great forward movement of the native and white proletariat is inevitable in the near future, and we have done and are doing all we know to help it on. Perhaps, after all, it is a pity that a general strike was not allowed to mature. It will come anyhow some day. Nor must the probation period be exaggerated. Solidarity is natural to natives and their position as bottom dogs needs little teaching to bring home. The movement is coming quickly, in time to participate in the coming general overthrow of capitalism in this country. It will take just that form of the emancipation of the native wage slaves, co-operating with the class-conscious white wage slaves. It is because the ruling class see this coming that they adopt their monstrous panic tactics, from which they will, as heretofore, be obliged in the long run to withdraw in shame and ignominy. The industrial prole-tariat of South Africa need no "agitators; their own agitation is spontaneous and natural. . . "

Forerunner of the Treason Trial

Arrests and police raids followed swiftly on the heels of the Transvaal strike. Eight progressive leaders — D.S. Letanka, L.J. Mvabaza, J.D. Ngojo, H. Kraai and A. Cetyiwe (all ANC officials) and Bunting, Tinker and Hanscombe (leading ISL members) — were raided and arrested.

Their trial was in many ways an embryo of the 1956 Treason Trial. A former secretary of the ANC, Mweli Skota in his *Black Folks Who's Who* wrote: "For the first time in South Africa, members of the European and Native races, in common cause united, were arrested and charged together because of their political activities" (p.171).

Letanka was the Vice-President of the ANC (Transvaal) and Secretary of its Council of Chiefs. Mvabaza was later one of the members of the 1919 ANC deputation to the King. Both were founders of newspapers which later merged into *Abantu-Batho,* of which they were managing directors. Ngojo, Kraai and Cetyiwe were members of the old IWA, Cetyiwe being active in the Cape Western ANC in after years.

70 People's History

All the accused were held in jail for 12 days before being allowed bail, an earlier application in the Supreme Court being refused when the accused men were described by the prosecution as "dangerous" and the charge as "very serious" almost amounting to one of "treasonable conspiracy." They were charged with incitement to public violence.

The main crown witness was one Luke Massina, who had been sent into the IWA by the Native Affairs Department and paid by the week for his efforts. But Massina's case was an illustration of one of the government's biggest handicaps in its struggle with the liberatory movement. As spies it must employ Africans. But the actions and policies of the liberatory movement are so appealing to any African that no one of intelligence and integrity can fail to be won over by them. Only the most miserable specimen of non-European could serve a non-European-hating government as a spy on non-Europeans. Massina turned out to be not such a miserable specimen.

An unsuspecting prosecutor led Massina through all his evidence- in-chief in which he alleged that the accused had incited the public to violence. Then under cross-examination, Massina repudiated his entire evidence and described to the court how the statement from which the prosecutor had led his evidence had been written out for him by the police. Of an affidavit allegedly signed by him testifying to ISL implication in the strike he said: "I know nothing about that statement. It was given to me today and I read it, I know nothing of what is written in it where the papers says 'Massina his mark'. . . I never made that mark. I can sign my own name . . . All my evidence-in-chief was false" (*International,* 20 July 1918).

He was promptly arrested and charged with perjury. But at his trial six months later, the crown was reluctant to open the way for a real investigation of Massina's perjury and he was acquitted. Going on the attack at the Preparatory Examination, the defence took every opportunity to show up the oppressive conditions under which the workers suffered. A compound manager who came to testify to the work stoppage at his mine was dramatically confronted with evidence of a man with weals on his back to show that he had the habit of hitting the workers with a sjambok.

In his statement to the court, Bunting said that while he would advocate a strike when organisations and circumstances warranted it, he had not done so directly or indirectly in the present instance. But for the rest, the statement was a vigorous repudiation of the notion that African strikes necessarily involved violence. Bunting showed how much more peaceful had been African strikes than those of white workers in recent years and said that it was not African workers but the government and employers with their sjamboks who resorted to violence.

Without even the pretence of adjourning to consider the evidence and the argument, the magistrate committed all the accused to trial. There was not a shred of evidence against any of the accused. The Attorney-General did not act on the magistrate's committal and the charge was withdrawn against all the accused.

Thus it was in the closing days of the First World War that the first bonds of unity between democrats of all races were forged.

4. The Communist Party and the ANC, 1921-50: The Background to the National Question in South Africa

In July 1921, delegates from the ISL and other socialist groups in Johannesburg, Cape Town and Durban decided to merge into a single working-class party, the Communist Party of South Africa.

The ISL's application for affiliation to the Third International had been accepted in 1920 and a conference of left-wing organisations met in Johannesburg on 2 January 1921 to discuss unity on the basis of 21 points set out by the Second Congress of the Comintern in July 1920 as the requirements for affiliation.

Discussions were held with Labour Party leaders, including Creswell and Waterston, but the gulf between Labour policy and marxist theory was, of course, unbridgeable in South Africa as it was everywhere else.

Representatives of Cape Town's three main socialist groups, the Social Democratic Federation, the Communist Party and the Constitutional Socialist League, had also met several times early in 1921 to discuss unity. Only the Social Democratic Federation was willing to accept the 21 points, and it, together with individuals from other organisations, therefore agreed to form a new Cape Town-based party on adherence to the Third International.

This United Communist Party of South Africa was established in Cape Town in March 1921, and it was a source of pride to Capetonians that they had beaten Johannesburg to it. Cape Town also led in the formation of a Young Communist League, and it was on the suggestion of Cape Town YCL Secretary Rochlin that a Johannesburg YCL was inaugurated on 22 May 1921.

Later that month, on Easter Sunday, in Johannesburg, delegates from Durban's Social Democratic Party and its Marxism Club, Cape Town's United Communist Party and Johannesburg's ISL and Jewish Socialist Society had agreed on the principle of forming a single Communist Party.

The inaugural Congress of the Communist Party of South Africa was held in the Cape Town City Hall on 29 July 1921. The hall was packed with about 2,000 supporters and there was great excitement and enthusiasm. It was also swarming with detectives and police.

D.L. Dryburgh was in the chair and Bill Andrews was Conference Secretary. The first executive committee of the Party, elected from the Transvaal only, consisted of C.B. Tyler (Chairman), W.H. Andrews (Secretary), S.P. Bunting (Treasurer), and G. Arnold, Mrs. R. Bunting, T. Chapman, J. den Bakker, R. Geldblum, A. Goldman, H. Lee, E.M. Pincus and R. Rabb, together with one each from the Cape, Natal and OFS branches.

In South Africa, where the Africans, Coloureds and Indians who constitute 80 per cent of the population enjoy almost no political rights, and are held in a state of subjection and poverty by the ruling white minority, one of the key questions faced by the Party from its formation was the formulation of a correct policy on the national question — that is, a policy which would most effectively rally the African rural masses and oppressed Indian and Coloured minorities into alliance with the proletariat of all nationalities under the leadership of their party in the struggle to end national oppression, as an essential part of the fight to end capitalist exploitation.

The hammering out of a correct policy has been made more difficult by the fact that, unlike the struggle characteristic of the rest of Africa, in South Africa it is not simply a question of fighting for independence from foreign white rule. The substantial white minority is far from being merely the direct agent of an overseas imperialist government. The whites as a whole, and in particular the Afrikaners who constitute the majority of them, have their roots deep in South Africa and know no other home. They are white Africans.

To add to the difficulty, the oppressed people, far from being a homogeneous community, are themselves divided into a large number of different national groups — the African "pre-nations" and the Indians. The oppressing whites are themselves divided into Afrikaner and English groups with very severe economic conflicts straining their unity both internally and in relation to one another. Then there are the Coloureds (a Coloured person is curiously defined in law as "a person who is not a white person, or a Native, or an Indian") who, because of their peculiar legal status form a single political but not national community.[1]

Looking back at the long and difficult road covered by the pioneers of South African communism, it is not surprising to find that in the search for a correct policy on the national question they stumbled often, did not always point out the best route, and sometimes even had wearily to retrace their footsteps down alleys which they had not perceived to be dead ends. Because in a small movement like ours such a description of our past history might weaken the confidence of those who look to us for a lead, it is worth repeating the words of D.N. Aidit, Secretary of the Indonesian Communist Party, in a review in *Marxism Today* (April 1959, p. 109) of the history of that great party, now the biggest in the capitalist world:

If we today, recall the entire period of the 1920s and even if we recall the entire period up to 1951, we will realise just how shallow the communists' knowledge of Marxism-Leninism was at that time. This is why we should not be surprised if, during the period prior to 1951, the welding of Marxism-Leninism with the practice of the Indonesian

74 People's History

Revolution did not proceed well and rapidly and some serious mistakes were committed in leading the Indonesian Revolution.

But it was due to the fact that Marxism-Leninism had entered into the Indonesian independence movement that these serious mistakes and failures did not weaken and certainly did not destroy the revolutionary movement of the Indonesian people. Marxism-Leninism helps the working class to analyse and draw conclusions from mistakes and failures, and in this way to raise the struggle of the Indonesian people to a higher level.

These words are fully applicable to the history of the South African Communist Party and in particular to its striving for a correct policy with regard to the national liberatory movement.

The South African Communist Party is by far the oldest in Africa. Its pioneers of Marxism-Leninism in South Africa were all white men, predominantly British immigrant workers on the big industrial complex that had developed around the mines in Johannesburg and its vicinity. They were men whose political experience was mainly confined to that of the British trade union and labour movement, and the organisations they formed were modelled on those in Britain. Although their militancy and working-class consciousness made them seize eagerly on Marxist-Leninist ideas when the Russian revolution brought these within their ken, the founders of the ISL were, at the time of its formation, by no means marxists. Most were militant socialist internationalists who perceived that the First World War was a struggle between rival capitalist power blocs and refused to support it, but they were socialists of all hues, including fabians, co-operators, syndicalists, anarchists and the like.

At the time of the formation of the ISL, African workers in the Transvaal, the nerve centre of industry, were completely unorganised and voiceless. Migrant labourers, they were men from the reserves — backward rural areas, where the farms were too small and impoverished and overcrowded to support them without the supplement of mine wages. Forming the majority of the labour force, they were unskilled labourers paid at starvation wages, and the main source of profits.

The whites were the skilled men and overseers. They had fought hard battles with the employers and their bitter strikes had won them gains. But they were well aware that they were in constant danger because, as the African acquired industrial skills, whites would be replaced by blacks, or would have to accept the far lower African wage rates. The white trade union movement, therefore, was dominated by the fear of competition from African workers, and determination to keep the Africans out of the skilled jobs. Many argued that they should be kept out of industry altogether, and that unskilled work should be reserved for whites.

The men who formed the ISL were an integral part of the Transvaal white labour movement. The task which now faced them was to break from the hostility of the Labour Party to Africans, and to discover the first principle of South African communism — that the African worker and the white worker must be brothers.

In the period between 1916 and 1919 — the years of international revolutionary upsurge highlighted by the great October revolution — the ISL believed that revolution was imminent in South Africa too. It believed that the white proletariat would seize power, but that it could only succeed with the backing of the Africans, and it must guarantee to them the "fullest rights they are capable of exercising."

These years saw co-operation between the ISL and the ANC in order, by combined effort and united political organisation, to defend their "freedom, rights and privileges." In July 1917, the ISL was instrumental in forming the first African working-class organisation, the Industrial Workers of Africa. In 1918 three ISL and five ANC leaders were charged jointly with incitement to public violence as a result of their part in an African mine strike. With its affiliation to the Third International, and with the formation in 1919 of the Industrial and Commercial Workers' Union (the ICU), a mass organisation of African workers which swiftly drew tens of thousands of militant workers into its ranks, the situation was ripe for a great advance by the ISL — for its transformation from a body with roots in the white aristocracy of labour only, into one drawing its main membership from the masses of unskilled workers, the Africans.

The communists were far ahead of anyone else in realising the might of the awakening African peoples. "The influence of the Russian Revolution is felt far beyond the boundaries of the vast Soviet Republic and probably has an even more immediate appeal to the enslaved Coloured races of the earth than to Europeans" wrote W.H. Andrews one of the pioneers of Marxism-Leninism in South Africa in an article in *International* (22 July 1921) on the 1921 Pan-African Conference convened by the great W.E.B. du Bois and attended by three ANC delegates. "Capitalism is tottering to its fall, and as it was in backward Russia, with its illiterate millions, which delivered the first staggering blow, so it may be that the humblest and most despised worker, who has been the slave of each succeeding civilisation for thousands of years, is destined to launch the final onslaught which will send this latest phase of human exploitation staggering into the abyss of infamy which has engulfed all preceding tyrannies."[2]

But the Party still believed that whites were the main revolutionary force. "The African revolution will be led by white workers," the South African delegate, David Ivon Jones, told the Third Congress of the Communist International in 1921. This belief in the leading role of the white proletariat was reinforced by the militancy of the white mineworkers of the Transvaal in the face of the threat by the mine-owners to replace some white labour with cheap black labour. As a result, in 1922, the Communist Party became submerged in the struggle of white workers, and, at a crucial period, neglected the demands of unskilled workers and oppressed masses. In the strike of white mineworkers which stopped the mines for two months and was only ended by full-scale military action, the communists (although

76 People's History

they attempted to convince the white workers that the Africans were not their enemies, but potentially their allies) became identified with a struggle which produced that notorious slogan of the aristocrats of labour: "Workers of the World, Unite and Fight for a White South Africa."

Though the strike was beaten, the white workers won their demand for a white labour policy in the general election of 1924. The Labour Party united with the Nationalist Party to defeat Smuts. The Nationalist-Labour coalition, the ideological predecessor of Verwoerd's party, entrenched the mining colour bar for which the 1922 strikers had fought. As a result, the mine-owners were forced to reconcile themselves to the colour bar and to switch their policy to one of transforming the white miners into bribed policemen over the blacks, ensuring continued high profits by the super-exploitation of the Africans.

It cannot, unfortunately, be said that the Party leadership learnt all the lessons of the strike. The account by the central committee was completely devoid of self-criticism, and it clung to the belief that the repeal of the industrial colour bar "will not benefit the Native worker, rather the reverse." It criticised Africans for failing to support the white strikers and claimed that this was because they were "taught" by the rulers that the colour bar was against the interests of the Africans. In fact, the Party claimed:

> Though it is theoretically fair that no sort of work should be closed to native workers, yet the practical result of just abolishing the colour bar, as the Chamber would do, without replacing it by something better for all workers, white and black, would not be to the benefit of the native but only to harm the white worker — and harm him very seriously, for remember, he is hurt by a closing of an avenue of employment to him far more than the native workers can benefit by an opening of those avenues to them. The native so far can usually get a job, the white man can in comparison, ill afford to lose his. So that at best the Chamber's policy, even if it would benefit some native workers, would on the whole do more harm than good.

> But as a matter of fact the Chamber's policy will not only not benefit the native workers, it will hurt them. The policy of the capitalist class is to use low (native) wages as a lever to bring down higher (white) wages. The converse is also true: higher wages operate as a lever to bring up lower wages. If the scale of wages now drawn by the white artisan is reduced, it will be easier for the capitalists to reduce even the native scale too. (S.P. Bunting in *The Red Revolt*.)

Although *The Red Revolt* does not indicate that the strike brought a conscious advance in theoretical approach, events made practice outstrip theory. The communists, although they gave qualified electoral support to the Labour-Nationalist coalition, now found that they could no longer obtain a hearing among white workers, demoralised by the crushing of their strike, and more hostile than ever to Africans. That wing of the Party which had continually urged that the main task was the "awakening" of the African proletariat, now came into its own. It found strong allies in the communists of the Western Cape, where, unlike the Transvaal, the main labour force was Coloured.

The Cape Coloured workers were permanent city residents, not migrant labourers. Unlike Africans, they had a long artisan tradition, and were organised into trade unions and political organisations. And unlike their Transvaal brethren, they had the vote and were wooed by political parties. In these circumstances, socialists at the Cape, some of the most outstanding of whom were Coloured, had a better consciousness of class solidarity than did those of the Transvaal, and they were far less prone to the racial prejudices of the North.

At the conference of the Party in 1924, the Cape delegates, who had witnessed, and were participating in, the rise of the ICU, united with the most advanced section of the Transvaal delegation, and, by narrowly defeating the proposal by General Secretary Andrews, that the Party should apply for affiliation to the thoroughly reactionary white Labour Party, placed the Party's main emphasis on work among Africans. It should be mentioned that the arrival at this decision was aided by a letter from the Young Communist International to the YCL supporting such a new orientation.

Africans were recruited in numbers into the Party for the first time. As a result opportunities were created for the emergence of African communist leaders, among them Moses Kotane, Albert Nzula, J.B. Marks, Edwin Mofutsunyana and Johannes Nkosi. But as communism grew, so also grew bourgeois reaction. At the end of 1926, the ICU leadership, corrupt and opportunist, and fearful of the communist call to militant action, turned against the Party on the rallying-call that it was white-dominated and expelled all communists from the ICU. Because of its late entry into the ICU and the Party's unpopular and incorrect role in the 1922 events, communists did not have sufficient support among the ICU rank and file to challenge the anti-communist leadership and resist the expulsions.

While the Party suffered this defeat in the ICU, it succeeded in making progress in the ANC which agreed to send its President, J.T. Gumede, to the anti-Imperialist Conference in Brussels in 1927, from which he proceeded to tour the Soviet Union, returning a vigorous ally of co-operation with the communists.

Majority not proletarian

Although the Party had made great advances, and had contributed very greatly indeed to raising the general level of the political consciousness of the South African people, it had not yet developed a correct policy with regard to the national question. It tended to see the struggle in terms only of the mobilisation of the proletariat and the organisation of the trade unions, and not pay proper attention to the fact that the overwhelming majority of the South African people were not proletarians and could not be reached by the slogans of the class struggle.

During 1927, one of the Cape communists expelled from the ICU executive, James La Guma, discussed the situation with Bukharin, from whom he obtained a new perspective — that the purely national struggle uniting the oppressed people of all classes against white domination was itself of great revolutionary importance in the struggle against imperialism, and that the wresting of national freedom was an essential stage to the winning of socialism.

The International therefore put forward to the South African Party for discussion the adoption of the slogan "an independent Native Republic as a stage towards a workers' and peasants' government." Today when the vital importance of the national struggle is seen by marxists as axiomatic, the correctness of the analysis brought back by La Guma is easy to see.

At the same time it seemed to the Party leadership to be a complete reversal of their policy. They had urged proletarian unity as the only way to socialism, as the only way, in turn, to the equality of nations. Now they were called upon to support the African National movement; and that movement, which they had previously condemned as diverting the attention of the African workers away from the class struggle, was to be the path to socialism. The Party leadership of the time was still ideologically extremely weak and paid little attention to the study of Marxist theory, and, if Roux's description in *Time Longer than Rope* (p.89) is correct, they failed completely to understand the proposed resolution:

Was it not similar, we said, to Marcus Garvey's slogan "Africa for the Africans" which the C.P. had always opposed as the exact opposite of internationalism? How could we reconcile such a cry with our steadfast aim and slogan: Workers of the World, Unite!? We, as South African communists, had claimed to represent the aspirations of all workers, black and white: and now we were being asked to go before the masses as a purely black, even, as we saw it, as an anti-white Party. Almost all the white communists were indignant, and the black communists like Thibedi who had been trained in the old tradition, equally so.

The Party majority rejected the draft resolution. Three delegates, Bunting, Mrs Rebecca Bunting and Roux, went to Moscow to the 6th Congress of the Communist International in 1928 to argue against it on the main ground that the slogan would antagonise white workers. To the charge that they were falling into the error of white chauvinism, they replied that of the Party's 1,750 members, 1,600 were Africans — but the significance of the fact that in these circumstances all three delegates were white, as had been the two previous representatives at the Comintern (Andrews and Jones), must have struck other delegates. (As late as 1942 the Party was still faced with this very real problem: "In a party like ours, where whites and blacks come together, the general tendency of non-European members is to take

The Communist Party and the ANC, 1921-50 79

back seats and leave the leadership to the Europeans. They feel themselves inferior to the European comrades." (Moses Kotene, writing in *Freedom,* September 1942) It is only in the post-war years that the situation has changed, and the tendency, at least in the political leadership, is the reverse, the Europeans being inclined to "take the back seats" and defer to the judgement of the Africans because of their closer direct contact with the masses.)

The *International* agreed, with only the South Africans dissenting, that the correct slogan was "A South African Native Republic, as a stage towards a Workers' and Peasants' Government, with full protection and equal rights for all national minorities."

Entering fully now into the national struggle, the Party introduced a new spirit of courage and militancy at a time when oppression was reaching new heights. In June 1929, the Nationalist Party, after discarding its Labour Party crutch, won power for the first time on its own, following an election in which the promise to crush the "Black Peril" was its main slogan. The Nazi Pirow became Minister of Justice, and the Riotous Assemblies Act was amended to give him the power to banish militants without trial.

The communists broke through their isolation from the leadership of the ANC and ICU and joined with them in a mass campaign against Pirow's amendment, and Dingane's Day (16 December 1929) was the occasion for the first time of big united front demonstrations of the communist and national movements. The new approach was to bring the Party ever greater support. Branches were being set up in all the main towns, including Bloemfontein, and the Party now decided to call for a national pass-burning campaign on Dingane's Day 1930. The support it won from the widest section of the national movement showed what strides were being taken. Not only did Congress and ICU leaders respond to the call to the preparation conference in October 1930, but even *Imvo Zabantsundu* wished the campaign success.

Needless to say, reaction did not sit idle. Pirow's police launched a terror campaign against the militant ANC of the Cape, which had all but adopted the Party newspaper *Umsebenzi,* then being produced in Cape Town, as its organ. The right-winger Thaele rallied support for an anti-communist crusade, again relying, as Kadalie had done in 1926, on the charge that the communists were dominated by whites. Kadalie was brought into battle to address meetings in the Free State against the anti- pass campaign.

The anti-pass campaign proved too ambitious. A successful national pass burning would have shaken the very foundation of the oppressor state and this could not be achieved in a campaign of a few months. In Durban, where the communist, Johannes Nkosi, led a most successful burning, Pirow's retaliation was immediate. The martyr, Nkosi, was brutally done to death on the spot by the police. Thousands of recruits had been won by Nkosi in a few months before the campaign. Pirow lost no time in using terror on a scale unknown in Natal since the war against Bambata in 1906. Mass arrests and deportations succeeded in crushing the Party in Natal.

During 1932, the Party intensified its propaganda, aimed at arousing action on national liberatory demands and the executive committee of the Communist International recorded at the end of that year that "The national revolutionary movement in South Africa has moved considerably forward during the recent period. The framework of the slave regime is beginning to burst under the pressure of the masses who are seeking in the Communist Party their guide and leader" (*Umsebenzi* 25 December 1931).

The *International* now proposed a further elaboration of the programme on the national question, declaring part of the fundamental task of the Party to be the furtherance of the slogan "Down with the British and Afrikaner Imperialists. Drive out the Imperialists. Complete and immediate national independence for the people of South Africa. For the right of the Zulu, Basotho, etc. nations to form their Independent Republics. For the voluntary uniting of the African nations in a Federation of Independent Native Republics. The establishment of a workers' and peasants' government. Full guarantees of the rights of all national minorities, for the Coloured, Indian and White toiling masses."

This was a programme for a national movement on the upsurge. But the parties of the Afrikaner and the English, or of agriculture and mining, previously at loggerheads, had now united precisely in order to prevent the framework of the slave regime from bursting, and with a new coalition government, the state was strong and firm. On the other hand, the national movement was in a state of quiescence. The leadership had not been able to withstand the assault launched by Pirow from 1929, and the organisations themselves were too amorphous and inchoate to exist in semi-illegality.

"The Congress of 1917 to 1920 that organised strikes on the mines, that led the pass-burning campaign, is no more," *Umsebenzi* (13 January 1934) noted. "Its leaders are corrupt; its fighting strength is gone, and it has lost practically all its membership." And Moses Kotane declared flatly: "The once formidable ANC and the ICU have disappeared" (*Umsebenzi* 27 January 1934).

Not that the Party mourned what appeared to be the passing of the ANC and the ICU. The communists, while ready to unite with the ANC on specific campaigns, still saw Congress as a basically reactionary body, serving the interest of an African bourgeoisie and there was no question of communists working to build and strengthen the ANC. The Party believed it was necessary to rally the masses on national slogans but under its own banner. Experience had still to teach the vital leasson that it was not in spite of Congress but in alliance with Congress that the Party would lead the struggle against national oppression.

The Party was also going through a difficult period. Before 1931 it too had been very loosely organised, a member being anyone who had taken out a membership card, irrespective of whether or not he or she attended meetings. From 1931, the Party had reorganised to meet the new conditions, but had gone to the other extreme, purging itself not only of the undisciplined and the waverers, but also, in an unbridled campaign against right-wing deviation, expelling some of its most loyal members, among them S.P. Bunting. And here it is necessary to note that the influence of the Communist International was a contributory factor to the Party's error, which had its parallels in other countries too in this period.

With the Party weakened and the national organisations virtually non-existent, the call for the right to self-determination of the "Zulu, Basotho, etc. nations" died stillborn. There is no record of its having been discussed in the Party, nor any sign that it made any impact on the national organisations.

In 1934, a new factor began to loom large on the South African scene — the fight against fascism. Nazism had triumphed in Germany, and everywhere democrats rallied to form popular fronts to prevent the same thing from happening to them. There was an increase in the activity of the white trade union movement in response to the fascist threat.

Anxious to build a strong anti-fascist front, the Party found itself confronted with its old dilemma in a new form. As it saw the situation, the world was divided into fascist countries and countries in danger from fascism. But exceptional South Africa fell into both categories. Africans lived under fascism. But whites enjoyed democracy which was threatened by fascism. White fascists drew their strength from whites only, and it seemed that the battlefield therefore was mainly among whites. Large sections of the white population were willing to resist this fascism, while not being willing to form a united front with Africans. At the same time, Africans could not be called upon to fight against something that did not affect them directly.

In fact there did begin to develop a parallel struggle. On the one hand, Africans were uniting against the Hertzog Bills to deprive Africans of the Cape of their vote (the Cape was the only province where they were enfranchised). In the 1935 campaign for the calling of a truly representative All-African Convention, African communists played an important role. On the other hand, there was the predominantly white Anti-Fascist League, in which the Party was a driving force, and in which some of the white ex-Party members who had been expelled as right-wing deviators now returned to activity.

Although in the League the Party consistently urged that non-Europeans must be drawn into the anti-fascist struggle, the Party now found itself fighting on two fronts — with Africans in the AAC (All-African Convention) and Europeans in the Anti-Fascist League.

The Hertzog Bills went through with little real popular opposition. This, combined with the shock resulting from the defeat of Ethiopia by Italy, led to a falling-off of African political activity in 1936. The emphasis of Party work swung disastrously once more towards the Europeans. Until then the Party newspaper had been called *Umsebenzi*, with the translation, *South*

82   *People's History*

African Worker as a sub-title. Now the paper was called the *South African Worker*, and *Umsebenzi* became the sub-title.

Propaganda material was produced in Afrikaans and directed at the Afrikaans worker and there was a tendency to underemphasise the question of equality for the African. The directing of activity towards the African diminished.

This switch of policy, like the previous one, was accompanied by an intense internal struggle and new expulsions, but unlike the previous occasion, its bad features were not compensated for by the fact that they merely marred a basically correct line. When the Party of 1926 had swung its attention from white workers to Africans, the new support it won more than compensated for the loss of white support. But the shift back brought only disaster. The newspaper closed down in 1937 for lack of support; so low did morale sink that Party secretary Mofutsanyana was actually able to find a seconder for his proposal to a depleted Party Conference that the Party should divide into two — a white Party and a black one. In 1939, with the Johannesburg Party members demoralised and divided, headquarters moved to the calmer atmosphere of Cape Town.

At the time public attention was increasingly becoming focused on international affairs. At last there was a realisation of the threat of Nazi domination. In its clear analysis — unplagued by the "national question" — of the international alignment of forces, its forthright condemnation of Munich and its call for military defensive alliance with the Soviet Union, the Party slowly took on a new lease of life.

The crippling preponderance of white membership was halted in 1939, when, in the first, imperialist phase of the war, the Party refused to support it, and as a consequence, lost the backing of Europeans and won increased backing from non-Europeans.

Once again discussion on the national question began, and now the influence of the Soviet example was clearly perceptible. But there was a tendency to follow that example a little mechanically. South Africa was not thought of as a predominantly African country, but as one with some "predominantly African areas where, with the addition of more land, African republics may be set up. Industries could be established in these areas, agriculture put on an economic footing; towns, schools, and training institutions built", wrote Moses Kotane (*Freedom* 7 November 1940).

In a draft constitution for a People's Republic published as a basis for discussion in *Freedom* two months later, a writer suggested a bicameral legislature like that of the Soviet Union with each "national group" (undefined) equally represented in one house. Autonomous areas would be established for different national groups where they could develop along their "own cultural and national lines", Harry Snitcher suggested (*Freedom* January 1941).

With the Nazi attack on the Soviet Union in June 1941, the character of the war changed and the struggle for the rallying of the maximum possible support for the war to smash Nazism became the main task of the

Party. It called for the proper arming of African troops (who throughout the war were never permitted to carry anything more lethal than assegaais) and for the accordance to them of some instalments of the democracy for which they were alleged to be fighting. This policy won the Party great support. From 1942, it switched its organisational basis from that of a tightly-knit body of cadres to one of a mass party, and, by 1944, as South Africa cheered the breathtaking achievements of the Red Army, the Party was probably stronger than it had ever been before.

The ANC, which (like the Party) had fallen on bad days after the failure of the 1935-36 campaign against the Hertzog Bills, pulled itself together, (again like the Party) in the early war years. In 1940 a more vigorous leadership, under Dr Alfred Xuma, replaced that of the moribund Mahabane. Close co-operation was once again established between the Party and the ANC, the two organisations which with all their ups and downs and differences had, since 1917, been sisters and brothers in the South African freedom struggle.

With war's end, new theoretical assessments became necessary. Once more the national question and the relations with the national organisations came to the fore. Here one is struck by the lack of continuity between the discussions in this period and those of the pre-war years. While in its work in the trade union field there is a continuous thread, there is none with regard to the national question. It is as if a veil had been drawn over the period before the war. The "native republic" slogan is not referred to, its correctness or otherwise not discussed.

This is unfortunate, for the old discussions were in many respects relevant to the new situation. Where lay the main sphere of Party activity — among whites or among blacks? And to offer, as was sometimes done, the facile answer that it was wrong to pose the question at all — that the Party must work everywhere where it could gain support — did not provide sufficient guidance. The Party was getting a hearing among a section of the middle-class urban Europeans — and especially from Jews who had seen with joy the smashing by the Red Army of the Nazi murderers of six million of their kin. A communist candidate was returned in the Johannesburg Town Council and an exuberant Party official declared that she was the first of many. But a writer in *Freedom* noted: "A Johannesburg municipal election aroused the District Committee to a height of activity which it never achieves at any other time of the year. On the other hand, elections for Advisory Boards in the locations pass almost unnoticed by the bulk of the members. This is something which has been commented on bitterly by African Party members. . . " (*Freedom* February 1946). And in the same issue of *Freedom*, a member of the central committee criticised the Pretoria District for issuing a leaflet to the Afrikaner workers which, while obviously well intentioned, pandered in certain respects to their race prejudices.

There was an echo of the "Native Republic" controversy when a minority in the Party criticised the slogan "Votes for All" adopted in 1948.

84 People's History

One comrade declared: "While the slogans of the Party must be in advance of the general consciousness of the working class, this slogan is so far in advance that it does not bring the Party into the position of leading the working class but leaves us out on a limb far ahead of the working class. To the average worker, even to the average non-European worker, the slogan represents a dream, an ideal which does not appear possible" (*Freedom,* 6 December 1948).

In a reply in the same edition, the Party Secretary, Moses Kotane, made clear the incorrectness of this view and its dangers. He pointed out that for Africans the winning of the vote was not an unattainable dream and that to drop the slogan would mean the abandonment of the whole basis of the struggle against the colour bar.

In the following year, the Party issued its first detailed post-war analysis of the national question, an analysis in which one is particularly struck by the absence of any references to the decisions of the past. A report prepared by the central committee for the January 1950 National Conference argued that:

South Africa is entering a period of bitter national conflict. An intensive racial oppression, an aggressive and virulent Afrikaner nationalism are provoking an exclusive nationalist consciousness among the Indians, Africans and Coloured, and even among the English-speaking whites, whose former unchallenged pre-eminence is now being threatened. On all sides the national and racial differences are being emphasised, and the realities of the class divisions are being obscured. All but a small minority of class-conscious South Africans view the clash of interests, not as one between worker and employer, but as a clash between white and black, or between English and Afrikaner (*Freedom,* 15 December 1949).

Just as the Party in 1937 had seen South Africa as two countries in one — a South Africa which fell into both of the world categories, "fascist" and "menaced by fascism" — it now saw South Africa as a country which combined "the characteristic of both an imperialist state and a colony within a single, indivisible, geographical, political and economic entity . . . The non-European population, while reduced to the status of a colonial people, has no territory of its own, no independent existence, but is almost wholly integrated in the political and economic institutions of the ruling class."

Although in communist literature national movements had been identified with an actual and rising bourgeois class, this description, it argued, could not be applied to the black bourgeoisie. "It is small, fragmentary, pinned down in the poorest areas, forced to use subterfuge and illegalities to evade discriminating laws, starved of capital, and exposed to constant insecurity. It is not a class that could provide effective, militant leadership." In fact, the leadership was petit-bourgeois and in keeping with its character, the aims of the national organisations were usually vague, often contradictory, and at times conciliatory. Whenever an attempt was made to formulate specific aims, other than immediate demands, the leaders "show a tremendous capacity for evasiveness and ambiguity."

The report went on to note that there could be detected "the beginnings of a non-European racialism, matching the racialism of the Europeans. . . . Nationalism need not be synonymous with racialism, but it can avoid being so only if it recognises the class alignments that cut across the racial divisions." The conclusions drawn were:

> that the national organisations can develop into powerful mass movements only to the extent that their content and aims are determined by the interests of the workers and peasants. To be sure, no clear line can be drawn between the bourgeois and working-class demands; pass laws, residential segregation, prohibition on the buying of land, the exclusion from employment, the whole range of colour bars, affect every section of the non-Europeans, and therefore constitute national issues. Moreover, since the non-European bourgeoisie is weak, no serious divergences can develop between it and the non-European working class. The orientation of the national movements on the basis of the workers and peasants is to be brought about by relating the struggle against racial discrimination to the struggle against capitalism. By showing that the colour bar is primarily a technique of exploitation for private profit, by emphasising the unity of interests that exists between the workers of all races, and by ensuring the dominant role of the class-conscious workers in the national organisations.

> The national organisations, to be effective, must be transformed into a revolutionary party of workers, peasants, intellectuals and petty bourgeoisie, linked together in a firm organisation, subject to a strict discipline, and guided by a definite programme of struggle against all forms of racial discrimination in alliance with class-conscious European workers and intellectuals. Such a party would be distinguished from the Communist Party in that its objective is national liberation, that is, the abolition of race discrimination, but it would co-operate closely with the Communist Party. In this party the class-conscious workers and peasants of the national group concerned would constitute the main leadership. It would be their task to develop an adequate organisational apparatus, to conduct mass struggles against race discrimination, to combat chauvinism and racialism in the national movement, to develop class consciousness in the people, and to forge unity in action between the oppressed peoples and between them and the European working class.

> Our Party must give much more attention to the ideological struggle in the national movements than it has been receiving. In particular, we must make a practice of issuing immediate and critical comment

86 People's History

on the statements of the bourgeois leaders, draw attention to the vague and inconsistent formulations, and expose those that betray a tendency to conciliate. We must no longer allow the bourgeois elements in the national movements to attack, without challenge, the working-class movement, to slander the Party, and to adopt a negative or hostile attitude to international working-class forces. We must set the pace for the national movements, by taking positive action on concrete instances of race discrimination, such as the industrial colour bar, or the denial of the right to buy land. Above all, it is for us to develop in the workers of all races a positive class consciousness, based on the unity of the African, Indian, European and Coloured proletariat against capitalism and for socialism.

The Party's analysis reveals very clearly how far ahead of any other body in South Africa were the communists in their understanding of their country and its needs. Nevertheless, from the vantage-point gained by our knowledge of subsequent events, it is possible to see that in this analysis, though at a far more advanced level, there are defects of a similar type to those of the period before the "Native Republic" slogan — principally a tendency to underrate and underemphasise the revolutionary character of the national struggle.

While it is absolutely correct that basic to everything in South Africa is the class struggle, and that it is because of imperialist exploitation that there is national oppression in South Africa, the fact that the overwhelming majority of the people see their immediate enemy as the national oppressor of all classes rather than the class oppressor of all nationalities, is not because of lack of political consciousness, but because their experience shows them, just as their Marxist-Leninist understanding showed the delegates at the 1927 Congress of the International, that the first task is the winning of national freedom. As the first stage to a socialist South Africa, we must have an independent African republic with full protection and equal rights for all minorities.[3]

That the 1949 analysis tended somewhat to underrate the revolutionary nature of the national movement is evidenced by the declaration that it could avoid racialism only if it recognised the class alignments that cut across racial divisions; and by the belief that petit-bourgeois leadership was by its nature "irresolute and timid" and best described as "an intellectual revolt." In fact in the very week that the analysis was published in *Freedom*, the militants of Congress, rallied by the Youth League, were deposing Xuma precisely because of his irresolution and timidity, and were setting Congress firmly on its militant course with their famous *Programme of Action*.

These Youth Leaguers were students and teachers and professional men — as petit-bourgeois as their predecessors. They were men thrown up by the national struggle, and not the class struggle. And more significant still, although they were not communists when they initiated and carried through their militant policies, many of them were afterwards drawn towards marxism and the Communist Party.

Part of the explanation for this underestimation of the national movement may be that the Party's analysis erred when it saw the purpose of South African national oppression to be, like that of the national oppression in pre-socialist Eastern Europe, the attempt to prevent the development of a racial bourgeoisie. In fact, our oppressive laws have the purpose first and foremost of driving African workers to the factories and farms. Whereas in Eastern Europe the national oppression suffered by the workers flowed from the laws designed to shackle their bourgeoisie, in South Africa the restrictions on the bourgeoisie, crippling as they are, are secondary to the enslavement of the African worker.

For this reason, the African worker, when he fights the pass laws and all other oppressive chains, is fighting directly in his own class interests against the capitalist class; for this reason the national movement is not merely the movement of a bourgeois class attempting to arise, but a movement putting forward urgent class demands of the African proletariat.

One further point about the 1949 analysis needs to be made. Although in previous periods one of the cardinal questions had been the thorny issue of self-determination, this statement said nothing at all about it — except to criticise the Youth League's Programme of Action for claiming the right to self-determination. The analysis made the astonishing comment:

> Here is the familiar objective of nationalist movements. But what meaning must be ascribed to it in South Africa? The "right of self-determination" can only mean the "right of political secession" i.e., to set up a separate state. To be politically "independent" to "secede" would mean the dividing of South Africa into a "black" and a "white" state — would mean apartheid. Is that to be the aim, or must one understand the Programme to mean that the whites should be expelled from South Africa?

The Programme of 1949 brings us to the end of the survey of communist discussion of the national question. In 1950, shortly before the promulgation of a law making membership of the Communist Party illegal, the central committee, faced with an extremely difficult situation, took what was, in the view of this writer, an incorrect course, and decided on the liquidation of the Party. As one result there has not, since that time, been a journal for the discussion and development of Marxist-Leninist theory in this country.

At the present time, when the national liberatory movement is more militant and more politically conscious than ever before, with the working class acknowledged by all to be the leading force in it, the need is growing for further theoretical advances to show the way to swift victory. While the proletariat and urban petit-bourgeoisie are already in the arena of combat, their great and indispensable allies, the agrarian masses on the farms and in the reserves, are not.

88 People's History

In the sense that it is not a class slogan, but a national slogan, which will bring these masses into alliance with the proletariat, it may be said that the national question in South Africa is now primarily an agrarian question. And not only is this the case with regard to the content of the slogan, it is true also of the form in which our call is delivered. The rural people do not understand our newspapers and pamphlets, which, in the main, are produced in English. Most are illiterate or only slightly literate, and must be approached in their own language, but also through their own national idiom and culture.

This is mainly a practical problem, but it also has a political undertone, for in the very necessary struggle to overcome national antagonism and to build a united African political organisation, there has in the past been a hesitancy to foster separate nationalisms.

Dr. Potekhin, in his book on South Africa entitled *Formation of a National Community among the South African Bantu*, comments on the fact that an article opening discussion on the national question (which appeared over my initials in *Advance* in 1954) was never followed up. This was not accidental. Further discussion was not encouraged precisely because there was a fear among some that the raising of the "national question" might somehow adversely affect our international political unity.

The time has come to consider whether, under the leadership of the working class, a healthy, peoples' nationalism, within the framework of our firm multi-national political unity, need any longer be feared; or if indeed, this might be the best way to raise the political consciousness of the rural people.

Linked with this problem too, is the question which is going to be raised more and more frequently as the realisation grows that the Freedom Charter is neither treason nor a dream. Already a body of thinking and sincere white people believe that votes for all would simply mean the replacement of white tyranny by black tyranny.[4] It will be desirable to be able to explain to people what the Charter means when it says "All national groups shall have equal rights," and what is meant by "There shall be equal status in the bodies of state. . . for all national groups and races." Does this, for example, contemplate a bi-cameral legislature, like that of the USSR or China in which there is one house where all nationalities, irrespective of size, have an equal vote, or does it simply mean one person, one vote? And what do we mean by the term "national group"?

One answer we may give is that these are things which must be thrashed out at a national convention to plan the new state form, and that if people want to know the answer, they must urge the holding of such a convention.

But such a reply is not one that can be given by the vanguard party. The new state may not come about as the result of a round-table conference! We must have our answers ready now — not fixed and inflexible answers, for conditions change, but answers nevertheless.

Notes

1. In fact, they form part of the Afrikaner and English national groups. This statement would, of course, be hotly denied by the present spokesmen of Afrikaner nationalism. One of the facts hidden by the "race" smokescreen, which a more detailed study of the national question will reveal, is that the "Coloureds" are probably Afrikanerdom's richest national asset. I have expressed the view in an earlier article ("The Development of Nations in South Africa," *Marxism Today*, April 1959) that the Afrikaners (meaning the white Afrikaners) do not constitute a nation. This did not paint the picture adequately. When the Afrikaans-speaking Coloureds are included, the Afrikaners are a nation, dispersed throughout South Africa, but with their own territory, i.e., a territory where they constitute the majority of the population, in a part of the Western Province. At the same time it must be noted that the position is by no means static. The political discrimination against the Coloureds is in fact creating something akin to a Coloured "national consciousness", comparable perhaps with that of the Negro's of the United States, and the South African Coloured Peoples' Organisation is thought of as a national organisation like those of its African and Indian allies in the Congress Alliance. But any reasonably optimistic estimate of the time required for the winning of freedom precludes the development of a Coloured nation born of "race" oppression.

2. *International* 22.July 1921. Stalin's thesis on the national question had just become available in South Africa (it was reprinted in the following issue of the *International*) and its influence is seen throughout Andrews's article.

3. But, of course, this does not mean that there must be "two revolutions". Under the correct leadership of the working class, the national revolution merges with the socialist revolution and the assertion of national independence is immediately accompanied by the building of socialism. This the Chinese Communists have shown us.

4. See, for example, the pamphlet *The Betrayal of Native Representation* by D.B. Molteno Q.C., p.16.

5. The Congress Alliance and the Turn to Mass Action: The People's Reply

In the political upsurge of the war against Nazi Germany, a consciousness of their common interest developed among the African and Indian peoples of South Africa. The Indians in their passive resistance against Smuts' "Ghetto Act" in 1946, had the moral support of the ANC, and in turn, in the post-war anti-pass campaign the Africans were supported by the Indians. The move towards unity was signposted in 1947 by a formal pact of co-operation between the Presidents of the Indian and African Congresses.

Both organisations gained immeasurably from their unity and in the course of the continual state of hostilities between the Nationalists and the rest of South Africa, the South African Coloured People's Organisation, the Congress of Democrats (an organisation of Europeans) and the South African Congress of Trade Unions — the only non-colour-bar trade union federation — were formed and joined in the Congress Alliance.

The non-European organisations have adhered very strictly to a policy of non-violence in their opposition to the Nationalists. Although their every striving for freedom is met by Government force, although every time a legal channel of activity becomes effective the Government makes it illegal, with ingenuity the Congresses have sought out new methods of peaceful and lawful struggle. When the Government has blocked the last channel, new problems will arise but the people will certainly not be kept in thrall.

At the annual conference of the ANC in December 1949, faced with a stream of anti-African legislation, the leaders of the African people decided for the first time in their history to call for a one-day general strike as a protest against Nationalist tyranny. The delegates made it clear that they were determined to halt the Nationalists, and a new President, Dr Moroka, was elected to make a break with the somewhat somnolent leadership of the past. In the months ahead, Dr Moroka, in all his speeches, spread the theme which was to be the basis of the new militant Congress policy — unity with the Indians and Coloureds in a common struggle. "We are fighting for the freedom of the Indian people, of the Coloured people. We shall join hands even with those Europeans who are prepared to fight with us — and there are many of them," he told enthusiastic audiences.

With the spirit of unity shared by all, it was not difficult to find an issue for its practical expression. It came when the Nationalists banned Dr Dadoo, President of the South African Indian Congress, from attending any meetings on the Rand and at once the Transvaal regions of the Indian Congress, ANC, African People's Organisation (predecessor of the South African Coloured People's Organisation) and the Communist Party came

The Congress Alliance and the Turn to Mass Action: The People's Reply 91

together to call a "Defend Free Speech" Convention for the end of March, 1950.

Dr Moroka agreed to open the Convention. The enthusiastic turn-out to greet Dr Moroka on the day of the Convention was the first mass crowd of Africans in the streets of Johannesburg since the Nationalist elections — and probably one of the biggest until then. Met at the station by a huge crowd, Moroka was festooned with garlands — an idea that Africans had taken over from the welcome given by Indians to their leaders every time they came out of jail — and conducted to a flower-bedecked carriage, flanked by horsemen. A huge crowd lined up behind and the procession marched to the city hall steps, bringing traffic to a standstill on the main streets of the city.

The Convention decided to appoint May 1st that year as Freedom Day, when the people would be called upon to stay away from work as a protest against unjust laws.

The issue of the *Guardian*, a weekly newspaper later banned by ministerial decree, which came out on the Thursday before May Day had a strange appearance. The main front-page headline "Mass Rallies for Freedom Day" could be read only if the paper was held up to a sharp light. Over it was pasted — the *Guardian* staff had glued feverishly through the night — a strip of paper headed "Important Notice": It read:

Transvaal political meetings and processions for April 29th, 30th and May 1st have been banned by the Government. All such meetings have been cancelled. All announcements of such meetings in this issue are cancelled. The public is prohibited from attending.

So, instead, the people stayed at home. The Rand's industries came to a standstill. It was estimated that eighty per cent of non-European workers struck.

Towards afternoon the police began to take revenge. The offices of the Transvaal Indian Congress, with well-situated balconies on the first floor of the corner of Market and Diagonal Streets, Johannesburg, were the Freedom Day headquarters, and thirty or forty striking posters were displayed along the balcony of the street below, serving as a focus for small crowds all day.

The authorities had imported a chieftainess from Swaziland to condemn the protest day and had launched a terrific propaganda campaign to get the people to work — in the morning the radio reported falsely that everyone was at work as usual — and as the factories stood silent the rows of posters and jubilant crowds around them were too much for the police to bear.

Several squad cars screamed up in the afternoon, police poured into the Congress offices and tore the posters down and threw them into the street. For good measure, they seized a Moslem priest who was in the offices and bundled him out by the scruff of his neck. A few minutes later, without warning, a baton charge was launched against the crowd.

92 People's History

A *Guardian* reporter [it was Lionel Forman] crouched in the roadway taking photographs as the batons swung at the heads around him — but they never swung at his. A white skin still gave one immunity in a baton charge. Two police hustled the reporter to a squad car and the sergeant radioed headquarters.

"I have arrested a Jew communist," he reported in Afrikaans.

"What for?" crackled a voice back over the radio.

"He is taking pictures here."

"What?"

"Pictures."

"Pictures?"

"He's taking pictures."

"No, man," the voice laughed in a superior manner. "You can't arrest a man for taking pictures."

Things have changed since then.

That evening the police took their revenge on the people for their defiance. There were mass armed forays into the areas where the strike had been most complete. In Benoni, when the police arrived, a small number of people gathered round them out of curiosity, and no hostility was shown by either side. This small group of unarmed people was suddenly given three minutes to disperse. A woman who was an eye-witness described what followed in these words:

> I have never seen anything so horrible in all my life. The people were dispersing and walking unhurriedly away from the police in all directions. Some who had not heard the order were still standing together talking. It was not three minutes — it was more like three seconds — when suddenly the order was given to charge into the people. The police rushed into the crowd — some police with fixed bayonets. They slaughtered the people like cattle, stabbing them from behind and shooting them in their backs as they ran. I swear that there was no provocation from the people.

Third Avenue, Alexandra, a very narrow lane was the scene of more shooting. A pick-up van and troop carrier were passing through and the people had dispersed. One solitary stone was thrown by a woman as the pick-up van passed. It bounced harmlessly from the roof. There was no other stone-throwing or threat. But immediately the police opened fire with sten-guns. In a few seconds eight people were dead, including one fifteen-year-old schoolgirl.

In Sophiatown, the police instructed a small crowd to disperse. An eighteen-year-old boy, Brown Mpome, stood leading against a pole. A close friend of Brown told the *Guardian*:

> When the police told us to disperse, we all ran away. Brown just stood there against the pole. The police opened fire and I got a bullet in my arm. When the firing stopped, I saw Brown still standing there.

The Congress Alliance and the Turn to Mass Action: The People's Reply   93

I went to him and saw blood streaming from his neck. As I reached him, a policeman struck me down with a baton and arrested me. He raised his baton to hit Brown but before he could do so Brown fell to the ground. The back of his head had been shot away.

As the people gathered during the weekend at the funerals of those who had been killed, it was clear there was very great bitterness in their hearts. At the funeral in Alexandra Township, where Mr Moroka, President-General of the African National Congress, addressed the enormous gathering, one speaker said: "We have not made this a political funeral, but the people know that those whom we are burying did not die of taking poison."

There was mourning but it was not enough to mourn.

Meeting three weeks after the killings, the ANC national executive decided to call upon the other Congresses to set aside a day of mourning and to couple it with protests against Government oppression, and particularly against the "Suppression of Communism Bill, Group Areas Bill and all discriminatory laws in South Africa."

The Suppression of Communism Bill was then passing through its last stages in Parliament, and was seen by all the Congresses as an attack not only on communists, but on all expression of democratic opinion. The day fixed was June 26, the week in which the Communist Party dissolved itself, banned by the Suppression of Communism Act.

In centres where there had been no violence on May Day, the strike on June 26 was most solid. In Port Elizabeth, Durban and most Natal areas there was a complete work stoppage. On the Rand, scene of the recent bloodshed, it was less complete this time, but about fifty per cent of the workers heeded the call.

June 26 — day of mourning for those killed on the preceding May Day, day of protest against unjust laws — became a national day of the African people. With the years ahead it was to take on enhanced significance.

The 1951 Conference of the ANC decided, after consultation with the other Congresses, that the time had come to embark on a mass campaign of peaceful civil disobedience.

In a letter to the Prime Minister, informing him of the decision, Dr Moroka and ANC Secretary Walter Sisulu said:

The struggle which our people are about to begin is not directed against any race or national group but against the unjust laws which keep in perpetual subjection and misery vast sections of the population. It is a source of supreme satisfaction to us to know that we have the full support and sympathy of enlightened and honest men and women, black and white, in our country and across the seas, and that the present tension and crises have been brought about not by the African leaders but by the Government themselves. . . Posterity will judge that this action we are about to begin was in the interest of all in our country and will inspire our people for long ages to come.

94 People's History

The letter was not ignored. A gentleman by the name of Aucamp, the Prime Minister's secretary, answered it. "Resolutions adopted by the African National Congress at its annual meetings were, in the past, he said, sent to and dealt with by the Minister of Native Affairs and his Department. On this occasion, however, there has been a definite departure from the traditional procedure inasmuch as you have addressed yourself directly to the Prime Minister in order to present him with an ultimatum. This new approach is probably accounted for by the recent rift or purge in Congress circles, after which it is doubtful whether you can claim to speak authoritatively on behalf of the body known to the Government as the African National Congress."

However, Aucamp pointed out, the Prime Minister would waive this point so as to explain to Congress "that it is self-contradictory to claim as an inherent right of the Bantu, who differ in many ways from the Europeans, that they should be regarded as not different, especially when it is borne in mind that these differences are permanent and not man-made. .

It should be understood clearly that the Government will under no circumstances entertain the idea of giving administrative or executive or legislative powers over Europeans to Bantu men and women."

To describe the "differentiating" laws as being of an oppressive and degrading nature was to be guilty of a "totally incorrect statement. The laws are largely of a protective nature. Even those laws which are regarded as particularly irksome by the Bantu population have not been made in order to persecute them, but for the purpose of training them in the performance of those duties which must be fully observed by all who wish to claim rights."

Mr. Aucamp advised the ANC leaders to reconsider their decision, because the Government would "deal adequately with those responsible for initiating subversive activities." Instead they should decide to "work for the welfare of the people in a constructive way by helping the Government to carry out its programme."

The ANC considered this magnificent epistle and found itself unconvinced.

On 6 April, 1952, while white South Africans were celebrating the tercentenary of the arrival of Jan van Riebeeck — "founder of white civilisation in South Africa" — with extraordinary apathy, a crowd of 15,000 people of all races at a mass rally in Johannesburg repeated after Dr Moroka the pledge and dedication to struggle against unjust laws. Similar huge meetings were taking place all over the country. The campaign was on. The registration of volunteers began. June 26 — second anniversary of the day of mourning and protest which had followed the Rand May Day killings — was the day chosen for the commencement of defiance.

A week before, the Government carried out a long-standing threat to ban the *Guardian* by a ministerial decree in spite of a massive freedom of the press campaign backed by most English-language newspapers in defence of that paper. The *Guardian* had acquired the status of unofficial spokesman of the whole Congress movement, and its absence as an organiser and morale-booster would have been a disaster for the Defiance Campaign. But, without a week being missed, from the same offices and the same printer the same editor issued through the same circulation organisation to the same subscribers and readers a new newspaper called the *Clarion* without an issue being missed. It sold 8,000 more copies that week than the *Guardian* had sold the week before. The *Clarion* was the forerunner of *New Age*.

The six months from June 26 were among the most glorious in South Africa's history. In disciplined groups, inviting arrest and imprisonment, the defiance volunteers went about the business of breaking South Africa's unjust laws. Eight-and-a-half thousand had gone to jail for varying terms during those six months — serving probably one thousand man-years in the cause of freedom. They sat on benches in post offices and stations marked "Europeans Only". They walked the streets without passes. They went into locations without permission. They sat in "white" coaches on trains. And in every case they first made certain that they would be caught red-handed, making their appointments with the police as meticulously as they normally would with their dentists.

In Worcester the nine volunteers were nearly frustrated. After standing for half an hour in the European queue at the post office, all that happened was that the white post office clerk served them on that side! They had to repeat the performance the next day before the police could be made to co-operate and put them in jail.

There were some unexpected results of the campaign. Seventy-three Port Elizabeth defiers, also arrested for standing in the white queue at the post office, were set free when the magistrate held that there was no law authorising post office apartheid. In Cape Town it was similarly held that apartheid on railway waiting rooms had no legal foundation. The resisters had to find other means of defiance.

In the first month 1,200 volunteers defied the unjust laws. The police then launched raids on all Congress offices and those of Congress leaders, dwarfing any raid that had gone before. Simultaneously, sentences became more vicious. Some magistrates, having no power to order whippings for adults, began to make a point of sentencing all volunteers under twenty-one years old to be whipped. In jail, solitary confinement and spare diet was imposed at the slightest opportunity and prisoners were beaten up by the warders.

In the middle of August, the members of the Campaign's national action committee, headed by Moroka and Dadoo, were arrested. They were charged with having contravened the Suppression of Communism Act, by attempting to bring about a change in the country's social structure through unconstitutional and illegal means.

On 2 December, Justice Rumpff gave his verdict. To call upon the people to defy the law was communism and was punishable by the full rigours of the Act. All were sentenced to nine months imprisonment, suspended on

96   People's History

condition that they did not commit another breach of the Suppression of Communism Act.

At the same time, the Nationalists and the United Party united to pass new legislation providing for the most vicious punishment of defiers. With the political wisdom which has been a feature of the Congress Alliance, the Defiance Campaign was brought to a close, with the progressive forces still intact and enthusiastic. The 40th Conference of the ANC, meeting in Johannesburg in December, was already charting new campaigns.

In the course of six months, the Defiance Campaign transformed the entire South African scene. There was no Congress member now who did not know that it was direct action and nothing else which brought strength and new membership to the organisation. The paid-up membership of the ANC a few months before Defiance was 7,000. Less that a year later it was 100,000.

The campaign gave birth to two new organisations which took their place in the Congress Alliance: the Congress of Democrats, an organisation of whites, and the South African Coloured Peoples' Organisation. Above all, the complete unity between the leaders of these groups — steeled under fire — was an accomplished fact.

For the December Conference of the ANC it was a matter of "The Defiance Campaign is over. Long live the Campaign for the Freedom Charter!" At once the plans were begun for the next great campaign. Within a week of the ANC Conference, at which Albert John Luthuli, Nationalist deposed chief of the Amakholwa tribe, was elected President, the three other Congresses had all intimated their support for a Congress of the People to draw up a Freedom Charter.

The determination of the Congress leaders that there should be no break in the continuity of mass activity is shown by the fact that, although the Defiance Campaign had only just ended, the report of the National Action Committee to the ANC Conference on December 5 recommending the Congress of the People, complained of the "lull in Congress activities".

The sense of urgency was shared by the other Congresses. By the end of March, they had already accepted the ANC invitation to them to act as co-sponsors, and their delegates had met at the little town of Tongaat in Natal to make the first preparations. Tongaat was chosen because Chief Luthuli was confined to that district by a ministerial decree.

A National Action Committee was appointed, and it at once tried to win support from other organisations. Letters were sent to trade unions, churches, sports bodies, to the Liberal, Labour, United, and even Nationalist Parties inviting them to appoint representatives to participate in its preparation. A wheel with four spokes, symbolic of the four sponsoring organisations and the four main racial groups, rolling swiftly along, was adopted as the symbol of the Congress of the People. Soon the symbol was to be seen chalked and painted on walls in all of the cities, and the owners of the walls were giving evidence, against young people charged with malicious injury to property, of "a thing like a hot cross bun", or a "nought

The Congress Alliance and the Turn to Mass Action: The People's Reply 97

crossed out" or a "shield with a cross on it", which had appeared on their walls. Sentences were not light. Worst was four months imprisonment without the option of a fine imposed on two Coloured youths in Cape Town.

The main emphasis of the campaign was the call for demands which were to be incorporated into the Freedom Charter. The Charter was not a document prepared in advance — it was based on thousands of ideas and suggestions forwarded from all over the country.

On the fourth anniversary of the first Day of Protest and Mourning — 26 June 1955 — nearly 3,000 delegates gathered beneath a great green four-spoked wheel in Kliptown, a village just outside Johannesburg specially chosen because it was not an urban area and people of all races were therefore entitled to be there without permits. The Congress was on specially leased private ground, open to delegates only so that it could not be banned as a public gathering.

The delegates came from every centre of the country, converging on Kliptown by car, cart, lorry and bus. The national roads into Johannesburg were blockaded by the police, and delegates were stopped for pass and tax inspections. The Western Cape's 90 delegates fared worst. Two lorries in their convoy were found not to have the necessary transport permits, and 60 delegates were held up at Beaufort West and had to organise their own little Congress of the People there. Delegates from little country dorps in the Northern Transvaal were simply refused train tickets by the railway clerks.

At the Congress itself, each section of the Freedom Charter drafted on the basis of the demands submitted, was introduced, opened for discussion, and voted upon. Throughout the Congress scores of plain-clothes detectives lined the hessian fence surrounding the meeting site, recording the speeches and photographing the delegates. Shortly before four o'clock, when the last sections of the Charter were under discussion, Congress of Democrats President Piet Beyleveld jumped on to the platform and announced: "Armed police are approaching. We don't know what they want. Please keep your seats".

The crowd rose as one, and standing still in their places, began to sing "Nkosi Sikelele, Afrika". Armed with sten-guns, the police mounted the platform and began methodically to stack up for removal every document, book, and paper in sight, even the kitchen posters marked "Soup with meat" and "Soup without meat". Cordoning the Conference square, they then moved in among the delegates, searching them and taking down their names and addresses, after announcing from the platform that they were acting on the suspicion that treason had been committed.

"Shall we proceed?" said the chairman, and he called upon the women's leader Helen Joseph to introduce the section dealing with houses, security, and comfort for the people. And so, while the police methodically interrogated and searched the delegates in groups, the Congress of the People continued its work, the creation of an affirmation of faith, hope, confidence and freedom from police intimidation — the Freedom Charter. It was not until eight at night that the police finished and permitted the delegates to leave.

Eighteen months later, when the Freedom Charter had spread to the four corners of the land, came the dawn raids, the imprisonment without bail, the solemn declaration by the prosecutor that he intended to prove treason.

Part Two:
The Treason Trial

The excerpts from *The South African Treason Trial* reproduced here provide one of the few contemporary records of an important event in the political history of South Africa. Forman's insider account recreates the atmosphere at the Treason Trial and gives some inkling of how the Preparatory Examination was conducted and why the trial was eventually thrown out of court after four years. Forman and Solly Sachs had planned a follow-up book but before the trial ended Lionel died. Helen Joseph took on the task and in her Author's Note to *If This be Treason*, she wrote "This brilliant young journalist and barrister described the drama and comedy of the long drawn out Preparatory Examination, and his book came to us on the very day that we were committed for trial. We sat in the cells under the Magistrate's Court waiting for our new bail to be arranged autographing each others' copies."

6. "You Can Hang for Treason"

> He believes in democracy because he so believed he is called by the Government a Kaffir Boetie and Communist but more those things are said he is more determined to side with the oppressed.
>
> (Extract from a speech by accused No. 12, Jack Hodgson as recorded in the notebook of Detective Sergeant Isaac Sharp)

At dawn one morning in 1956, twenty days before Christmas, police knuckles and police batons hammered at the doors of 140 homes all over the Union of South Africa; the doors of luxury flats and the tin entrances of hessian shanty *pondokkies* (huts), the oak of a parson's manse and the stable-openings of farm labourers; doors in comfortable white suburbs, in grim African locations, in Indian ghettoes, in cities, in villages and on farms far out on the veld.

One hundred and forty families were wakened that morning — Africans, Indians, Whites, Coloureds; doctors and labourers, teachers and students, a university principal, a tribal chief. And if the names and occupations were analysed, here was a complete cross-section of South Africa. Afrikaners, English, Jews, Zulu, Xhosa, Basotho, Hindi, Moslem, young and old; sick and healthy; university graduate and illiterate . . .

Those who asked for them were shown warrants of arrest. The crime charged in every single case — high treason — *hoogveraad*. What does it feel like to be hauled out of bed at dawn and arrested for treason?

Here is how it was for accused number 83, cell number 13 and co-writer of this book.

On the Monday before the arrests, *New Age*, the weekly newspaper of which I am the editor, went to the printers. The front page carried a warning that the government was preparing "some drastic action . . . The attack is likely to take the form of nationwide arrests."

And our editorial began: "It is becoming increasingly clear that the Government is planning its own version of the notorious Reichstag fire trial of Nazi Germany as a means of eliminating the most consistent and determined opponents of its apartheid policy. If it is treason to demand these rights for all South Africans, then we are proud to plead guilty to the charge of treason."

But one can know perfectly well that one is going to be arrested without really believing that it will happen. "The maid's probably lost the key and wants us to open up for her," I thought when the knocking woke me, two days after the editorial was written. But I knew perfectly well that the maid wouldn't hammer as loudly as that. My wife went to the front door and let them in.

"You Can Hang for Treason" 101

I had my gown and slippers on when the two Special Branch men came into the bedroom. "I am Sergeant Du Pisanie . . . I have a warrant for your arrest." I looked at the warrant and saw the words "High Treason, *Hoogveraad.*" That relieved the first tension. I often break Strijdom's laws. I read and own illegal literature — books like Aldridge's *The Diplomat*, Richard Wright's *Native Son*, and even *Black Beauty*. I serve my African guests with liquor — maximum penalty three years. I invite non-European friends to spend a week-end at my home — maximum penalty five years.

But high treason! "You can laugh," said Sergeant Du Pisanie. "But you get hanged for treason." And having delivered this friendly thought, the Sergeant and his companion from the Diamond Squad began to pull the books off the bookshelves.

The noises had woken our three-year-old, Karl, and he toddled in to see what the visitors had to offer by way of entertainment.

Du Pisanie pushed him away. "Get this thing out of here and leave us in peace," he said to Sadie.

"This is my house and don't you tell me what to do in it."

"You be polite when you speak to my wife," I joined in, trying to speak like a barrister and a gentleman, and not like a prisoner in pyjamas.

"I'll go down on my knees to her," said Du Pisanie a little defensively.

"Careful," I warned. "You just be careful." But I'd pushed the attack too far. He rushed at me and held a big fist under my nose. Don't threaten me!" he shouted. "Just don't threaten me! You're just a prisoner like any other prisoner and I'll break your bloody neck!"

I'm no hero. That was quite enough for me. I shut up . . .

The phone rang, Du Pisanie took away his fist, and I went to answer it.

It was an African National Congressman phoning from a public telephone in Langa Native Township. "Sorry to get you up so early," he said. "The police have raided in Langa this morning and they've taken Ngugunyeko and Annie Silinga away. Can you go and fix their bail?"

When I climbed into the police car, I still had a vague idea that I would appear before the magistrate, kick my heels for an hour or two while bail arrangements were made and get to my chambers a little late. I even suggested to Du Pisanie that I should drive down to the court in my own car so that I could go straight to town as soon as things were fixed up.

The idea didn't impress him. "You'll ride with us," he said. "And you'd better pack him a suitcase and bring it to Caledon Square," he told Sadie.

At the Court, three sets of fingerprints and palmprints were taken and my physical characteristics were entered on a card by a bored policeman. My hands were black from the fingerprint ink. I saw some Africans in an adjoining room rubbing their fingers through their hair to get the ink off. My hair was the wrong colour. The third policeman I asked took me to a tap and I got some of the ink off. He was astonished when I talked about a towel. "Use your handkerchief," he said. I did.

102   The Treason Trial

Then they took away all my worldly possessions. Cash, pen, watch, the notepaper I'd thoughtfully slipped into my pocket before leaving — everything.

Annie Silinga and David Ngugunyeko (President of the ANC in the Western Cape) were already in the dock when I was ushered into the court. We were the last batch. I was not permitted to go into the dock with them. Apartheid.

The magistrate came in looking cross and weary. He'd also been pulled out of bed at dawn for this top-secret court . . . "Are you Lionel Forman?"

"Yes," I said.

"I order your removal under arrest to Johannesburg to face a charge of high treason. The court is adjourned."

Johannesburg is a thousand miles away from Cape Town. This thing was getting more unreal by the hour.

"Johannesburg better than Transkei," said Annie "No-sentence" Silinga philosophically. Mrs Silinga, a fat, jovial woman, chuckled delightedly at me. "My lawyer is coming with me," she said. "That's good."

This was far from being the first time we'd been in court together. The Native Affairs Department had been trying to deport Annie from Cape Town for three years now.

The enforcement of the hated pass system is a relatively new thing to Cape Town, and when a few years earlier it was announced that in future all Africans in Cape Town would have to be in possession of a pass — a permit authorising them to remain in the area — there had been anger among the people. For the pass laws provide that any black person who stays without a permit for more than seventy-two hours in an urban area — and that includes the smallest village — commits an offence and can be sent to jail.

The women are particularly militant on the question of pass-carrying, and Annie Silinga, an almost illiterate Langa housewife, had come to the fore as one of the leaders of the women's anti-pass campaign.

"I will never carry a pass!" Mrs Silinga had told cheering men and women at meetings all over the Peninsula. And so, inevitably, the police came at dawn to the home in Langa where Annie and her husband Matthew and their three children had lived for many, many years.

"Where's your pass?" the policeman asked Annie.

"I don't carry a pass," said Annie. So she was bundled into the *kwela*, as the police vans are called, from the police cry *kwela! kwela!* — jump in! jump in!

The next day she came before the court of the Native Commissioner. "You are charged with being in the urban area without a pass," said the prosecutor. "Guilty or not guilty?"

"I do not carry a pass."

"Enter a plea of guilty," snapped the Native Commissioner. But the Congresses had got Mrs Silinga legal representation and a long battle was begun.

"You Can Hang for Treason" 103

A tiny group of people were at the time exempted from carrying permits — those who could prove to a court that they had lived lawfully and continuously in Cape Town for 15 years before the Act was passed in 1952, and those who had worked for the same employer for the whole of the past ten years. These people, the bountiful Nationalists conceded, were entitled to consider Cape Town their home, as long as they broke no laws. (This concession smacked of liberalism and in 1957 the Nationalists amended the law so that no Africans could consider themselves secure in an urban area.)

"We plead not guilty, your worship," said the attorney. "Mrs Silinga has remained here lawfully and continuously for over 15 years."

"The onus is on you to prove that," said the Native Commissioner.

And so Annie Silinga and her friends tried to satisfy the Native Commissioner that she had lived in Cape Town for the 15 years before the Act was passed and the three years since.

The magistrate did not believe her or her witnesses.

On appeal, the Supreme Court found it clear that she had been in Cape Town at least since 1939 — 15 long years. But that was not enough. The key date was 1937, and the court having only the written record before it must rely on the Native Commissioner's findings on credibility. The appeal was dismissed and the Appellate Division saw no reason to interfere.

So after 15 years of residence in Langa, it was held that Annie Silinga had not established her right to remain — and she was sent under escort to her "home", the area in the parched, famine-stricken Transkei reserve where she had been born, and where she no longer knew a single person or had a single relative.

In a phrase used by Annie herself, her three children in Langa were orphans whose mother lived and Matthew was a widower though his wife was alive.

Then one day Annie Silinga arrived back at her home. She made no secret of it. She came back and mothered her children and cared for her husband.

The Special Branch looked in their law books and scratched their heads. It seemed that they had to begin all over again.

A policeman went to the Silinga home. "Where's your pass?" the policeman asked Annie . . .

The second prosecution was still before the Appellate Division when Mrs Silinga was arrested for treason and taken to Johannesburg.

Apartheid came into operation for the trip from Wynberg to Caledon Square, so we had to have two cars.

There were 18 of us at Caledon Square and I was pleased to see them all. There's safety in numbers. Then the *kwela-kwela* drew up and we all piled in . . . There was no apartheid in the *kwela-kwela* and we all sat jammed together with nine armed policemen. The police were polite and restrained and everyone was in the highest of spirits. An African accused, Greenwood Ngotyana, even asked one of the white policemen for a match.

104   The Treason Trial

And to the general surprise the policeman took out a box and handed it to him. Encouraged, Greenwood felt in his pocket and offered a fruit drop. But this was taking good relations too far and the policeman snorted and turned away.

At the airport we sat locked in the lorry for over half-an-hour, the policemen prisoners with us. The *kwela* had been locked from the outside and the Special Branch had the key.

When the Special Branch men arrived, they had four more prisoners with them. First came old John Mtini, veteran African Congressman, walking along between the detectives, his back, as always, held as straight as it could possibly be. Uncle John is over seventy years old. He has been over seventy years old ever since I first met him about ten years ago, and he has not changed a scrap. His face creased into a happy toothless smile when he saw us all locked up in our cage.

What a rotten piece of work to drag old John Mtini out of bed at dawn.

The other three new arrivals were from Worcester — Asa Dawood, a young Indian woman, Julius Busa, secretary of the Worcester branch of the Textile Workers' Union, and Joseph Mposa, another trade unionist.

Asa had been in the wars before. Two years ago the Worcester magistrate held that an anti-apartheid speech of hers amounted to the incitement of hostility between Europeans and non-Europeans, and sentenced her to nine months. The Appeal Court disagreed.

Busa's last brush with the law was even more recent. He and five other Textile Union leaders had been charged with the incitement of workers to go out on strike. It is a crime punishable by three years in jail for an African to go on strike for any reason whatsoever, and an even worse crime for a trade union leader to urge such a strike.

Coloureds, unlike Africans, may still, under very limited conditions, use the strike weapon, and the Coloured workers at the Worcester textile factory had come out for higher wages.

The African workers refused to cross the picket-lines of the striking Coloureds. Not a single African gave ground and the strike was won. In turn, the Coloured workers refused to go back unless the wages of the Africans were also raised. The employers agreed.

But every one of the 300 Africans who had refused to go to work was arrested and charged. Each was fined £16, of which £12 was suspended on condition that he never struck again! They were allowed time to pay off the £4. It was a carefully balanced punishment. The workers could not be sent to jail because the factory would then come to a halt. For the same reason the fine had to be within their ability to pay, otherwise the factory owners would have had to fork out to keep their labour. And the workers, for their part, were not distressed by their punishment. Their wage increases more than covered the loss.

But if the workers en masse could not be punished, the trade union leaders certainly could. Busa and the other union leaders were jailed and held without bail for nearly a month before their case came on.

"You Can Hang for Treason"   105

Four men were called to give evidence that at a public meeting Busa and the others had called on the workers to strike. They would all have gone to jail had the frame-up not been an unusually clumsy one. The factory time-clock showed that at the time of the alleged meeting Busa had been at his machine in the factory, and two white foremen came to court to swear that he had indeed been at the job. "Case against all the accused dismissed," said the magistrate.

In the course of the strike, Mposa had also been arrested for "obstructing the police" — but this case against him, too, had collapsed. This time it was treason.

On the aeroplanes, apartheid once more. Blacks in one plane, whites in another. Apartheid is quite expensive. We could easily have fitted into one aeroplane . . .

The military airport near Pretoria where we landed was bustling with soldiers armed as for war. The Government was taking no chances with us 18 Capetonians . . . It was now late afternoon and most of us had had nothing to eat since the day before. So we were, perhaps, just a little less boisterous than we had been on our previous *kwela* ride as we sped along on the 30 miles to Johannesburg. As we entered the city, we saw the first newspaper posters — "140 Arrested in Treason Swoop."

At a robot an elderly gentleman ambled past the *kwela* with his newspaper. "Give us your paper, sir," Fred Carneson called out, dropping a *tickey* (a threepenny piece) into the gutter. Without any hesitation, the man pushed his paper through the wire mesh, picked up the *tickey* and ambled back to the news vendor to buy another.

We swarmed round. "We certainly are front-page news," said Fred, former member of the Cape Provincial Council, elected by the Africans of the Western Cape and unseated in terms of the Suppression of Communism Act.

"The Nats. seem to have gone completely crazy. Chief Luthuli, Professor Matthews, Reverend D.C. Thompson, Dr Naicker" Cape Town land surveyor Ben Turok read out the names. During the course of the coming preparatory examination, Turok was to stand for election to the Cape Provincial Council in Fred's old constituency as a treason trial candidate. He was to be elected, unopposed.

One thing stood out as clear as the pimple on the end of Strijdom's nose as we read through the astonishing list of names of the alleged traitors. The Nationalists had bitten off more than they could chew.

When we pulled up outside the Fort, we got our smiles ready and held our thumbs high for the photographers who were milling around the *kwela*.

But the big gates of the Fort were opened and the *kwela* drove right in. The gates were slammed shut in the face of the photographers. The authorities had been playing a frantic game of hide-and-seek with the press the whole day — and within the week photographers were to find themselves assaulted by the police and placed under arrest for daring to take pictures.

106 *The Treason Trial*

We climbed out of the *kwela* and looked about us. You get an unpleasant feeling when you go to jail for the first time . . .

Public Support: The Origins of the Defence and Aid Fund

Traitors are not usually popular with the public. Treason is a crime which arouses the most intense indignation and anger in the breasts of the people. And from the moment the news of the arrests flashed to the furthest corners of the country it became clear that these emotions had indeed been aroused.

Everywhere there was seething indignation. Everywhere there was smouldering anger. But the indignation and the anger were not directed at the accused people. They were directed at the accusers.

There is no doubt at all that the Government hoped that the wave of arrests would serve to smash the non-European political organisations and intimidate white opponents of Government policies into silence. The Nationalists were to be disappointed. The nationwide reaction was, during the first days after the arrests, one of revulsion against the Government's methods, and sympathy for the accused people.

A National Defence Fund was brought into being on the day of the arrests and its sponsors came from those very sections of the white community who in the past years have been reluctant to be associated with "political" issues. The list of people who identified themselves with the Fund could hardly have been more impressive. It included the Archbishop of Cape Town, the Bishops of Johannesburg, Natal and Grahamstown, the Dean of Cape Town, and a large number of other prominent Church leaders, the Hon. Richard Feetham, Chancellor of the Witwatersrand University and a former judge in the Appellate Division, The Hon. F.A.W. Lucas, another former judge of the Supreme Court, all the Liberal and Labour Party members of Parliament, Mr G. Heaton Nicholls, former South African High Commissioner in London, several distinguished university professors and even a general — A.R. Selby.

The Liberal Party issued an uncompromising statement urging the people of South Africa "not to be intimidated by these events nor to be misled into believing that there is something sinister about uncompromising opposition to apartheid and totalitarian rule".

The Labour Party immediately offered its Trades Hall offices as the headquarters of the Treason Trial Defence Fund.

In Durban, Alan Paton, Liberal Party President and author of the best-selling *Cry the Beloved Country*, together with other Liberal leaders gathered on the same platform with representatives of the Congresses — the very Congresses whose policies were being arraigned as treason. (Months afterwards, with the sort of fizzling anti-climax for which the Nationalists are famous, they were all brought to court and charged with the offence of holding a meeting without the permission of the city council.)

On the day after the arrests, Father Jarret-Kerr, who had come to South Africa to replace Father Huddleston as the head of the Community of the Resurrection, presided over a meeting of members of a number of organisations and a "Stand By Our Leaders Committee" was formed. "Let us show the Government and the whole world that we, the people of South Africa, of all races, stand by our leaders in this hour of trial. As they have been faithful to us, so we shall be faithful to them," Father Jarret-Kerr declared.

Over the week-end men and women bearing placards "We Stand By Our Leaders" silently took up positions at bus stops and other public places.

And from the very day of the arrests food and gifts poured into the Fort. Three times a day full meals were brought for all the "treason" prisoners; newspapers, books, clothes, washing material — even special foods for prisoners on diet — were all sent in.

African, Indian and European women took turns at the catering. Groups sat up late through the night preparing sandwiches for the six o'clock breakfasts, and men and women together carried heavy steaming coffee urns into the Fort.

In Fordsburg, several Indian homes were all but converted into bustling kitchens where the gigantic task of turning out hot meals for the 153 prisoners was efficiently carried out — a woman doctor, Zainap Asvat, acting as O.C. Food. Africans in jail who had never before been introduced to curry had an education. Twice a day they ate curried fish or curried eggs or curried meat or curried beans. Water consumption at the Fort rocketed.

African washerwomen at Orlando offered to do all the prisoners' laundry, and stood singing at their tubs as the bundles piled up around them. Non-European shop-keepers supplied the committees with generous quantities of fruit, vegetables and meat. A butcher supplied a whole sheep daily. And, anonymously, many white businessmen — even one or two big wholesalers — made large donations.

It was surely a remarkable thing: 153 people were fed — well fed — for sixteen days, and not a single penny was spent [by the Fund] on the food.

7. The Evidence Begins — Soup Without Meat

It is long that we have been demanding freedom from Europeans and they have been refusing and we are going to fetch it now.

(Extract from a speech by T. Mqotha as recorded in the notebook of Detective-Sergeant N. Sogoni.)

For the first six weeks of the examination the prosecution did nothing but hand in the thousands of documents seized in the frequent raids on homes, offices and meetings.

A notice over the kitchen at the Congress of the People, "Soup without meat", was solemnly read, marked as an exhibit and handed in. The next exhibit was, logically enough, "Soup with meat". Even Sergeant von Papendorp, who had seized this evidence of treason, and who had been brought to court to swear to that fact, could not restrain a shamefaced laugh. Perhaps those posters were really disguised communist slogans? Almost as if the thought had crossed his mind, von Papendorp volunteered, as the magistrate studied the exhibit, "There was two kinds of soup, your Worship."

Most of the documents were newspapers, magazines and books which had been seized. And, handing them in, the prosecutor doggedly maintained the pace of an ox. When for example a two-year series of issues of the monthly *Fighting Talk* were dealt with, instead of having the whole collection identified as a single exhibit, he handed them in one by one . . .

And if that wasn't enough to make a man scream, an identical pile of the identical magazines, seized from another accused, would be handed in, in the same drip, drip, drip fashion.

Invitations to dinners and to weddings. Letters to girl-friends. Almost every kind of document you could think of finding in a person's pocket. The rumour spread that the Government was determined to keep the affair going until right after the 1958 elections.

Some of the documents brought one up with a start as an illustration of the nature of this battle of ideas. The United Nations Charter was handed in. It was found on a table at the Congress of the People. "Read the opening section to the court," said Mr van Niekerk in the solemn tone normally reserved for "Show the jury the murder weapon".

The detective read, stumbling over the words: "Whereas it is essential, if man is not compelled to have recourse, as the last resort, to rebellion against tyranny and oppression, that human rights should be protected by law . . . "

The magistrate made a note . . .

The Evidence Begins — Soup Without Meat 109

Two seats away from me sat fellow Capetonian Alex La Guma, Coloured leader and son of a Coloured leader, who is on the staff of *New Age* and has blossomed in to a first-rate journalist and story writer. This is how La Guma captured the atmosphere for *Fighting Talk* . . .

The cop at the door looks bored. He tilts his chair back and eases his gun harness, stares at the hessian ceiling as if he sees something hypnotic up there. In front of me a ladybird crawls carefully up the back of Archie Patel's chair, hesitates about six inches from the top and decides to turn back. You can cut the heat with a knife. 156 bodies stir uncomfortably in the diamond-wire dock. Somewhere voices clack metallically.

Duplicated copy of a speech by Lilian Ngoyi.
Yes, your worship, I hand in this document.
. . . Peace Council . . .
. . . Worship . . . document . . .
Do you know a man named Stanley Lollan?
I am surrounded by South Africa. Damons, Nthite, Hoogendijk, Horvitch, Moonsamy, Shanley. Workers, housewives, clerks, lawyers, journalists, doctors, priests, trade unionsts.
Pamphlet called "New Life in China" by Ruth First.
I hand in this document, your Worship.

There is Dr. Motala, who cannot find somebody to replace him, so many of the sick in Maritzburg must go unattended. And there is Sibande, the Lion of the East, whose home has been the country roads ever since he was deported from the area where he had lived and his house sold for ten pounds at a public auction.

The ladybird has reached a paling across the back of the chair and advances cautiously along it, waving its tiny antennae.

The court orderly is a youth in a khaki uniform, with a gun as big as a plough-handle at his waist. He carries the exhibits from the prosecutor across about twenty yards of floor to the witness in the wooden frame box.

Is this an invitation to a dinner . . . ?
Yes, your worship. I hand it in.

In the wire dock the accused spend five and a quarter hours each day. Five and a quarter hours taken from one hundred and fifty-six lives every day. Five and a quarter hours wondering whether the folks at home are all right. Whether the baby will recognise his daddy when he gets back home. Whether the Defence Fund has collected enough money to support one hundred and fifty-six families.

One hundred and fifty-six families to feed.

110   The Treason Trial

The ladybird has encountered an obstacle in a projecting fold in Archie Patel's coat. The antennae feel forward cautiously. The tiny oval body goes into reverse for a few minute paces.

Did you, on the 26th September, search . . . ?
That's correct, your Worship.

The heat beats down in waves. Heads nod. Eyelids struggle to keep open. Ears strain to listen. In Nazi Germany the Gestapo used a deadly, vicious and ridiculously simple method of torture in order to force confessions. They didn't allow the prisoner to fall asleep. Night and day. Day and night.

Twelve million people to liberate, and one hundred and fifty-six families to feed. What is the price of freedom? The thunder on the door in the early dawn? A ride in an aeroplane? The roaring swaying drive in a steel truck? The roar of the crowds? *Afrika Mayibuye!* All these small instalments . . .

The magistrate is grey-haired and dapper, the prosecutor smooth-shaven and suave, and the defence counsel alert under the fluorescent lights. And beyond the battery of microphones, the recording apparatus and the gin-bottles full of drinking water, the accused perspire in their wire pen.

To the magistrate on his platform the 156 people in the dock form a conglomeration of faces, each one different, skin, clothes and hair forming an irregular pattern of colours, brown, black, white, tan, pink. Each face is a name and a number . . .

Let us put flesh and blood to some of those names and numbers.

Stout, chubby, Bertha Mkize of Durban is accused No. 132. "I'm sixty-seven years old. I hope they make this business short and sweet. I've got lots to do back home." A member of the ANC, Mrs Mkize does sewing for a living. She is worried about the rent for the little shop she occupies. "And the house rent, and the monthly instalments." She clucks faintly, and then shrugs and her eyes are merry behind the spectacles. "We shouldn't worry too much. I am prepared to take what comes. No, I have no regrets. Never."

William Mini, New Brighton, Port Elizabeth, age 37. He is a magnificent bass and in the Fort his voice rolled above the combined effort of all the others, singing a song he himself had introduced: *Iza unyatele Afrika, Strydom shoo . . .* ("Strydom, beware, Africa will trample you"). Tall and hefty, with a tan-coloured, freckled face, he is a veteran of the Defiance Campaign, who served three months for breaking railway apartheid regulations. He has lost his job as a packer in a battery factory because of his arrest.

"I earned £3 15s. a week. I'm not sure about what is happening to my wife and three children." Then he adds with a grin. "But we have many

The Evidence Begins — Soup Without Meat   111

friends. I am not sorry I'm here. Right now I'm taking part in the bus boycott. I walk to and from Sophiatown where I'm staying. Get a lift sometimes."

In Newclare where he lives, and to everybody in the Congress movement, Andries Chamile is affectionately known as "General China". He is fifty-nine years old and sells *New Age* for a living. While he was in the Fort thieves broke into his home and stole all his clothes. "There was nothing I could do about it. Anyway, I've got some other clothes, and many friends came to my assistance. That's life."

Things are not so good with his family, and the Fund has promised to pay his rent. "But," he says, blinking and looking a little sad, "it's my gramophone I'm worried about. I still owe some money on that and I don't want to lose it. I hope they'll agree to pay the instalments." Then he brightens as he tells with pride how he was arrested during the Bantu Education school boycott and again during a bus boycott. "Now I'm ready to pass a higher examination."

The youngest among all the 156 accused is Mosie Moolla. At twenty-two he is joint secretary of the Transvaal Indian Youth Congress, with a premature moustache and a perpetual grin on his baby-face. Mosie was expelled from school for participating in the Defiance Campaign, and now has lost his job as a clerk as a result of his arrest. A little worried about the fact that he cannot help to support the family, the grin nevertheless remains. In the cells he was one of the most enthusiastic singers, but with the worst voice.

Simon Nkalipe, intense face and burning eyes, finds the grim old Drill Hall a pleasant change from his normal surroundings. He has been serving eighteen months in the Grahamstown jail for addressing a gathering although banned by ministerial decree from doing so. "A religious meeting," he says, "but even that was forbidden." Now he travels in daily from the Fort, has a decent meal and a smoke with his friends. Treason has its silver lining.

At the other end of the scale are Bob Asmal, V. Maake and Joe Molefi, who were committed by a magistrate for trial on charges of murder exactly two days after they were arrested in the dawn "treason" raids. They had been part of the leadership of the boycott committee which had won transport improvements for the people of Evaton after a long and bitter battle, in which anti-boycott thugs had been let loose to terrorise the township into surrender, but had failed. Lives had been lost, and to nobody's surprise the terror gangs were not charged. The boycott leaders were.

During the June adjournment of the treason hearing, Asmal, Maake and Molefi appeared in the Supreme Court, where charges were reduced to "public violence". Judge Kuper found them not guilty, which was an eminently just decision, because they were not guilty . . .

Flesh and blood. Lawrence Nkosi sits for a few weeks, coughing tuberculous blood into his handkerchief. Finally he is allowed to go to

112 The Treason Trial

hospital for the duration of the case, as long as he undertakes to read the record of the evidence.

Even the magistrate looks concerned when he hears that one of the Shanley children, whose parents are accused numbers 133 and 134, has been taken to the Fever Hospital as a polio suspect. Everyone is happy when the boy is found not guilty of polio and is detained only a short time for 'flu.

Accused No. 111 is a lively, talkative, bespectacled woman, Florence Matomela of Port Elizabeth. She walks upright and energetically and as she chatters, arm in arm with her friends, she curls her lips in speech, as though to give full and proper effect to every syllable. The many struggles in which she has participated, and her equally numerous arrests — for she has been in and out of gaol for one political offence after another — have not dampened her ardour. Yet, strangely enough, she first chose the quiet and sedate calling of a school teacher.

She remained sedate until 1950, when, fully forty years old, she was roused into action by the decision of the Port Elizabeth municipality to permit no African to remain in the area unless he or she was given permission by the town council. That day, 4 November 1950, remains clear in Florence's mind, for she passed her apprenticeship then. The women, singing *Lizabise Idingalakho Nkosi* ("Lord, may thy promise be fulfilled"), marched to the superintendent's office, led by Florence Matomela, and on that day the permits were burnt.

In the Defiance Campaign she was the first woman volunteer and went to jail for two months. A year later, on the same campaign, she got nine months, suspended for three years.

As the evidence is led a faint smile flits across her face as she recalls her exploits as provincial organiser of the Women's League of the African National Congress, how she carried her message deep into the Eastern Province, her shawl tied around her waist and her bag containing her few belongings resting on her head, going from village to village, talking and explaining till the early hours of the morning. The secret police would be on her trail, but always too late. They would arrest her finally at her home in Korsten. *Afrika! Mayibuye!* her little nine-year old daughter would cry, raising her thumb, and Mr Matomela would return from his job at the chemical factory and learn that the police had been there.

For, besides her political work, Florence Matomela is a mother of five to whom she is devoted. She is a sick woman too, suffering from diabetes. "I was in bed for three weeks with pneumonia, when they came for me on December 5. And here I am. *Ndilindele umayonzeke.* They will never put out the fire that is sweeping through the country" (From a profile on Florence Matomela by accused Henry Makgothi, *Fighting Talk*, June 1957).

In the middle of everything, three of the accused — Oliver Tambo, medical student Syd Shall, and trade union secretary Doctor (of Chemistry) Ronnie Press — took the opportunity, on the same day, during a short adjournment, to get married. Never in the history of South Africa have so many people accused of high treason gathered together to celebrate a wedding of so many people accused of high treason . . .

Robert Resha, who worked very closely with Father Huddleston in the campaign against the Western Areas Removal Scheme, and who is now sports editor of *New Age*, is also hard at work on his notepad. While the images are flowing easily from La Guma's pen, Resha works hard at his writing. But he gets his picture too: this matter-of-fact practical one from *New Age*, February 1957:

> The authorities have been at pains trying to implement apartheid. One entrance to the Drill Hall was reserved for "Europeans Only", but this has failed. All prisoners use the "Non-Europeans Only entrance". Attempts to separate the women prisoners in the use of lavatories have also failed. All the women are using toilets originally reserved for "European Women Only", and the officials have got used to the idea.

> Seating accommodation for prisoners is arranged alphabetically. You find Helen Joseph (European) sitting next to Paul Joseph (Indian), Isaac Bokala (African) beside Piet Beyleveld (European), Asa Dawood (Indian) next to Fred Carneson (European), Reverend Calata (African) next to Stella Damons (Coloured).

> The messenger policeman who delivers documents from the prosecutor to the witness and then to the defence counsel table and back to the prosecutor is the centre of amusement. He travels a distance of twenty yards to complete the delivery of one document. So that he walks two and a half miles each day and thirteen miles a week. The prisoners who stay in the areas that are boycotting the buses refer to him as a fellow boycotter . . .

While the Congress leaders sat in court, great things were happening outside. The arrests were the Government's show of strength. The people smiled and began to show their strength. From out of the early morning mist which enshrouds Alexandra Township came an army to deal the Strijdom Government its first defeat.

Alexandra is a dreadful slum nine miles from Johannesburg. In its one square mile are jammed over 60,000 people, almost all of them Johannesburg workers and their families. Nearly all the men and most of the women make the daily eighteen-mile trip to and from the city, which would falter and die if they did not come. The people of "Alex" do not live there because they want to. They live there because the apartheid laws do not permit them to live nearer their jobs, and they must live somewhere. Their earnings keep them well below the poverty datum line, so every penny counts.

Every penny counts. The bus fare to Johannesburg is fourpence each way. A fair price for nine miles, but all that the people can afford. With

114   The Treason Trial

effect from 7 January 1957, four weeks and two days after the arrests, PUTCO, the bus company, announced that it was raising the fare by one penny. It had been trying to do this for fourteen years. In 1943, when Smuts was premier and the war was still on, "Alex" had walked for nine days and the penny rise had been defeated. In 1944 the people had had to walk for seven weeks. But they won.

Now PUTCO tried again. And this time the company had the whole might of the Nationalist Government behind it. Schoeman, the Minister of Transport, said flatly that the Government would see to it that the boycott was defeated. The people had no genuine grievance, he said, the whole thing was "a trial of strength by the ANC." The Minister was to regret his words. For if it was a trial of strength, the ANC won hands down.

For three months nobody rode on the buses. And as a sign of the nationwide sympathy, there were short spontaneous boycotts of the buses in centres all over the country.

Nobody planned for months ahead. There was no preparation or propaganda campaign. The people knew they couldn't afford the penny and they wouldn't pay it. They couldn't afford the penny so they walked their shoe-leather down. They couldn't afford the penny so they paid more for taxis. But, come what may, they weren't riding the buses at fivepence. The police blocked the roads and stopped the walking men and women. Thousands were arrested for not having passes or not paying taxes. Africans who gave their fellows lifts on their bicycles were fined, cyclists were trapped for a variety of traffic offences.

And the Europeans who rallied to give lifts were harassed and hunted. Their cars were stopped, their licences were examined, their names were taken, their passengers were bundled out and searched. An Afrikaans-speaking university employee was stopped with Africans in his car. He lost his job.

Ironically, an African Security Branch man who had given evidence in the treason trial was caught operating a boycott taxi service and convicted.

The South African police force was used with the minimum of pretence as a PUTCO strong-arm squad. But *Azikwelwa* — "We shall not ride" — the people said and they walked the daily eighteen miles. Industry was dislocated. Workers cannot walk eighteen miles a day on a starvation diet and run the factories at top speed. Commerce went into a slump. No one dallied in town to buy — there was too long a walk ahead. And no woman was going to walk to the city just to do her shopping.

The Chamber of Commerce and the Chamber of Industries and the mayor set up a howl, and when Schoeman still would not listen, they sat round a table with the ANC agitators and worked out a solution. They put up the money themselves to subsidise the company and bring the fare down to fourpence.

The fare was fourpence. The people rode the buses.

The Evidence Begins — Soup Without Meat   115

And everyone knew that somehow the arrest of 156 people for treason had something to do with this first victory of the people against the Strijdom Government.

Nor was the boycott victory the only evidence that the "treason" arrests had not only failed to frighten the people, but that they had served as a spur to the anti-Nationalist upsurge.

In Johannesburg and Cape Town, almost the entire teaching staffs and student bodies of the universities, led by their principals and chancellors — in the case of Cape Town by the recently retired Chief Justice of South Africa, Centlivres — marched, gowned and hooded, in solemn procession through the streets of the city in the fight to stop the Nationalists from destroying the only two universities in the country worthy of the name, by prohibiting them from teaching non-European students.

Nurses marched in the streets in the fight against apartheid in healing. It was to be a criminal offence for a white nurse to co-operate on a case with a black doctor, or even a black sister . . .

The African trade unions, spurred on by the evidence of economic hardship spotlighted by the bus boycott, began a campaign for a minimum wage of a pound a day, and the whole Congress movement backed them.

A man on trial for his life (Ben Turok) on a charge of treason was elected unopposed, by the Africans in the area in which he lived to the Provincial Council. Unopposed!

All the bishops and prelates of all the Churches except the Dutch Reformed Church came out fighting against the introduction of church apartheid, and bishops solemnly announced that they would go to jail rather than carry out the law. The Defiance Campaign of 1953, when ten thousand went to jail, was being carried forward by the Anglican bishops. The Springs Methodist Circuit passed a unanimous vote of full confidence in the Reverend D.C. Thompson (one of the accused).

The Congresses announced, more or less from the Drill Hall, that the people's economic might would be used in a boycott of companies whose directors were Nationalists, and the air became loud with frantic cries from boards of directors that they had nothing to do with the Nationalists. Rembrandt, producers of cigarettes and tobaccos, even swore Supreme Court affidavits to that effect when they were the first to be named by the Congresses as Nationalists . . .

There was an immediate result of immense significance. Chapman's, a tobacco firm, half of whose shares were owned by Rembrandt, was included in the boycott list. Its directors at once approached the Congresses and gave them the written assurance that theirs was a family company and that Rembrandt exercised no control at all over the policy of the directors — non-Nationalists — who had run the firm before Rembrandt bought the shares.

The boycott of Chapman's was withdrawn. And a week later there appeared in *New Age* — which had long been completely boycotted by advertisers although its large circulation makes it an acknowledgedly ex-

116 The Treason Trial

cellent medium — a large advertisement for Chapman's tobaccos. The firm had signed a long-term advertising contract. The dike of Nationalist intimidation which makes advertisers afraid to use the pages of *New Age* had been breached.

Throughout the examination, a secret policeman called Kruger sat at the prosecutor's side, passing him the documents and whispering in his ear. The case was the handiwork of the Secret Police and they knew that on its success depended their future . . . They are jittery, edgy, vicious. They do not like being under the microscope and they have good reason for their fear.

The Secret Police

The secret police have humble origins. Long ago, some time in 1935, there was set up at Marshall Square a small group of five or ten detectives — a Special Branch of the CID — whose function was to keep track, secretly, of illicit gold and diamond dealings and tax and customs evasions.

The training the Special Branch men obtained in detective techniques at Scotland Yard fitted them for work during the Second World War investigating the Broederbond, the secret fascist brotherhood of which many Nationalist Cabinet Ministers are members, and the Nazi Fifth Column in this country.

After the war, the character of the Special Branch was completely changed. The new spying techniques, which had been rapidly expanded during the war years, were put to use against the Communist Party, trade unions and the Congresses. In 1946, following a week-long strike of the Rand's African mineworkers, there came the first Special Branch raids, on the offices of the Communist Party, and the trial of the Central Committee of that Party, on a charge of sedition. In this first public effort the Special Branch failed miserably. After a long preparatory examination, the Crown's indictment was thrown out by the Supreme Court. The prosecution, although given additional time, found itself unable to frame any charge.

When the Nationalists came to power, they had, already bequeathed to them by the United Party, an apparatus which could be built into the powerful secret police organisation which was essential to them if they were to retain power. They wasted no time. The Special Branch was swiftly transformed on the pattern of Himmler's secret police. The Branch had previously been part of normal police organisation, answerable to the Commissioner of Police. Swart (Minister of Justice) changed that. The Special Branch — which was renamed the Security Branch — was separated from all the other branches of the force, and made directly responsible to Swart himself.

By 1953 the secret force was so large that the *Rand Daily Mail* reported there were members even in little villages like Bethlehem in the Orange Free State. Not only was the secret police force expanded and huge additional undisclosed amounts spent on its organisation and expansion,

The Evidence Begins — Soup Without Meat   117

but, perhaps most important, under Swart's protection the secret police gained so great an aura of power that no civil servant dared question its dictates.

In spite of strict Post Office regulations forbidding postal officials to allow access to the mails, the secret police were allowed to intercept, read and copy letters in the custody of the Post Office. And the presentation in Parliament by the Liberal Party of clear proof of this illegal activity did not give Swart's secret police the slightest pause.

There are clear prison regulations requiring the admission of visitors, but the Superintendent of the Fort did not dare to question secret police chief Spengler's instructions that the "treason" prisoners were not to be permitted visitors. Nor did he refuse to attempt to impose an illegal political censorship on the prisoners' letters.

Even magistrates can be influenced by the Secret Police. A magistrate who refused bail to trade unionists charged with incitement to strike — they were acquitted at the end of the Crown case — admitted quite frankly that he had felt that he had no option to grant bail "if the Security Police are against it".

Not unnaturally the men of the Secret Police have tended to become drunk with power . . .

At first the Security Branch kept tabs only on trade unionists, "named" communists, Congress leaders. But now the police photographers and the men with the official notebooks travel further afield. Once they took the speeches of the Luthulis, the Dadoos and the Sisulus. Now Huddleston, Alan Paton, and former Chief Justice Centlivres himself are on police files. Once it was Congress demonstrations behind the green, black and gold flag that were watched by the Security Branch. Now the same force photographs and reports on an academic procession, led by the Chancellor of the largest South African university.

What is the purpose behind this wide-cast net? Partly, no doubt, it is that the Security Branch, like the Nationalist politicians who have let them loose, follows the standard fascist practice of dubbing all opposition "communist" and subversive, irrespective of the nature or content of the opposition. On this basis, Professor MacCrone's participation in a university protest is indistinguishable from a gunpowder plot. It is here that the Security Branch reveals its true character, as the straitjacket of opposition to the government, rather than guardian of the national security from subversion . . .

For a time, precariously, the courts seem to control the worst and most flagrant excesses of the Security Branch, but the government steps in to pass new laws which make legal what was formerly illegal. So, for example, Justice Blackwell's decision that the police cannot enter a private meeting without cause was speedily regulated by a new law which says in effect that the police can do what they like.

Strijdom's Government — hated by the great majority of the people, and facing a powerful and, in the long run irresistible liberatory movement

118 The Treason Trial

— is forced to rely to a greater and greater extent on brute force to remain in power.

Such a government cannot exist without a strong and lawless secret police, with comprehensive dossiers on all the government's political opponents and unbridled powers of intimidation.

But history has shown that when governments are forced into dependence on a secret police organisation, they find that they have created a Frankenstein monster which they can no longer control, and which, running wild, destroys both them and itself.

Part Three: "The Youngest and Proudest Card-Holder": Action Years 1947-59.

In a sense this section of the book reflects Forman's political development. A few of the surving chapters of *A Book for Karl* are reproduced in Chapter Eight. They are meant to give the reader a feel for the grassroots politics in the late 1940s when apartheid became institutionalised. Although an autobiography, the book was written in the third person when Forman lived in Sussex for a few months. One copy of the manuscript was burnt by his father who feared that it might fall into the hands of the police and another was lost after having been sent to Harry Pollitt of the Communist Party of Great Britain, whom Lionel hoped might publish the book. Pollitt wrote to say that he could not publish it, as it was too critical of "a brother party". Chapter Nine on imperialism is a selection of articles written by Forman in 1954 in *Advance* in a column entitled "International Summary" by "Commentator". They reflect South African left perspectives on world politics at the height of the Cold War, when local Liberals and Communists adopted almost without refinement the language of the superpower adversaries. However, Forman's independent view, as expressed in "Lessons from Hungary" was sometimes critical of the practical application of theoretical pronouncements from the Eastern bloc, but he maintained his pro-Soviet position. Throughout the 1950s he was concerned that unless socialism continued to be discussed, its ideals would be lost in South Africa. Chapter Ten contains some of his articles attempting to initiate and keep the discussion going. With foresight Forman wrote, "smashing apartheid will lift a very great burden from our shoulders. But it will not mean an end to our problems. Far from it. A new and greater challenge will face us — the building of a nation free from want. Both in the flight against apartheid and the planning of the future, the congress movement needs a partner in struggle — a multi-national socialist party. The article on "Stalin and Dictatorship" was not published, but "Lessons from Hungary" appeared in *New Age* on 1 November 1956 under the title "The Revolt from Hungary".

8. A Book for Karl

"Talking their Tongues Away"

One of the things it's hard to be much of a communist without doing a lot of, is talking to people. To one person at a time, to small groups or to the whole of Market Square or the Grand Parade. And you have not only got to talk, but to convince. To do that, understanding of your case and a calm voice are the best, but sometimes you've got to shout loud, sometimes even haggle. What a weapon speech is to the good communist. Think of Lenin saying calmly, "We shall now proceed to build a socialist state"; of Dimitrov shouting defiance at a Nazi court, or the thousands of councillors or shop stewards talking their tongues away to wrest every ounce of benefit for the people from the bosses' tribunals.

Get used to speaking to people, and practice doing it. It's no good reading to them. You must be able to speak without paper. There's a simple way to learn how to do that, which only requires hard work. Write out your first speeches and learn them by heart, word-perfect to every turn of phrase. People will be impressed with your gift of the gab and that will give you confidence and get you more opportunities to speak. After a little while, when you've studied enough to know how communists judge whether an argument is good or bad, whether it helps the people or harms them — you'll see that it's not difficult to get up and put in the simplest and most straightforward way possible what you think.

There wouldn't be any story . . . for you if it weren't that I got involved by our English master in the opening meeting of the Forest High School Debating Society. He was too intimidated by the big boys to press-gang any of them, so he told me that I was to speak on a motion "That the bus curfew should be lifted". The curfew was a wartime measure suspending bus services at ten every night as an economy effort. I don't remember which side I was on, but it was definitely a great success and the English master was very pleased, and told me I should read *The Grammarian's Funeral* by Browning.

My powers were immediately pressed into use on a more serious subject and I was made to move, the next week, "That the Natives Cannot Benefit from Education." What I said, luckily, I haven't the faintest idea, but a mental picture painted by Master Evans, seconder, with enormous appreciation from the audience, stands out clearly. "If you educate the Natives," he pointed out, "in no time you'll have some big fat Native woman coming and sitting next to you in the bioscope and taking out a greasy packet of fish and chips."

The fame of my powers having spread to the YCL (Young Communist League), I was asked once more to speak at an inaugural debate — the establishment of our YCL speakers' class. For the opening theme, four

A Book for Karl 121

strangely chosen characters were placed in a sinking ship with only one lifebelt. The sailors in this predicament were Pasteur, Stalin, George Bernard Shaw and Trotsky. I was Trotsky, and I regret to say that the other three were permitted to drown.

Immediately I floated ashore, I was given the job of organising the YCL Debating Club. The YCL Debating Club and Speakers' Training Course met every Wednesday at 5.30 p.m. in a room on the second floor of the Left Club in Commissioner Street . . . Except for me, the members were African workers in town who came in straight from their jobs. There were four of us when the group began, but within three or four weeks we had blossomed out to between 30-40 members, divided up into four main political parties, with prime minister, cabinet, regular motions and bills, exactly like our hazy idea of the real parliament.

We had a United Party government in coalition with Labour and a Nationalist opposition. A United Party member would move whatever motion was actually before the house and give official reasons for the motion. We made only one improvement in the actual parliamentary set-up. We added a strong Communist Party to the opposition.

As the fame of our parliament spread, we began to get bigger and bigger audiences listening to the debates each week. It was never long before voices in the audience were to be heard denouncing or approving a speech, and at half-time we would invite the audience to join the groups and affiliate to one of the parties. After half-time, the audience always completely disappeared and the ranks of parliament bulged on all sides.

It says sufficient for the unanswerable policy of the Communist Party among the African people that, after hearing the speeches, the audience all always insisted on becoming Communist parliamentarians, in spite of everything we did to keep up the strength of the other parties and to win reinforcements for the hardy few who had at the beginning volunteered to put the case for white "civilisation".

These comrades never lampooned the government case, but stuck very closely to the kind of arguments put forward by the eminent ministers themselves. These arguments, which to the European farmers, businessmen, teachers, university professors, were clear and logical always caused the audience to roar with delighted mirth when put forward by an African in a tone of utmost seriousness.

The United Party managed to retain three or four of its original members, who each chose one United Party luminary and modelled themselves on him, reading up his speeches and imitating the reports of his style.

But the Nationalist Party was able to retain only one — Seperepere. He soon became the star attraction of the meeting. Calmly and reasonably putting forward the Nationalist race theories, arguing the merits of apartheid, pausing severely at the waves of laughter and interruption to say as a weary aside: "You see what happens when they let ignorant kaffirs sit in Parliament."

Comrade Seperepere subtly offered just the right amount of provocation to be the cause of bringing some comrade to his feet with a pertinent answer or joke who would otherwise have been reticent at speaking publicly.

Seperepere's speeches did not require quite the brilliance and subtlety which went into arguments for the United Party. For that Party, Comrade Mopeli, a chauffeur, excelled himself in the role of Jan Hofmeyer, the typical bosses' hypocrite, who as Smuts' deputy would often put up a shadow fight against the more vicious of the racialist laws, to quieten popular protest, and then sell out at the crucial moment. Such is the desire of white liberals to be gullible that Jan Hofmeyer is still mourned among them as a heroic champion of freedom.

The audience listened carefully as Mopeli made his introduction to some bill. "Everyone in Parliament must realise that the day must come when Africans will have direct representation in this House. It is our task as Christians to prepare the Africans for that day, by providing better educational facilities, better . . . "

"Kaffirboetie", Seperepere interjected.

"As a Christian I am a lover of all mankind", replied Mopeli urbanely.

"And womankind. A lover of Kaffir womankind".

Seperepere's sally was so typically Nationalist that it could have come right out of Hansard, and the audience laughed its appreciation.

Like Hofmeyer, Mopeli was Minister of Finance, and like Hofmeyer, his budget didn't exactly reflect his appeal for better educational, health and housing conditions.

It wasn't long before we had a revolution. The Communists became tired of merely exposing what was wrong with the United Party government. They called for a vote and the House enthusiastically elected a Communist government.

The three-man United Party and Seperepere became a vocal little opposition, and Parliament set about laying the foundations for a five-year plan for South Africa. Soon everyone was so interested in working on this that even the four arch-reactionaries lost interest in their interjections and became recruits to the Parliamentary Communist Party. The dictatorship of the proletariat was established.

These were great evenings for us, and the debating group was for a long while the biggest source of new African YCLers.

These were the first Africans I had met. In my last months at school, I learned from a group of people, most of whom were barely literate, far more of value than I did in years at Forest High . . .

"Young and Immature"

If I seemed to stress at unnecessary length earlier on the paramount importance of discipline, it is because a single deviation from party discipline can be sufficient to do untold harm to your comrades, and because a person who persistently acts against the rules of the party is an enemy of the people. I hope this looks obvious to you, because indiscipline is the greatest hazard of the young communist, especially if he is self-confident and cocky and very sincere. Too often the young Turks think that they can put everyone else right, and they're prepared to use every opportunity to tell the world how wrong the wrong people are. Usually we sober down after the first once or twice we've had our heads soaked, but you should be one of the many that your comrades can trust implicitly not to do anything that will make them tear out their hair.

David [Lionel Forman] came back to Johannesburg for the few weeks before the new term began in March. It was much more than enough to make a great deal of trouble for himself. In fact all he really required was about two hours. Up to about seven p.m. Red Army Day, David was known by a small circle as a keen hard-working youngster who could make a good speech for his age. By ten o'clock he was known by a far wider group as a keen, hard-working, hot-headed irresponsible youngster who shouldn't be allowed near a party platform.

The YCL held a big celebration of Red Army Day at the Left Club, with Hilda Watts, City Councillor and first communist ever to be elected to public office in Johannesburg, as the star speaker. David was appointed to speak for the YCL. He prepared his speech in the usual way and didn't think that there was anything special about it . . .

Jenny [Ruth First] introduced David and announced that he would speak on what Red Army Day meant to youth. It was one of the biggest audiences he had ever spoken to, and he was nervous at first. He began by describing the enthusiasm of young people for the heroic achievements of the Red Army in the war against Nazism, and went on to talk of the great exploits of the Red Army in the infancy of the Soviet Union — how they drove out the invaders from the interventionist powers. The speech flowed smoothly and David gradually built it up for the declamatory climax.

> When we think of these heroic exploits and the amazing feats of these soldiers, defying and laughing to scorn the predictions of the military "experts" of all countries, it is necessary to understand why it was that this was a new kind of army. It wasn't because of a miracle. It wasn't any mystic reason. It was because they knew, and know, exactly what they were, and are, fighting for, and because this thing that they know is something that a man can willingly die for. It is for the right of a man to stand up straight and free, to live in brotherhood, to destroy exploitation and oppression.

> Out in battlefields, Soviet soldiers are giving their lives for that ideal.

> I sometimes wonder, if a Red Army man could witness the way we are choosing to fight the same fight, if he would be satisfied, or if rather, he would be amazed. What could he think if he was here for our celebration a little while ago, of the great October revolution?

124 *"The Youngest and Proudest Cardholder"*

What would he think if he stood and watched the women in fur coats going into the City Hall while crowds of Africans stood on the pavements and watched — barred from the hall because of their colour?

He who dies for the equality of man — what would he say if he knew that we held two celebrations — a big one for the whites in the City Hall and a little one for the non-Europeans in the Gandhi Hall?

What would he think if he knew that we were fighting white elections in colour-bar halls — that we trumpeted aloud our few hundred votes in Hillbrow and said nothing of the fact that we were defeated by the African voters of Orlando?

There was the usual applause when he finished and walked back to his seat. He noticed as he passed Hilda Watts that she was smiling at him and clapping also.

Then she went up and made her speech. She had a very good, toneful voice and she spoke as though David hadn't said anything out of the ordinary. Only once did she hint at it when she said, with a smile, that it was important that all sections of the population, including the "few hundred" if you could describe two thousand people as that, should be able to learn of the ideas that motivated the Red Army. Important enough for them to have the opportunity to learn about this, for people to be correct to tell them in colour-bar halls if that was the only way you could tell them.

"Why don't you just get out and join the Trotskyites?" said Eric [Eric Laufer] after the meeting. "You'll never speak again on a YCL platform if I have anything to do with it." David didn't take Eric very seriously because they had disliked each other for a long time.

He left for Cape Town on the same evening as the YCL Committee met, and he only heard that the matter had been discussed there a week later in a letter from Jenny.

"Eric was all for chucking you out on the spot," she wrote. "But I've still got a soft spot for you and put up a defence of how young and immature you are and that you should have another chance. All the Africans stuck up for you, but I can tell you that everyone is very angry."

But David was already very busy in Cape Town, and though he was shaken for a moment at the thought that, if it weren't for Jenny, they might have expelled him, he dismissed it as another nasty piece of work from Eric.

Students' Socialist Party

For the first time the Students' Socialist Party (at the University of Cape Town) had managed to have a non-European student, Lawrence, elected to the Students' Representative Council, and there had been a sharp reaction from the Nationalists.

A Book for Karl   125

Varsity (the student newspaper) always carried news of some new provocation. The Nationalists, who formed nearly half of the SRC, were now refusing to take tea together with Lawrence, now refusing to be in the official SRC photograph if he was in it, and generally being as vile as racialists are.

The SSP was very active in publicising the Nationalist actions as widely as possible, and mobilising opinion so as to be able to defeat them decisively at the next election. After one of the nastiest stunts of the Nats, David found when he arrived at the university that students were distributing leaflets at all the gates. "Take Care Lest These Insults to the non-European People Exact a Bloody Revenge," said the leaflets, which bore the stamp of the SSP.

"What on earth is this?" David asked Basil Jaffe, who was on the SSP Committee.

"Never seen it before," Basil replied puzzled. "My God, this will smash us."

Before long there was a spate of leaflets from all the other University groups. "Communists Threaten Murder" was the Nat. heading. "Inflammatory Statement by Student Extremists," said the United Party version.

A general meeting of the SSP was immediately called. In the meantime, it was discovered that the leaflet had been issued by two Trotskyist members of the committee, who claimed that an emergency had arisen and they had not had time to consult the other committee members.

The general meeting was the first experience he had had of the SSP and David could hardly believe his ears when he heard the discussion.

"That chap's talking as an open Trotskyist," he whispered to Max [Jack Schedrin].

"Of course — he's secretary of the local branch of the Fourth International."

"But he's on the SSP Committee."

"And what a bastard he is too," said Max.

"Do you mean to say party members are working together with them?"

"Always have."

David digested this information. If there was one thing he had learned, it was that to call a man a Trotskyite was the biggest insult possible. They did their dirty work from within the working-class movement. And this leaflet they'd issued was a classic example.

There was no doubt about the temper of the meeting, and it looked as though the Trotskyites had shown themselves up. There was a motion up calling for a statement denouncing the leaflet and it was clear that it would be carried. Josie Sandler and Hosea Jaffe, the two mainly responsible for the leaflet, put up a fierce argument in justification of it, but the motion rejecting the leaflet was carried by a two-to-one majority.

As one man, almost the entire group of about twenty people who had supported the leaflet got up and left the meeting.

126 "*The Youngest and Proudest Cardholder*"

The next day they distributed a statement at the university headlined: "SSP sells out Non-European Students — Backs White Chauvinists" announcing the formation of a new body, the Students' Socialist Democratic Party.

Shortly after this introduction to the university political scene, David was invited to attend the meetings of the students' group of the Communist Party. Discussion at the meeting centred on how unity was to be re-established in the SSP.

It was his first Party meeting and David was a little shy to argue, but he expressed it as his opinion that it was a good thing that the Trotskyites were out and now the SSP would be able to grow instead of being stifled by internal wrangling. He was the only one to express this view.

"There's a long tradition in Cape Town of the unity of all who call themselves socialist," Basil explained for him. "The position is that the SSP is not intended as an all-embracing popular front — it's for socialists, and the fact is that although we could increase our membership, we have got to consider what sort of new members we would get. We could draw in any number of white wishy-washy liberals — but the hard fact is that the non-European students like the stand the SSP has taken. It isn't very good that our meetings should be almost all white, and the SSDP people should be able to attract all the non-Europeans by seeming to be the only ones with a revolutionary policy. The SSP has 100 to their 31. But of 100, only 4 are non-Europeans and there are 22 with them."

David was not convinced but he said nothing.

As the last item of business, the Chair announced that she was sponsoring David's application for Party membership. There was a snag because he was seventeen and the constitution said eighteen but if the group agreed, there should be no difficulty.

A week later David was the youngest and proudest card-holder in the Party.

Nineteen Forty-Eight

May 1948 was one of those nasty elections where you worked like mad for a lesser evil which wasn't so very much less evil. David hated the meetings where he came to trot out the trite — we are for burying the Nats, not for praising Smuts. He expected the United Party to win, but only by three or four seats. The UP press was so bubbling with confident predictions of a majority of about fifty, that it was difficult not to be influenced.

The (Communist) Party was concentrating all its efforts in the Cape on the Flats, where Dick Sparks [Fred Carneson] was opposing the United Party candidate. There were 3,000 Coloured voters in the constituency, which was picked largely because it had the biggest non-European electorate in the Province.

A Book for Karl 127

The big initial drive was to get new voters on to the polls. There was a simple literacy test, involving the ability of the voter to sign his name, and David and tens of others spent every Sunday for months before the election going from house to house and signing them on.

Among the most virulent opponents of Dick's campaign was the Unity Movement, who tried to organise a boycott of the election with no success at all.

At the same time, the Springbok Legion was running a nation-wide sticker campaign against the Nats, and getting a great deal of publicity for plastering Nat strongholds with anti-fascist posters. A special university "sticker group" was organised when the time came for Cape Town itself to be dealt with. David, Irma and Dora went in one group, and setting out after midnight worked their way down Adderley Street. Each carried thousands of little gummed labels marked with a bayonet pinned through a squirming swastika. They developed a swift harmonious routine. Irma dipped a sponge into a tin of water and sponged the wall, David splattered stickers all over the wet surface, and Dora smoothed them down with another sponge.

They put on a big act when the police arrived in order to keep them occupied while other groups went on with their work.

"I wonder if you could help us, officer?" Irma asked sweetly. "Just wet this wall."

"Have you got permission for this?" demanded the policeman.

"Permission? What permission?" asked David.

"From the owners of these shops you"re defacing the walls of."

"Now, Officer, you know very well that you can't do anything unless the shopkeeper lays a charge," replied David, moving down with more stickers."

"I am warning you to stop this," said the policeman.

"Threatening us!" David whispered loudly to Irma, "Take his number!"

Irma went up to the policeman and peered short-sightedly at his hat.

"What is your number please, Constable?" she asked.

"None of this!" said the policeman, fingering his truncheon.

"Refuses his number!" Irma whispered to David.

"My number is 00769 and my name is Pretorius if you want to know. You wait here." And he got on his bicycle, and rode off.

They were a good few blocks further on when the police van arrived. This time it was a sergeant and he was much less impressed.

"Inside! Quick!" he said, and they got inside quick.

At the police station, they met Thelma [Naomi Kaplan] and Monty [H. Festenstein] and lots of other old friends. All the remaining leaflets and the brushes and tins were confiscated and when their names had been taken they were set loose. The police couldn't find any charge.

As one who knew the area, David was out at the Cape Flats on the whole of election day, visiting voters and bringing them into the polling booths.

"It doesn't look too good," was the general feeling at Dick's committee rooms.

The results came in the next day. David heard the first ones over the radio the next morning in the university tea room.

"Hillbrow: Bernard Friedman, United Party, 6,800 votes; Michael Harmel, Communist Party, 340 votes. Mr Harmel forfeits his deposit."

The students burst themselves with mirth.

At lunch, Mr Baskin came in rubbing his hands. "Looks good so far. The United Party has eighteen and the Nats two."

"Urban results," said David, "don't mean very much."

"You think so?" asked Mr Baskin, stopping the hand-rubbing.

David went to the Party office after lunch.

"Where's Dick?" he asked Lottie [Hettie McLeod] who was alone in the office.

"Poor Dick. He's been up all night watching the count."

Poor Dick slammed through the doors a few minutes later cursing admirably. "Lost my bloody deposit!" he said shamefacedly. They all roared with uncontrollable laughter.

David and Thelma spent the evening at Dick's flat listening to the last results. The announcer put on *Valse Triste* and announced the Standerton result.

Everything seemed terribly funny. "Smuts has gone, the old bastard. Serve him right," said Dick, and they all held their sides.

There was a United Party lead right up to the very last few returns and they sat tensely waiting for the inevitable and not believing it would come. Then they drove quickly to the Party offices, took out every paper there was and gave them to Thelma to hide at home in her wardrobe.

"The raids will begin tomorrow," said Dick.

Irma was waiting up when David got home. "Our summons has come," she said dramatically, reading him the letter: "That you did in Adderley Street unlawfully . . . "

She paused, and added with a shake in her voice, "We're the first political case under the fascist government."

What an anti-climax the case was. It was front-page news, and (Professor) Batson was startled to see that half his post-graduate class was in the dock. The Springbok Legion appointed two King's Counsel, and the Court was packed with newspapermen and accused. One of the King's Counsel made a speech on the law under which the accused were charged, which forbade the sticking of anything to any wall and demonstrated that it meant that you could be charged with putting up a picture in your own bedroom, which meant that the whole thing was *ultra vires*, and the prosecutor didn't even have a show-in.

Then he had a go at the second charge, which was that they had distributed election material without the address of the organisation and the second K.C. got them off on some other wangle.

"It's not taking the classical German form of fascism," Irma explained.

A Visit to Caledon Square

"Can you make the Parade meeting today?" Dick Sparks phoned to ask . . .

"Have a heart, Dick. This will be the sixth week in succession," David moaned.

"How are you for lectures today?"

"Oh, I can miss the bloody lecture, but the Parade must be getting a bit sick of me."

"I know," said Dick. "Actually Lottie was going to do it today, but the radio's just come through with the Moroka thing and there may be some provocations, so we need someone with a bit of experience. I've got a Central Committee meeting or I'd go. Lottie will be there to help."

"Hold on," said David. "Not so fast. What Moroka thing?"

"A few policemen have been killed there in a riot . . . The Nats are blaming the Party of course, so it's important that you should bring it into your speech."

"Righto. I'll be in for the loudspeaker in about half-an-hour."

There was a slightly larger group of policemen than usual around the statue which the Party used for a platform when David and Lottie arrived and set up the loudspeaker. The police were among the Party's best publicity agents at the time, because whenever they gathered in force the people knew that a Party meeting was about to begin, and hurried along to listen. The more police there were, the bigger the crowd was.

David weighed his words carefully when he came to the point where he'd decided to bring in the Moroka events.

"They're trying to say that the communists had something to do with the death of those policemen," he said. "Well, we didn't. Every night they raid the people's homes. Every night they arrest and beat up Africans in their own townships, and they are surprised when the people get to hate them with such a hatred that sometimes it cannot be controlled. The Minister of the Interior is the murderer of those policemen for sending them to the townships to maraud. Our Party is opposed to terror and the meaningless taking of life. We are against killing people, even if they're not really people, but policemen . . . "

"Watch out," Lottie whispered.

Two policemen were running up to the platform, and the others were closing in.

"That's the end of the meeting," said David trying very hard to sound as cool as a cucumber. "We'll be here again next week."

The police, whose instructions were to close the meeting without any violence, were a little nonplussed. The running policemen had been instructed to take away the loudspeaker, which was no more being used, and they felt like it was a bit of an anti-climax.

130 "The Youngest and Proudest Cardholder"

Inspector-Sergeant White of the political department of the CID restored official dignity. "Your name and address?" he said to David (information he had had for some years).

"Why do you want to know?" asked David innocently (he knew very well White knew very well).

"I'm asking you for your name and address."

"You can't do that unless you have a charge."

"Don't tell me my work!"

"I've studied the law," said David.

"Leave him alone," the crowd chanted. "Leave him . . . Police, *sies*, Police *sies*."

"I have information to charge you with sedition."

"Note that Lottie. Remember it for the court. Now, Sergeant," he said as pompously as he could. "Will you say clearly — are you charging me with sedition?"

But the detective was tired of the joke. He took David by the arm and they marched off to Caledon Square at the vanguard of a shouting procession.

The room occupied by the political squad had four desks with a man in plain clothes sitting behind each of them. It was Thursday, the delivery day of the *Guardian*, and a copy of the paper lay neatly in the centre of each desk. It was something like the *Guardian* editor's dream of a trade union office.

They told David to sit down and took no more notice. Tea was served and they drank it without offering David any. One turned to David finally, with a large sheet of paper.

"Name?"

"David Mann."

"Address?"

"Astley Street, Mowbray."

"Occupation?"

"I"m not going to say anything else until I've spoken to a lawyer."

The detective went away, and . . . the detective from the second nearest table came.

"We've got ways of making people talk," he informed David.

"I"m sure you have."

"One of those clever ones, are you?" the detective grunted. He looked at David for a long time and then went away . . .

After another while a head came through the door. "Mr Snitcher wants to know how long he has to wait," he announced. "Soon as you pick one of these bastards up you have the whole of the law industry hammering at the door," he remarked philosophically.

"You know what would happen to you if you weren't a white boy?" he asked David angrily. "We'd kick your balls into the middle of next week. . . . "

A Book for Karl   131

"You know what would happen to people like you if there was a communist government?" David asked in turn.

"No — tell us" said White, signalling behind his back for the words to be written down.

"We'd give you the chance to do honest work for decent pay, instead of crawling around like a rat for the pay of a mouse."

"You can go — but next time you won't walk out of here with that clever look on your face," said White.

Enemy of the State

"Wits Student Refused Passport by Donges"

A student of Witwatersrand University, Mr Lionel Forman, aged 21, has been refused a passport by the Minister of the Interior, Dr T.E. Donges, to visit Western Europe on an educational tour organised by the National Union of South African Students (NUSAS).

Mr Forman, who is co-editor of the *Witwatersrand Student*, believes the reason for the refusal is that he wrote an editorial in the paper last month protesting at the "callous and totally reprehensible action of the government in deporting" a Portuguese Native student at the University.

Mr Forman, who is a rank-and-file communist, gave Dr Donges a written assurance that he would not participate in political activity while on the tour.

He first applied for a passport on October 26. The party of 100 students are to leave on December 16.

No other student has had difficulty in obtaining a passport. They received them within a few days of making application.

Mr Forman called for his passport at the Immigration Office several times, but was told that it was not yet ready.

Early in November, at 7.30 one morning, he was telephoned by the CID who asked him to see them. A detective showed him the copy of *Witwatersrand Student* and said that he "should not do that sort of thing." Then a detective asked him where he was getting his money from to go on the tour.

Mr Forman said that his parents had given him the money. The police rang his mother to confirm that statement. They told her that they were "worried about youngsters being left without money when they were overseas."

Later he saw an immigration official who told him that he (the officer) had been informed that Mr Forman would apply for a passport, and had been told to send it to the department. He received a letter from the Minister "regretting that he was unable to grant a passport."

A Johannesburg Member of Parliament went to see the Minister, who said that Mr Forman should sign an undertaking not to take part in political activity. He sent a letter to this effect and also a doctor's certificate saying that he had been ill and needed a trip overseas.

132   "The Youngest and Proudest Cardholder"

The Minister said that he might reconsider the refusal and he now wanted a letter saying that Mr Forman, in spite of having been ill, would be able to do the trip.

This was sent, and later an amplified certificate from a specialist which had been asked for, was also sent last Monday.

Yesterday Mr Forman was told by an official of the Department that the refusal would not be reconsidered.

It is understood that at a meeting of the Students' Representative Council of the University tonight, a resolution will be moved protesting at the refusal of the passport.

Rand Daily Mail, 30 November 1949.

Act 44 of 1950

I have to invite your attention to the contents of my letters of the 18th September 1950, and 21st February 1951 in the above connection addressed to yourself and your attorneys, Messrs. Berrange & Wasserzug respectively, and which were left in abeyance owing to your absence overseas. For your convenience, the contents of the second letter giving particulars of the allegations against you are appended hereunder:

"I have to advise you that the allegations against your client are:

(1) that he has been a member of the Communist Party of South Africa since 1945;

(2) that he was a National Committee member of the Young Communist League during 1946;

(3) that he was a floating member of the Cape District Committee of the Communist Party of South Africa and that he attended meetings of that Committee on the 9th September 1946 and 15th September 1946;

(4) that he was appointed a member of the education sub-committee of the Cape District Committee of the Communist Party of South Africa on 14th April 1946;

(5) that he has addressed Communist Party meetings in Johannesburg and Cape Town during 1947, 1948, 1949 and 1950."

You are accordingly now afforded a further opportunity of making representations against the inclusion of your name on the list which I am compiling in terms of Section 4 (10) of the Act, and any representations which you may wish to make should reach me at the above address within fourteen days from the date hereof.

Signed: Liquidator, Act 44 of 1950, for Department of Justice, Dated: 28 July 1954, addressed to L. Forman.

9. Imperialism: "Commentator" on International Issues

How the Yanks Were Dragged to Berlin

In a few days' time, on 25 January 1954, the representatives of the four big powers — the Soviet Union, United States, Britain and France — will meet in Berlin. This will be the first such conference for over six years — since American Secretary of State George Marshall walked out of the London Big Four Conference in December 1947, breaking up the Foreign Ministers' Council which had been set up in Potsdam to facilitate the post-war co-operation of the anti-fascist nations.

The Americans walked out. They did everything conceivable to hot up the cold war. And the fact that they have now been forced to resume at least a pretence of diplomatic negotiation is a measure of the failure of US cold war policy. The defeat of this cold war policy is a triumph for all who have been working for better relations between peoples. It is a tribute to the strength of the still-growing public demand for negotiations and agreement, to which the peace movement all over the world has made so great a contribution.

The victory of the peace forces is all the more important because of the clear manner in which Washington expressed its determination to torpedo the Four-Power meeting and to spread the war mobilization of the imperialist world. With suave self-assurance, they induced Britain and France to join them in sending a note to the Soviet Union laying down incredibly cynical conditions for the meeting. They declared that it was to be understood that, whatever happened, the aggressive "North Atlantic" alliance against the Soviet Union was to continue, and Germany was to be re-armed. They refused to enter into discussions with the representative of People's China, the power with the largest population in the world.

But the Soviet Union did what the warmongers had feared most — it refused to be provoked. In a long note it exposed the hypocrisy of the proposals of the capitalist countries. The Soviet Union did not reject the meeting!

The war-makers made a last desperate effort. The capitalist press of the world blared headlines announcing that the Soviet Union had refused to attend the conference. But they published nothing of the actual Soviet note. It was too long, they said.

Their propaganda was too crudely false even for their friends. The *New Statesman and Nation* carried a leading article denouncing this colossal lie.

To put matters beyond doubt, the Soviet Union issued a new, short, clear note. They accepted the meeting.

134 "The Youngest and the Proudest Cardholder"

No alternative

The war-makers studied the Soviet reply sadly. The US "now have no alternative but to agree to Russia's bid for a conference" commented the *New York Herald Tribune* ruefully . . . the American press did not attempt to hide its chagrin. The New York journal *American* headlined its report: "Red's Big Four Bid Sabotage"; the US State Department called the Soviet move another effort to "impede progress on European unity . . . dishonest . . . phoney."

A number of important factors have contributed to the failure of the United States to split the world into hostile blocs. Chief of these is the economic crisis developing in the capitalist world. Writing in the *Manchester Guardian* recently, economist Colin Clark predicted a slump in the United States, with six or seven million unemployed before the end of this year. The US press said that Clark was talking bunk. But *Business Week* shook a warning finger: "Clark has been right too often to ignore", it said.

And everyone in Europe is very uneasily aware that even the slightest sign of a slump in America would be multiplied in Europe and set off a real depression there.

Contrasted with this, US economists are being forced to admit that production in the Socialist world — the Soviet Union, China and the People's Democracies — is growing at a much faster rate than that in the US and the Nato countries.

Sufficiency to Abundance

Soviet economic development has entered a new stage, in which it will pass from "sufficiency to abundance." Consumption by the people is to rise by two or three times in the next few years. There have been frequent price cuts, further raising the living standards of the people.

Washington realises that this new stage of Soviet development, together with China's planned drive for industrialisation, is having a momentous impact on the weakening capitalist world. Already the expected "psychological" effect of rising Soviet and Chinese living standards on the workers of Europe and Asia is being studied by a US Congressional Committee.

Sorely in need of freedom to trade with the Socialist countries, the West is chafing impatiently at the restraining US bit, getting ever more restless at the war policy.

Opposition to cold war

Opposition to the cold war by the overwhelming majority of people gets harder to overcome with each new conciliatory move on the part of the Soviet Union. Even in the United States, 79 per cent want talks with Moscow to end the cold war, according to a Gallup Poll.

In the anti-Soviet *New Leader*, diplomat George Catlin acknowledged that " . . . it would probably be political death for any British leader to urge full co-operation with Dulles' policy . . . The country is unanimously

Imperialism: "Commentator" on International Issues   135

opposed to war . . . There is no effective public sense in Britain or Western Europe of any danger from Malenkov . . . (but only of) the danger of being dragged unwillingly into a world war by a policy in Washington which they do not control . . . (They) will see America to hell first."

Another factor which weakened the hold of the US over its satellites was the exposure of Western "atomic supremacy" as a myth. Said the *Christian Science Monitor*: "It should not be at all surprising that the Russians have a lead or may be about to forge ahead. In the atomic field the Russians have been consistently underrated." . . . So, kicking and fighting all the way, the Yanks are being dragged to the Berlin meeting.

Danger of sabotage

That there will be a meeting is a great victory. But the victory is by no means unqualified. The US has stuck to its audacious preconditions and pulled its satellites along with it. And they will do their damnedest to hamstring and break up the conference itself. Even now, on the eve of the meeting, the warmongers have not given up hope of sabotaging it.

Berlin itself has been one of the centres of the plot to sabotage the conference. The map of West Berlin shows how the whole area is honeycombed with military spying and propaganda centres which organise sabotage in the socialist countries and manufacture the anti-Soviet horror tales which we read in the *Star* and the *Argus*.

As an obvious provocation, Field-Marshal Kesselring — a Nazi criminal sentenced by the Allied courts to death for his war atrocities and subsequently released by the British — was scheduled to speak in Berlin just one week before the conference opened.

The Christian Democratic Union paper *Neue Zeit* has published a warning from what it describes as responsible West Berlin circles about the dangerous position in the western part of the capital. Under the headline "No Security for the Four-power Conference in West Berlin?", it calls for sharp control — preferably Four-Power control — on all undesirable elements in West Berlin. "West Berlin is today the sporting ground of all subversive elements," states the article. "There are innumerable thieves and spy organisations, and the West Berlin security forces are in no position to prevent incidents during the conference."

Future task

Now, in the words of the British Peace Committee, "the task is to make the talks succeed. Their success will depend on public opinion."

> The main obstacle is the intention, openly declared, of the Government of the US, with British support, to bring Germany into a military alliance with the West. This means reviving German militarism. To seek to impose this policy against the wishes of the great majority of the people will endanger the success of this conference. We must guard against attempts to poison the atmosphere by such "incidents" as the spreading of highly coloured stories in the news-

136 *"The Youngest and the Proudest Cardholder"*

papers of one side about the other. Britain's future demands an agreed, peaceful solution to the German problem and the unification of Germany in a way acceptable to all Germany's neighbours and to the German people.

This would open the way to Four-Power agreement and to a future of peace for the people of Germany, of Europe and of the world. It can be achieved only by preventing the revival of German militarism in any form . . . (*Advance* 21 January 1954)

Commentator goes to Bioscope

I went with my wife to the bioscope the other evening and let Metro-Goldwyn-Mayer write my column for me while we relaxed. The moral of the film had puzzled me. The thing was called *Half a Hero*, and so help me, the moral was that it is a good thing to buy far more than you can afford — on credit! It seems that to be hopelessly in debt shows the spirit of the American pioneers — courage and determination and so forth.

Well, I didn't quite get it, until one of the team who did the research for this summary produced this insight into the capitalist morality.

Christian Science Monitor, 31 October 1953:

Chicago — a New York investment banker, Paul Mazur of Lehman Bros. said Americans must buy much more than they need in the next 10 years or face a possible economic setback.

Kalamazoo Gazette, 6 November 1953:

New York (U.P.) — Henry Ford II believes the auto industry should try to create more two-car families in America.

Los Angeles Daily News, 18 November 1953:

Robert Gros, President of the Advertising Association of the West and advertising and public relations director of Pacific Gas and Electric Co. said: "The Job of advertising is to create the demand to live beyond our means, and thus we make a real contribution to the economy."

So there, ladies and gentlemen, you have it. The official prescription for avoiding slumps. You just read the motor car advertisements, buy yourself a couple of cars, get the chauffeur to drive you to town, invest in a new radiogram, fridge, bedroom suite, swimming pool and what have you, all on credit, and there won't be a slump. It's the most wonderful discovery since eggs, this capitalist economic system.

The real culprits

No, the real reason for slumps is something different. The culprit who is making depression is not the Langa African who absolutely refuses to buy

Imperialism: "Commentator" on International Issues   137

himself a Cadillac. The culprit is the fat boss who doesn't pay his workers enough to live on.

There is only one possible explanation of why it happens that in a world where we have the skill and techniques to provide a comfortable life for every man, woman and child, millions are starving while the shop windows are full of food.

Look at it this way. Say a worker adds through his labour and skill £10 to a thing. He gets a pile of steel worth £2 at one end of the factory and when he is finished working on it, it comes out at the other end as a bicycle worth £12. The boss gives him £5 and keeps £5 for himself as profit.

If that is happening all over the country, the result is obvious. If the workers, who are the great majority of the people, are paid far less than the value of the goods they produce, they have not enough money to buy what is produced. So the shops get full of goods. The people have not enough money to buy the goods. (All the money has gone into the pockets of the bosses.) Because they cannot sell their products, the factories have to close down. When they close they sack the workers, who then have even less money to buy with. The workers starve.

That is a slump. Food in the shops and the people starving. Food being destroyed because the people cannot buy it — and the people starving.

Famous statement

A very famous economist put it like this last year:

> The main features and requirements of the basic economic law of modern capitalism might be formulated roughly in this way: the securing of the maximum capitalist profit through the exploitation, ruin and impoverishment of the majority of the population of the given country, through the enslavement and systematic robbery of the peoples of other countries, especially backward countries, and, lastly through wars and militarisation of the national economy, which are utilised for the obtaining of the highest profits.

The phrase "maximum capitalist profit" is the key to what is new in this statement.

> Until recently there were certain limitations on the size of profits. But today the accumulation of capital necessary for the huge expenditure of the giant monopolies, and the cost of the terrible struggles which are being fought all the time between the big capitalist groups would not be possible with the previous average rate of profit. For example, a sharp war is being waged in the US motor-car industry between General Motors (capital $4 billion) and Ford. Similarly, a major struggle is going on, as James S. Allen showed in his *Atomic Imperialism*, between Morgan, Mellon, Rockefeller and Du Pont interests for preponderant influence in the atomic energy industry.

Rich men battle

Such struggles require huge capital resources for victory. They involve a battle to control raw materials, production, technical and scientific developments, markets — every aspect of production, both in the US and all over the capitalist world.

All this costs money. How do they get it?

First of all, of course, they squeeze the workers. In the United States this has been done mainly by speeding up work and lowering real wages by increasing prices and by taxation.

The *New York Times* (29 October 1953) gave a striking example of the effect of the speed-up in the steel industry.

From 1946 to 1951 the amount of steel ingots produced per worker increased from 79.4 tons to 114 tons. Meanwhile profits soared from $590 per worker to $2,149.

Below the minimum

And as a result of the huge cost of living, two-thirds of US families now have incomes below the minimum health-and-decency budget prescribed by the US Bureau of Statistics.

Not only do the big capitalists starve the workers — they also hack at the throats of the smaller capitalists.

The US Department of Commerce reports that 800 businesses are notifying their bankruptcy each month. And while from the beginning of the Korean War to the middle of 1953 the larger manufacturing corporations reported profits averaging 36 per cent above the 1949 level, the smaller ones reported an average decrease of profits of 16 per cent.

So much for the plunder at home. What about the plunder abroad?

Forty per cent of all US private investment abroad is located in Latin America. Victor Perlo, in his *American Imperialism*, estimates that at least $2.5 billion in profits is realised annually by US imperialism from this one area of the world.

To this US big business is rapidly adding the exploitation of other colonies previously controlled by older imperialist powers. Notably is this the case in Africa, where US investment has increased by leaps and bounds.

Colonizers become colonies

Monopoly exploitation now includes not only the colonies but also the conversion of other capitalist countries into the US colonies.

This is accomplished in a variety of ways including penetration or outright taking over of capital investments in other relatively advanced capitalist countries (a characteristic of Nazi domination of Europe and of US "aid" today), domination of foreign trade so that prices of imports and exports can be dictated, outright crippling or destruction of rival industries, control of money policies through loans, and so on.

Imperialism: "Commentator" on International Issues 139

Perlo estimates that the total annual profits realised by US imperialism from foreign investment and trade is roughly $7.5 billion. And he estimates the rate of profits to be extremely high.

Europe (outside Marshall Plan countries), 7.6 per cent; Canada, 14 per cent; Marshall Plan countries 14.5 per cent; Latin America, 17.4 per cent; colonies of Marshall Plan countries, 20 per cent; Middle East, 31.3 per cent.

The third means of extracting maximum profit is through war. War contracts worth $73.8 billion were allotted by the US government from July 1950 to June 1952. The biggest war contract receiver was General Motors. A former director of the company, Charles Wilson, is in the US Cabinet!

The effect of war on the profits of US monopolies is graphically illustrated in the total profits reported by the largest corporations. According to a government survey in 1939, their aggregate profits were $1.2 billion dollars. During the war against Germany they rose to $3.5 billion. And with the Korean war they jumped to $8 billion.

Are we crazy?

Yes, for them war is business. There are millions of us ordinary people, and we let a handful of criminals sit at the top of this capitalist system and guide us to hell. Working people should own the factories they work in, and the things they produce should go to making our lives easier and fuller. Instead we let this little lot line their pockets and send us to war. If we allow them to go on much longer we must be crazy!
(*Advance*, 18 February, 1954)

"Dit Lyk nie of Dulles dit Maklik Gaan He Nie"

The Geneva Conference on April 26 between the three main capitalist powers and the Soviet Union and China to discuss peace in Korea and Vietnam will take place in a different atmosphere from that of the Berlin conference, precisely because of the immense moral victory the Soviet Union won at Berlin and the effect Molotov's statements have had on the peace-hungry people of the world.

Take the position in Vietnam. French war-makers are dead scared of peoples' leader Ho Chi-Minh, who "holds the political as well as military initiative" (*Argus* special correspondent 3 March 1954).

Writing as if this would be a terrible thing, he says: "Even mild concessions by the Viet-Minh might be most difficult for the French to turn down . . . Any sort of Viet-Minh offer to co-operate peacefully in a truly independent Vietnam would be especially hard to resist. It is this form of offer which well-informed French and Vietnamese sources in Saigon fear is coming." France is disappointing the Yanks bitterly. "Washington thought that France had agreed last year to drive for victory. But

140 *"The Youngest and the Proudest Cardholder"*

the agreement was only paper deep. Paris's heart simply is not in the Indo-China war" (*Time* 12 February 1954).

And in slow-changing Britain, Foreign Minister Anthony Eden has been forced to make a statement which puts *finis* to the whole basis of the frantic western armament drive. He said that he did not believe that the Soviet Union had any intention of attacking Europe.

US stooges in Britain, Labour leaders Morrison and Attlee, suffered their biggest defeat ever on a major issue when they were able to scrape a majority of only two in favour of German re-armament.

The itch for normal life is also present in the capitalist class. So many businessmen are going looking for trade that the Scandinavian Airlines have persuaded the Soviet Aeroflot to run a daily service from Helsinki to Moscow.

Developments make it more and more clear that for progressives the results of the Berlin Conference are an important victory. The open attempts of the most reactionary forces to incite a breaking-up of the meetings failed hopelessly. That negotiations are possible was established beyond doubt — and no one is going to follow the war-makers as long as this is clear. Above all, the conference set the stage for further discussions and negotiations — this time together with People's China. This is a most bitter pill for the war-makers.

What happened at Berlin

The press has, of course, not told anything like the truth about the reasons why agreement was not reached on the most important question — that of preventing Germany from launching another aggressive war.

Agreement was not reached because Dulles and Eden blocked all progress.

Here's a swift summary:

Soviet proposal	Western reply
East and West Germans should participate in Conference	No
Peace conference with Germany by October 1954; German armed forces to be limited	No
Form all-German government to supervise free elections; occupation troops to leave before elections	No
Reduction of occupation costs to 5 per cent of budget; cancellation of post-war debts	No
Germany to be neutralised; occupation troops to leave within six months; Four-Power control of strength of East and West police	No
Conclusion of 50-year All-Europe Security Pact, with participation of both halves of Germany	No

Terribly confusing

As the US war-makers get busy trying to sabotage their April conference they find their hands full elsewhere. Like, for example, the Middle East.

Are you just a little confused by all the Middle East presidents going in and out? Come on, admit it — you are. But don't be too worried. The US and British rulers, who pull all the strings, are also confused. They are pulling the strings in opposite directions, so it's not surprising that things do get a little tangled up. (One day a string will break, then heaven help imperialism.)

Take poor old Shishekly of Syria — or, rather, formerly of Syria. In the last *Summary* we saw how this United States puppet tried "to feed democracy to Syrians in small doses." The opposition, led by elements notorious for their connection with Britain, seized the opportunity and tried to chuck him out, so he arrested them and re-established martial law. That's where this column left him on 25 February. One up for the US.

Since then the story has continued. Shishekly is out. Britain's pals are in. One up for Britain.

There used to be talk of a "Middle East Command" as part of the anti-Soviet bloc. Britain and France were to be part of it. But now the US has new plans. It has gone off on a completely different tack with a US-financed Turkey-Pakistan military alliance. Britain and France no longer figure. Two up for the Yanks.

The US is very busy on another little grab from her British junior partner. She wants to grab the Suez Canal. As you can imagine, that has Britain very worried indeed. If the US wins this point, she must win the whole game.

The US plan is to oust Britain from Egypt and to conclude a military agreement with Cairo to bring the Canal Zone under US control. "Evacuation of the Suez garrison," remarks the *New York Times*, "would make one more instance in which the British packed up and left and the US moved in."

So it's a safe bet to watch for more fun in the Neguib merry-go-round. No wonder the British are a little gleeful about the wave of anger which has swept Asia at the arming of Pakistan and Turkey.

The comments of the government press in Iraq, which is still "British", are certainly worth looking at. The *Baghdad Akhbar Al-Masa*: "It means the return of imperialism to Asia, military intervention of America and Europe in affairs of Asian states and a check to the growth of the movement for the emancipation of Asian countries still struggling against imperialistic domination."

And here's some real hard punching. "The issue does not merely concern India but all Middle Eastern countries, since Pakistan will become an American base not only against India but also against any country desiring emancipation, freedom or self-respect."

The press of Egypt, another British outpost, gives more clues. Says the Cairo-based *Al Mussawar*: "America hopes that as a result of this link

142   "The Youngest and the Proudest Cardholder"

between Turkey and Pakistan, Iran and other Near East countries would
be tempted to join the Middle East defence bloc. This hope is not likely
to be realised. On the other hand, it will cause these countries to adopt a
policy of neutrality or even throw in their lot with the Russian camp,
however much they may dislike it."

The fight between the US and Britain is still basically one for control
of oil profits. A glance at the facts will show why Britain is now so
desperate. At the end of the war the two rival imperialist powers each
controlled an approximately equal share of oil production outside the
United States. The Yanks kept their eyes open for a chance to reduce Britain
to a second-rate oil power. The chance came. A powerful movement for
oil nationalisation developed in Iran, and Washington seized the chance to
push Britain out.

The loss of Iranian oil was a severe blow to Great Britain. It shattered
British dominance in Middle East oil production. Her share fell to 38.8
per cent against the US' 58 per cent.

As British imperialism struggles for life, the Middle East merry-go-
round will gather speed. But while the rivals swing at each other they
forget the most important thing about the Middle East — the fact that
people live there. And the people don't like having all their oil carted off
for someone else to make a profit out of. They don't like having to live in
hovels. They don't like the British or the Yanks. They are going to chuck
them out.

Easier fighting Africans than Yanks

British imperialism is not enjoying being battered about by the bigger and
stronger Yanks. They are armed and they've got dollars. Britain thought
that the unarmed Kikuyu of Kenya were easier meat. She sent tanks and
bombers against them at the call of the white settlers.

But a people fighting for liberation can perform miracles. Fighting
incredible odds, the liberatory movement of Kenya grew stronger, not
weaker. Last week Britain began to send out peace feelers. The white
settlers who started the war in order to wipe out every trace of democracy
and to subdue (or destroy) the Kikuyu people were horrified.

They had been demanding complete press censorship and a declaration
that "the whole Kikuyu tribe are in rebellion." Such a declaration would
have made it legal to kill Kikuyu on sight — an essential step in the settlers'
plans to kill off a whole people just as the Nazis planned to destroy the
Jews . . .

Shooting up the Congress

The attempt by Puerto Ricans to wipe out a sizeable portion of the United
States Chamber of Representatives draws attention to another heavy problem on the minds of the rulers — the problem of keeping in check their
Latin American colonies. The shooting has spotlighted the fact that the US
colony of Puerto Rico, whose people live in the most terrible poverty, is

Imperialism: "Commentator" on International Issues **143**

seething with discontent. The US is as vicious a coloniser as the worst of Europe's imperialist powers.

Forty per cent of all US foreign investment is concentrated in Latin America and US Foreign Secretary Dulles was busy in the dependent countries last week in the role of a Colonial Secretary at a Latin American conference in Caracas, Venezuela. The thoughtful Venezuelans provided Dulles with a bullet-proof car. "But," commented *Die Burger* (4 March 1954), "Dulles could land up in the middle of bullets against which his bullet-proof car will offer no protection. Figurative bullets — and it would not be surprising if the Venezuelans themselves open fire."

Wants to fight Guatemala

Dulles wants to conscript the Latin Americans into an army to defend US profits. He wants to start by attacking Guatemala, which has a progressive government with strong working-class support. The US United Fruit Company used to run Guatemala until the people decided to run the country themselves. The Fruit Company is angry, and wants to take the country back, and Dulles is in Caracas to try to do the job — or, rather, to get others to do the job.

"The US would like to take steps against the present regime, and would probably have done so long ago if it were not scared of the unfavourable reaction in the other American countries," notes *Die Burger,* whose foreign editor is generally far more shrewd (and frank) than our English press.

In fact, I'm so amazed, I'm going to give you the whole lot out of the mouth of *Die Burger*:

> Instead of taking action against Guatemala off its own bat the United States will try to get the conference of American countries to agree to measures against "infiltration by international communism". The choice of words is neat. If without beating about the bush the US had expressed its concern about Guatemala, it would have laid itself open to the charge that it was again interfering in the affairs of an American country.

But, notes *Die Burger*:

> the people of Central and South America are not nearly as worried about communism as is the US. There are, indeed, many non-communist left-wingers who think that the US is far too taken up with the actions of communists in Latin America and not sufficiently troubled about the many right-wing dictators . . . many people in Latin America, although they are not communists, cannot help liking the way little Guatemala is cocking a snook at the Yankee giant.

In short, "Dit lyk nie of Dulles dit maklik gaan he nie." ("No easy ride for Dulles.")

Advance, 11 March 1954.

Danger on the eve of Geneva

For weeks after the Berlin Conference between the Foreign Ministers of the United States, the Soviet Union, Britain and France the world knew an upsurge of hope. The tide of the peace forces was high. US attempts to prevent and then to disrupt the Berlin Conference had failed miserably. The ministers had met and negotiated. And that was what the people wanted. Negotiation, not war; discussion, not death.

Nor had the discussion been fruitless. The decision to call another meeting, this time with People's China also at the table, was a victory for the forces of peace.

But the US war-makers have summoned every ounce of their energy for the come-back punch. With the strength of desperation, they have thrown everything into sabotaging the Geneva Conference which begins this week. The fortnight before the Conference has been a dramatic one indeed, as the war-makers pulled every trick in the bag. First they concentrated everything on creating an atmosphere of war. You remember Korea. It was equally cynical. Dulles went to Korea, looked over the troop concentrations, conferred with Syngman Rhee. A few days later Syngman Rhee, his attacking troops already defeated, announced to the world that South Korea was being invaded. Within hours the US had her satellites lined up as the world capitalist press shrieked sensational lies about "Red aggression".

The US plan to occupy People's Democratic North Korea swung into action. Surprised by the fighting power of North Korean troops strengthened by the support of the liberated people of South Korea, the mighty US army was held and pushed back at first. The US always underestimates the fighting power of a "non-European" people fighting for freedom.

Then when MacArthur crossed the parallel and marched to the Chinese border, the Chinese People's Army stepped in and stopped his little game. MacArthur had never believed that a Chinese army could conceivably beat the US army on the battlefield. But it did.

MacArthur reached for the atom bomb. The US satellites revolted. Attlee flew to the US and told Truman — no atom bomb. The US Government was still sane enough to know that it could not ignore the wishes of its allies. So, angry with MacArthur for letting the Chinese armies humble him, and unable to swing to atom warfare, the US Government recalled MacArthur.

All the signs point now to the fact that the US Government today thinks that this "appeasement" was a mistake.

And they want a repetition

Now they are trying to repeat Korea. They are trying to draw the satellites into war in Vietnam. And if they succeed this time they will not stop short of all-out atomic war.

This is easier said than done. It's all very well for the US to learn from Korea. But other people also learn. "One Korea is enough", say the

Imperialism: "Commentator" on International Issues   145

conservative governments of Europe uneasily, pleadingly, to Dulles. "One Korea is enough", say the working people firmly, threateningly, to the conservative governments.

Like the *skolly* (hoodlum) who idly carves a piece of wood from the shop counter as he explains the protection racket, the US casually blew a three-mile crater into the Pacific and maimed a few fishermen as it prepared to explain its policy of "massive retaliatory power . . . We have made a basic decision to depend primarily upon a great capacity to retaliate instantly by means and at places of our choosing" (Dulles).

The implication was clear. If there was "aggression" as they said there had been in Korea, they would resort to atomic warfare. Having created a war atmosphere, the next US step was to prove that there was Chinese aggression in Vietnam. That has been a little difficult, because there isn't any. But that, of course, does not daunt Dulles.

Pressed to give evidence of Chinese intervention, Dulles produced this lame case. The communists besieging Dien Bien Phu, said Dulles, are using new radar-controlled anti-aircraft guns that are "operated by members of the Chinese military establishment." A Chinese general with "nearly a score of Chinese technical advisers" is at Viet Minh staff headquarters near Dien Bien Phu. Some 1,000 Red trucks in Indo-China are "driven by Chinese army personnel."

China promptly declared this a lying slander. (And the French in Vietnam clamped tight censorship on foreign correspondents who were bothering them by reporting that there was no sign of Chinese involvement.)

"Does this mean the Chinese are committing the direct aggression that you said might produce massive retaliation?" asked a US Congressman. "They are coming awful close to it," Dulles replied. And with this casual warning that the world was "awful close" to atomic destruction, Dulles set out to convince the satellites.

Relief too soon

Dulles went to see his friends in the British and French governments. He wanted from them outright agreement of support for US aggression in Vietnam in the guise of a "South-East Asia Security Pact." They would not agree. "Dulles Fails," declared a *Cape Argus* editorial with a sigh of relief that even the capitalist press could not help emitting. But Dulles' failure had not been complete. For, while he had obtained no more than a statement that the two governments would agree to consider the pact, he had not met with the direct rebuff which the people of these countries demanded.

The blow which cancelled out any triumph Dulles might have been inclined to feel followed with dramatic suddenness. A British Labour Party executive member, Mr Aneurin Bevan, who never makes a bold move unless he knows that the rank and file members of the Labour Party and the ordinary people of Britain will not tolerate silence, denounced Attlee's statements as "a surrender to American pressure." Dulles' moves were, he said, "tantamount to the diplomatic and military encirclement of Republican China," and he resigned from the shadow cabinet of the Labour Party.

Why he's in a hurry

The reason for Dulles' desperate measures is the terrible lack of time with which he is faced. For he knows that if he does not turn the Vietnam war into a world war quickly there will be no Vietnam war left at all. In the words of Peter Lessing, *Cape Times* correspondent (16 April 1954), "there is no longer a stalemate. The communists have broken the stalemate and are winning the war."

Seeking other methods of sabotaging the Geneva talks, Dulles declared last week that China would not be present at Geneva as an equal. Dulles hoped upon hope that the statement would lead to China refusing to be present as an inferior, thus making the Conference impossible. For the Americans know that the mere fact of the Conference taking place, just as was the case with the Berlin Conference, will itself be an immense victory for peace.

Advance, 22 April 1954.

Know the Facts on Vietnam

The United States war-makers gained nothing from their hydrogen bomb explosion and succeeded only in strengthening the camp of peace. Then why did they do it?

The answer was to be read in the speech last week of war-loving US Secretary of State Dulles to the Overseas Press Club of America.

While the people's armies of Vietnam were routing the invading French aggressors, Dulles declared that "the US does not intend to accept a communist victory in Indo-China. If China sends its own army into Indo-China the grave consequences might not be confined to Indo-China." Later he commented that this stage was "perilously close." He was threatening to try again what the world had stopped MacArthur from doing in Korea — declaring war on China.

The war-makers are gambling with our lives once more, not because they are in a stronger position than they were when they were defeated in Korea, but because their position has become weaker, and they can see it worsening from month to month. They are launching a desperate attempt to swing the United States into war against the Soviet Union before their last chance vanishes — before the people of the satellite nations force a complete break with the US. Before the slump hits the US and the unemployed turn on the war-makers who are the cause of their starvation.

That is the reason for their violent swing back to direct threats of aggression, the reason for their reckless explosion of the hydrogen bomb. That is why our capitalist newspapers, ever ready to take their cue from

Dulles, are back to "Atmosphere of War" headlines (*Cape Times* 8 April 1954).

The hidden facts

As the war-fever mounts, it is well to know the rights and wrongs of the war in Vietnam. Who are the aggressors? Who are defending liberty?

The leader of the Vietnam army is Ho Chi-minh. "Ho Chi-minh is Vietnam. That strange little figure, so meek in appearance yet so determined in purpose, embodies the spirit, the aspirations and probably the future of the new state. He moulded it, he put it through the fire and he will guide it" (*New York Times* editorial 21 November 1946).

Vietnam Do Clap Dong Minh (League of Independence for Vietnam) — composed of socialist, democratic, nationalist, marxist parties and Catholic, Buddhist, Confucian, landlord non-party organisations — was born during World War Two, when the people fought against joint Japanese-Vichy rule. In August 1945, Viet Minh overthrew the Japanese puppet government of former Annam Emperor Bao Dai, and proclaimed a Republic.

After Japan's surrender, Anglo-French forces tried to reconquer the colony. But after six months' warfare, France, in March 1946, was forced to recognise the Free Republic of Vietnam within the French Union. Ho had been elected President on 6 January 1946. His government had Bao Dai's official blessing. Bao moved to the French Riviera to concentrate on having a good time.

France the aggressor

The US loan to France in June 1946 bolstered its colonial ambitions. France broke the March agreement, poured troops into Vietnam and attacked Vietnamese troops. In February 1947, President Ho, in a letter to a Reuters correspondent, denied Vietnam's programme was socialist or communist, declaring:

> It is quite simply: (a) To produce enough so that every citizen has sufficient rice and cloth not to die of hunger and cold. Last year we avoided starvation; (b) to teach all citizens how to read and write. Last year 2,500,000 finished this course; (c) to make every citizen enjoy democratic freedom. Last year universal suffrage was granted — men and women above 18 years of age voted at the elections and a democratic constitution was adopted by the National Assembly. We have not gone as far in nationalisation as England or France.

Ho's National Assembly soon won recognition as the official Government of the country by the Soviet Union, China and the People's Democracies — of a representative, stable administration which had come to stay. He warned that France could go on fighting for 20 years and not win.

Before the end of 1948, newspaper correspondents from the *Associated Press*, the *Manchester Guardian* and the *Christian Science Monitor* had

148 *"The Youngest and the Proudest Cardholder"*

all reported the French situation in Indo-China to be hopeless. But by 1948 the US had begun to subsidise the war indirectly through the Marshall Plan, which also opened the colony to US exploitation. (US Rubber, Am Smelting and Refining, Am Metal Co., Caltex, Goodrich Rubber, International Telephone and Telegraph were among US trusts which subsequently won Indo-China concessions as the price of US aid, paid by the US taxpayer.)

By early 1950 the French Union Force in Indo-China was so completely US equipped it was "difficult to distinguish from an American military aggregation" (*New York Times* 28 May 1950). Indo-China had become one flank in the overall US plan to reconquer China, launched in Korea in June 1950. In May 1951, it received "priority on US arms second only to that given UN forces in the Korean war" (*US News* 18 January 1952) while US generals for the next year tried to mobilise the encircling assault on China.

Defeat in Korea blocked the plan, but it has never been abandoned, as Joint Chiefs Chairman Admiral Radford frequently states. Washington's goal remains that stated by the State Department in 1951: the Viet Minh "must be decisively conquered down to the last pocket of resistance," since otherwise the "free world" would lose 80 per cent of its rubber and 50 per cent of its tin.

In Jean-Paul Sartre's *Les Temps Modernes*, Guy de Chambre and Jean-Jacques Salomon wrote months ago:

Hardly are they (the Bao Dai Army) instructed and armed than they pass to the other side. It is to be believed that the General Staff of the Popular Army encourages Annamites to enlist in the French ranks; so many men whose defection will be that much more resounding and who, in going over to the Popular Army, will furnish it with free arms and ammunition . . .

In the same magazine Jean Clementin reported:

The territories controlled by the Expeditionary Force and "administered" by Bao Dai have returned to a feudal condition such as no Asian people has ever known . . . (The Bao Dai puppet regime installed by France in 1947) has been from the first to the last a foreign body in Vietnam . . . in the matter of falling apart it surpasses the Kuomintang . . . In this incredible regime of muck and infamy everything is for sale, from an orderly to the Chief of State . . . To pretend the Vietnam people could one day accept this regime — what an insult!

French opposition to the continuation of the "dirty war" has mounted steadily. The announcement at the Berlin Foreign Ministers' meeting of the Five-Power peace talks in Geneva to take place at the end of this month, which will discuss peace in Vietnam, produced in France a wave of enthusiasm which reflected the yearning of France to end the Indo-China

Imperialism: "Commentator" on International Issues 149

war. So strong was the feeling that the US began to panic at the signs that France might pull out of the war even before the Geneva agreement.

Then began the vivid illustration that the people cannot rest on the laurels of the Berlin Conference. The drive to turn Vietnam into a Korea and into a world war is well under way. Last week the US disclosed that one-third of its total foreign "aid" programme of $1.166 million will consist of military equipment for the French in Vietnam.

The plan of the US is clear. They are going all out to start a war. We must help to stop them. Not only must we protest at the US intervention, but by redoubling our efforts to throw out the Nats and establish a democratic South Africa in the camp of peace we help prevent world war and the mass murder of millions.

Advance, 15 April 1954

Angry Asia also Abhors American Atomic Weapon

. . . A glance at the Indian press today shows that the once slumbering feeling of resentment at American imperialist interference in her affairs has burst into the open. This development was, of course, inevitable because US policy comes into conflict with the interests of all its capitalist allies. But the bombshell which let loose the dammed up feeling was the US war pact with Pakistan. The pact came as the end of a desperately twisting US policy. At first the US hoped, when China won her liberation, that Nehru would become their Asian spokesman to replace Chiang. They worked very hard to achieve this. Enormous financial backing and publicity was given to Ambassador Chester Bowles in his attempt to tie India to the American side. Indian big business was more than willing to co-operate, and to read the papers you would have thought that Bowles was the wisest, kindest, cleverest chap there could be.

But the progressive movement in India was far too strong. Eisenhower realised that bribery would not be enough. So he went over to blackmail.

When Britain pulled out of India, on the old maxim of divide and rule, she left the country broken into two parts, India and Pakistan, hoping that the two countries would be weakened by quarrelling so that Britain could profit by pitting the one against the other. Quarrel the countries did. The US stepped in and tried to take the fruits that British imperialism had hoarded for itself. The *Newport Herald Tribune* gloated: "Britain is disturbed by the unpleasant thought that the US is replacing her in another Commonwealth country" (28 December 1953).

Danger of friendship

In April last year there seemed to be a danger for the imperialists that India and Pakistan might settle their differences. Prime Minister Nazimuddin of Pakistan and Nehru of India were finding agreement. The Americans could not let this happen . . . While the talks went on announcements began to appear of US military aid to Pakistan. Then suddenly the Pakistan

150 *"The Youngest and the Proudest Cardholder"*

Governor-General sacked Prime Minister Nazimuddin and his whole cabinet. In power he put Mohammed Ali, a former Ambassador to the United States.

Immediately secret US-Pakistan talks, involving bases in exchange for arms, began, the success of which "could provide Pakistan an offensive punch for a show-down fight with India in the dispute over Kashmir," the *Overseas News Agency* reported.

The Indian reaction was very sharp indeed. The official *India News* (6 February 1954), published by the Indian Public Relations Department, headlined its main front page story: "Military Aid to Pakistan will Disrupt Peace — Nehru Reiterates Views on Proposed US Move — Time to Choose Between War and Peace."

"Apart from the effect which the aid will have on a hot war, it will bring cold war here at once . . . We have expressed our opinion very strongly. In my opinion, this aid is fundamentally and utterly a wrong thing," Nehru said.

In an editorial, the semi-official Egyptian paper *Al Misri* (1 February 1954) commented on a statement by Neguib that the United States was trying to drive a wedge between India and the Arab countries: "We must concentrate all our efforts against this American trick before the events take us by surprise. We cannot ignore this danger and just let the future take its course. Implementation of this pact will undermine all chances of forming the third bloc with an independent and neutral policy."

"Military crescent"

Unconcerned by this opposition, the US is pushing for a joint pact with Turkey, Iraq, Iran, Saudi Arabia, Pakistan (*Herald Tribune* 17 January 1954). Vice-President Nixon has suggested a "military crescent" — Turkey, Iran, Pakistan, Indo-China, Formosa and Japan to "close the ring" around the USSR and China (*Newsweek* 4 January 1954).

Such a pact will serve as heavy aggressive pressure, and the Yanks hope for these results — force India into line, keep a sharp eye on Israel, take united action against the progressive movements of all the pact countries, increase the usefulness of Thailand as a supply base for disrupters, create a huge army of "Asians to fight Asians."

But all this is not easy. India's opposition has been paralleled by all the countries of Asia. So strong has been the opposition in Pakistan that the shaky Government has been holding widespread secret political trials, and has even taken action against such normally pro-Government newspapers as *Dawn* and *Evening Star*.

The dramatic arrest of Kashmir Prime Minister Sheik Abdullah last August focused attention on the resistance to American imperialism in this highly strategic area. (Kashmir is of key importance to US war plans. In the North, only a narrow strip of Afghan territory separates it from the USSR; to the East is a 300-mile-long border with China. The Kashmir

Imperialism: "Commentator" on International Issues 151

Valley forms the communications hub of the whole area, and is an ideal air base.)

This country, too, has a history of frustration for the imperialists and the plans Britain made when she left India. At the time of the partition of India, Britain instigated an attack on Kashmir by Pakistan, calculating that this was the most convenient way of ensuring continued British control. But the people of Kashmir rose against the invaders and, with the help of Indian troops, stopped them. The dispute came to the United Nations, and again the US seized the opportunity to grab the British loot.

Under the guise of a UN Commission, a large number of American military observers went to Kashmir "to supervise a truce." They enjoyed diplomatic privileges and had power to operate on both sides of the ceasefire line. But while these agents were busy, the Kashmir people were making important gains. Arising from the resistance to the invasion, their mass organisation, the National Conference, came to power.

Sheik Abdullah and the leaders of the Conference proved, however, to be traitors. They embarked on a policy of repression. After discussions with Adlai Stevenson, leader of the US Democratic Party, on his visit to Kashmir last year, Abdullah came out in support of a scheme to subject his country to the US.

The result was a shock for both Abdullah and the US. Under enormous pressure, the National Conference threw Abdullah out of Parliament and put him into gaol.

The new government, headed by Bakshi Ghulam Mohammed, has bluntly warned US "observers" against continued interference, and actually ordered the police to arrest any of them found in places where they have no business to be.

Ceylon is another country to biff the Yanks in the eye. The Ceylon Economic Research Association has just sent me a copy of S.P. Amarasingam's book, *Rice and Rubber*, which gives a vivid, detailed account of the struggle that went on in Ceylon between the United States and the people "anxious to break away from the economic stranglehold America wanted to impose on this country." The people won and Ceylon became one of the first countries of South-East Asia to enter into large-scale trade with China, in spite of frenzied and continuing US opposition.

After a long period of comparative quiet, the anti-imperialist movement in Indonesia has increased its strength greatly in recent months. Writing on that country, *The Times* (London) correspondent, quoted in the *Cape Argus* (17 February 1954) admits: "The Communists have gained ground in spite of the mass arrests of two years ago. They dominate the most powerful trades union group, which has about two million members . . . They control youth organisations . . . and their announced programme is a popular one, appealing to emotional nationalism and economic discontent."

Nor are matters much easier in the Middle East. Iran is under strict martial law, the last opposition newspaper, *Shahed*, has been suppressed,

152 *"The Youngest and the Proudest Cardholder"*

and many political parties have threatened to boycott the coming elections as necessarily farcical under the control of US-supported dictator General Zabedi.

In Syria dictator Shishelsky repealed martial law and decided that it was time to "feed democracy to Syrians in small doses and gave his people a US-type Constitution" (*Time* 8 February 1954). He quickly changed his mind as "Red-led university students battled his police and shouted "down with Shishelsky, agent of foreign imperialism'." Back came martial law.

In Iraq, the *Manchester Guardian* (7 February 1953) reported: "The gulf between the rulers and the people makes it difficult to obtain public co-operation . . . The secondary schoolboy who walks along the banks of the Tigris muttering aloud from a textbook is the demonstrator of tomorrow . . . On the fringe of Baghdad about 40,000 people live in hovels — a constant prey to Communism."

Even in that most backward of countries, Saudi Arabia, when the Aramco oil workers came out on strike last August and the Government clapped the strike leaders into prison. "13,000 of Aramco's 15,000 Native workers walked out in a surprisingly well-organised general strike . . . Crown Prince (now King) Saud said he would ship them back to their villages, where they used to enjoy . . . 7.5 cents a day wages" (*Time*, 2 October 1953) . . .

And in Israel, as in India, the Government is angry at the arming by the US of her hostile neighbours, Iraq and Saudi Arabia, who are still technically at war with her. While Egypt is shaky as long as she quarrels with British occupation.

The poor old Americans are finding life hard in Europe and Asia . . .
Advance, 25 February 1954

Power Through Violence

It would hardly be possible to make a more incorrect statement than that made by a writer to *Advance Post* that the African people do not agree with the stand *Advance* has taken in support of the people of Kenya against the invading British Imperialist Army. At meetings up and down our country the African people have made their stand known, and only last week we reported the speech of ANC Secretary-General Walter Sisulu at a mass rally, which unanimously expressed solidarity with the people of Kenya and condemned the aggressive war there.

Does this mean that we support violence? It means exactly the opposite. The whole policy of *Advance*, like that of the entire liberatory movement, is one which hates violence and loves peace. Not only because we are morally opposed to the use of unnecessary force, but also because senseless violence has never been the means of winning the struggle for freedom.

It is precisely because of this firm hatred of violence and aggression that we back the people of Kenya. Our paper has given full documentation to the dreadful events there. Greedy imperialists stole the best land of the

Imperialism: "Commentator" on International Issues   153

Kikuyu people. In support of their just grievances, the people organised behind leaders like Jomo Kenyatta in a completely legal and peaceful manner.

Fearing the strength of the people, the imperialists decided to use violence against them. The oppressors wished to break the laws — to kill and intimidate. They looked for an excuse. Just as in South Africa the oppressors create a fake "scare" every time they want to break old laws, so in Kenya the settlers blew up an unimportant secret society — Mau-Mau — into a big horror story.

The oppressors used this as an excuse to do away with laws that prevented them from using violence against the freedom movements in Kenya. They used it to put Kenyatta, the leader of the Kenya Africa Union, which had nothing to do with Mau-Mau, in prison for seven years. They used it to destroy the trade unions and every vestige of democracy.

They called in the British Army. Against unarmed people they used bombing aeroplanes, tanks, machine-guns. They have killed thousands of innocent people. Violence! Cases of terror by the "uncivilised, savage Mau-Mau", though they are magnified 10,000 times by our newspapers, are rare and are no part of the real struggle for freedom.

But violence, torture, burnings by young "civilised" products of the advanced British educational system are reported with grim regularity — and are known and fostered by the leaders of the invading army.

The writer of the letter remarks that the daily papers do not tell the truth in matters about the non-European people of South Africa. He must also know that he does his brothers in Kenya, fighting for existence, a great injustice by believing those same papers when they describe them as terrorists.

Advance stands wholeheartedly with the African National Congress and all lovers of freedom in support of the struggle of the people of Kenya, and all other colonial peoples, for freedom.

Advance Editorial, 4 March 1954.

10. Keeping Alive Socialist Debate

Why do we Write and Argue so Little about Socialism?

In recent years there has been very little discussion in South Africa in progressive — or other — journals about socialism. This is surprising because in other countries articles on the advantages — or disadvantages — of socialism, and the best way of achieving — or preventing — it, are a continual source of lively controversy.

It is all the more remarkable that journals read by and supported by the Congress movement should contain so little on the pros and cons of a system which in one form or another, for example Nkrumah's liberatory movement in the Gold Coast, has adopted as the very first article of its constitution; or which Nehru's Indian Congress has declared is "the only path India can follow"; or which was the basis of China's liberation — a system which, in fact, has the following of the majority of the world's population.

I suppose the main reason people aren't writing and arguing about socialism is the Suppression of Communism Act. Now what exactly the weird rigmarole of things is which the Act bans, it certainly does not ban all discussion of socialism. Dead letter as it may be, the Labour Party still has as an objective in its constitution the achievement of socialism and there is no doubt that this is perfectly legal.

What you can't do is advocate that there should be dictatorship of the proletariat (defined in a manner which is an obvious travesty of the real meaning of that concept as a system "under which one political organisation only is recognised and all other political organisations are suppressed or eliminated.") Nor can you advocate or threaten law-breaking, violence or disturbances, or aim to bring about changes under the guidance or in co-operation with foreign governments or institutions which aim to bring about "communism" in the Union; nor can you encourage hostility between Europeans and non-Europeans.

There is hardly anything in this crude mix-up of misconceptions (which needless to say is not communism) which any writer on socialism today would advocate, and writers have been over-timid if they have allowed the Act to frighten them off from all discussion of socialism.

In fact, if by the long silence many, many readers have no real knowledge of even the fundamental principles of this immensely important political system, what a great victory we have allowed — quite unnecessarily — Strijdom and other Nat. obscurantists!

What is common to all socialists?

Socialists of widely differing general outlooks all have this in common:

Keeping Alive Socialist Debate 155

1) They believe that capitalism is unjust and unworkable because it is based on the exploitation of the workers by the rich;

2) The capitalist — the factory owner, mine-owner, big farmer — gets his profit by paying the worker less than the value of the goods he produces. Apart from the injustice of this, it is unworkable because if the worker is not paid the value of what he produces, the general public, which is mainly composed of working people, is unable to buy back the immense supply of goods flowing from the factories to the stores. Huge stocks accumulate, there is a slump, the factories close down, the workers are unemployed and there is immense misery;

3) Socialists believe there should be a planned society, in which individuals are not left to run the factories for their own profit. Those who make the factories possible — the workers — should, together with the rest of the people, have control of them. Only when this is achieved and private profit is eliminated, will it be possible to ensure the fair distribution of goods and the ending of the evils of capitalism.

On these rudiments there is an immense range of agreement (though some socialists soft pedal sometimes). Where the differences have come is in the means of achieving socialism.

In the first political study-class I attended, about fifteen years ago, our textbook asked: "What is the fundamental difference between Labour Parties and the Communists ?" and answered, "Labour Parties believe that socialism can be achieved through gradual reforms by parliamentary means. Communists hold that parliamentary power cannot achieve socialism as long as the capitalists control the state machinery which can corrupt or forcibly destroy the achievements of parliament — as for example, the Spanish army was used to destroy the Popular Front parliament — and that therefore socialism can only be achieved by the revolutionary seizure of state power."

That was a correct statement of the difference between the Labour and Communist Parties at the time. Today, however, when world capitalism is immeasurably weaker and world socialism immeasurably stronger, it no longer holds true for all countries.

In Britain, France, Italy, and the US, for example, almost all socialists are agreed that a decisive parliamentary victory by a popular front could pave the way for a peaceful transition to socialism because world capitalism is no longer in any position to intervene in those countries, as it did on behalf of Franco in 1936 or in Guatemala last year.

Because of that, the realisation is growing that as old differences on the correct road to socialism disappear, the time is rapidly approaching when all socialists will be able to come together on a common programme, as indeed is already proposed by the leading British Labour Party writer, G.D.H. Cole.

156 *"The Youngest and Proudest Cardholder"*

What stands out in the world situation today is that socialists agree that each country will follow its own road to socialism — that what is done in one land will not necessarily be correct in another.

Would socialism be a good thing for South Africa? My own view, of course, is not only that it would be — but that it will be. I think we will have a socialist South Africa in which there will not only be full voting equality but also full economic equality.

What do other *Fighting Talk* readers think?

"Readers' Views" (Lionel Forman), *Fighting Talk*, November 1956

Socialism not Treason

Lest certain proceedings be unnecessarily lengthened by the addition of another exhibit, the editor of the *South African Socialist Review* (Lionel Forman) wishes to place on record that he alone is responsible for this production. None of the organisations against whom allegations have been made in the "Treason" preparatory examination is in any way involved in this publication, nor indeed has any individual, whether accused or not, conspired with, combined with, or assisted the editor in its production.

That having been said, it is necessary to add that the *South African Socialist Review* has taken pains in the attempt to ensure that it contains no treason, sedition, arson or rape and that it does not infringe even the lunatic provisions of the Suppression of Communism Act. In his evidence before the Select Committee of Parliament which unseated him, Communist MP Sam Kahn went much further than to affirm merely that socialist ideas remained legal. He maintained that one would still be legally entitled to put forward the views set out in the aims of the Constitution of the Communist Party of South Africa.

The following is an extract from the official government *Blue Book* "Report of the Select Committee on Suppression of Communism Act Enquiry"(April 1952, p. 226):

Mr P.J. Wessels, (cross-examining Mr Kahn): "You say that you as an individual would be entitled to propagate the aims as set out in Clause 2 of the Constitution of the Communist Party of South Africa without bringing yourself into conflict with this Act; you yourself, personally in Parliament and outside of Parliament, would be entitled having regard to the terms of the Suppression of Communism Act, to continue to propagate those aims?"

Mr Kahn: "In my view, any person would be entitled to propagate the views set forth in Clause 2 (a), (b), (c), and (d) of the Constitution."(The aims of the Communist Party of South Africa referred to above, are set out on page 9 of the Report as follows:

The Communist Party is a political party of the working class. Its aims are:

Keeping Alive Socialist Debate 157

(a) To establish working-class rule and a socialist republic based on the common ownership of the means of production;

(b) To prepare the way for socialism and to defend and promote the interests of the workers and oppressed nationalities by organising, educating and leading them in political and industrial struggle;

(c) To strive for equal rights for all sections of the people of South Africa, to break down race barriers and to promote unity of the workers of South Africa and throughout the world;

(d) To work for the extension to all adults, regardless of race, colour, or sex, of the right to vote and be elected to parliamentary, provincial, municipal and other representative institutions.

Mr Wessels: "Then I want to follow that up by asking you, if that is lawful, is that what you intend doing, if you were to remain on as a member of Parliament?"

Mr Kahn: "Whether or not I remain on as a member of Parliament, I will continue to stand for the aims set out in Clause 2 (a), (b), (c) and (d)."

Mr Wessels: "And not only to stand for those, but to propagate those views by exressing them in public, and trying to persuade members of the public generally to adopt those views?"

Mr Kahn: "I have been doing so since the passing of this Act and I have not been called to account by the law for having done so. I have done so both in Parliament and outside. I have declared that I still stand for these things. I do not regard it — and apparently the officers of the law do not regard it — as a contravention of the Act."

This was said six years ago, and there has still been no prosecution. One is therefore, even if one is very cautious, probably entitled to assume that Mr Kahn was correct.

It is, nevertheless, not the purpose or intention of this *Review* to propagate the policy of any particular party. Its purpose is to serve as a forum for South African socialist viewpoints, and as a propagator of the general principles of socialism. It will support enthusiastically the national liberatory struggle being waged by the African National Congress and its allied Congresses.

If this trial issue meets with favour, it is hoped that the *South African Socialist Review* will evolve in time into a regular periodical. At present it is planned as a quarterly. Contributions are invited.

South African Socialist Review, Editorial, November 1958.

158 "The Youngest and Proudest Cardholder"

Revive Socialist Discussion!

Socialism has an immense following all over the world. Huge nations are led by socialist governments, and there is no country, except the most backward, which has no socialist political party, publicly putting forward a socialist policy.

But in South Africa, although there is no law that prohibits socialist propaganda (and the Labour Party has at least nominally a socialist constitution), there is no organisation, no club, no forum where socialists can get together, exchange ideas, and win new adherents to their cause.

Is this because there is no interest in socialism in South Africa?

Certainly not! Support for socialist ideas has probably never been so widespread in our country as it is now. It is almost certainly correct to say that the majority of those active in the Congress movement are supporters of socialism in some form or to some degree.

How then has it come about that public discussion of, and propaganda for, socialism has come to a halt? How has a state of affairs unknown in any other country in the world come about in South Africa?

Some socialists seem to feel that socialist discussions and activity would mean taking time off from Congress work and would result in weakening it. But the experience of other countries has shown that this is not the case. In India, China, Indonesia, Ghana — the national movements have all, though in vastly different degrees, absorbed and integrated socialist thinking — and immensely strengthened themselves in the process.

For people who have learned about socialism often become the most active fighters for freedom, the most ready to sacrifice. They are strengthened by the vision of the future which socialism gives them; more able leaders because of the understanding of how society develops which socialist theory gives them.

Through socialist propaganda too, it is possible to win recruits for the Congress movement, for no one can become a true socialist without becoming a wholehearted participant in the liberatory struggle.

The blending of the international concepts of socialist thought and struggle with the ideas and forms which are developing in the national movements today would lead to immense advances towards the South Africa of the Freedom Charter.

Editorial, *South African Socialist Review*, November 1958.

Has May Day Become the Forgotten Day?

"May Day" — the mention of which is sufficient to stir the blood of the politically conscious worker in most countries — often seems to pass almost unnoticed in South Africa. May 1st is the day of international working-class solidarity, the day on which the workers of all the world pledge their unity.

Keeping Alive Socialist Debate   159

In our country, where the most urgent call is for workers, artificially divided by racialist propaganda, to throw aside their differences and stand united, May Day is a day heavy with significance.

The First International, in July 1889, decided to set May 1st aside as the annual day of workers' unity; so May Day has been celebrated since 1890.

Remember that in 1890 Johannesburg was only six years old and was nothing more than a mining camp. Kimberley, where the diamonds were being dug out, was the country's industrial centre, and the black and white diamond diggers were rudely awakening the sleepy villages of Cape Town and Durban and transforming the country from a collection of semi-bankrupt farming communities into a single industrialised state.

When was May Day first celebrated in South Africa? The date has not yet been fixed with certainty. Ray Alexander has found records of a May Day demonstration organised by a body called the Johannesburg District Trades Council as long ago as 1895, and she fixes that as the first South African celebration.

But perhaps in the end the honour may go to Cape Town, Durban or Kimberley. For Cape Town's first trade union branch (the Carpenters and Joiners) was already fourteen years old in 1895, the Durban Typo's (South Africa's first independent trade union) was seven, and Kimberley's early working-class organisation (the details of which still have to be pulled out through the mists of history) may have beaten the Jo'burg workers as the May Day pioneers.

In spite of Johannesburg's promisingly early start, the annual celebration of May Day does not seem to have caught on in that city. This is not altogether surprising, for the organised working-class movement was confined to whites and one of its main preoccupations was ensuring that Africans were kept out of skilled jobs. Speeches devoted to the lesson of the unity of all labouring men irrespective of nationality raised certain problems.

Jack Cope records, however, in his biography of Bill Andrews, that during the visit to South Africa of the famous British Labour leader, Tom Mann, in 1910, he aroused such enthusiasm and "the spirit of solidarity was so great that all sections of the labour movement from the Trades Council to the Socialist Society turned out again for a mass demonstration on the Market Square on May Day."

But this was an exceptional occasion. May Day was not again celebrated in Johannesburg until 1915 when the left-wingers who were to be among the founders of the Communist Party six years later . . . broke from the Labour Party in protest against its support of the imperialist war and formed the War-on-War League.

"An attenuated procession"

In that year, in the words of a writer of a "May Day History" published in the *International* in 1921, "a little band of War-on-Warites organised a

160 *"The Youngest and Proudest Cardholder"*

picturesque but, as the press would say, attenuated procession through the streets of Johannesburg, ending with a meeting in the rain on the Market Square addressed by a number of stalwarts and enlivened by a small band."

An interesting thing about this account is that it begins: "Labour May Day was first observed in South Africa, to the best of our recollection, in 1915 . . . " Bill Andrews was editor of the *International* at this time and as he had for many years been closely involved in Labour developments, it is probably fairly safe to assume that the Tom Mann affair was an isolated instance.

As patriotic war fervour gripped the white citizens of Johannesburg, the follow-up to the 1915 procession became impossible. In 1916, May Day was celebrated by a social and a visit to the graves of the workers killed in the 1914 strike.

But 1917 was a year of importance. The War-on-Warites, who had now formed the International Socialist League, were increasingly becoming aware of the meaning of international socialism, and they were beginning to work for the unity of all workers, black and white. On May Day 1917, for the first time in the Rand's history, they announced that one of the speakers at their May Day rally would be an African — Horatio Mbelle. Mbelle was an articled clerk who was active in the Transvaal ANC. But the meeting never took place. Mobs of soldiers and civilians who gathered in the streets and at the meeting place saw to that.

With the white workers so war-fevered that they would not listen to any talk about international workers' unity, the International Socialist League (ISL) again broke new ground in 1918. It held its meeting, not on the City Hall steps or the Market Square — traditional gathering places of white labour — but outside the Pilkington Hall in Ferreirastown where the Coloureds usually met. A Coloured leader, Talbot Williams, of the APO, and William Thebedi were among the speakers.

It was a small meeting, with an audience of between one and two hundred, mainly Coloured, but the ISL was pleased with this first breaking of new ground. "Altogether a May Day demonstration with more in it than ever before."

But — and there is no excuse for it — with the war's end and with the resurgence of the militancy of the white labour movement so that May Day became a huge affair with paid holidays and big marches and drums, the ISL forgot all about the Pilkington Hall and the demonstration "with more in it than ever before."

Its speakers got in there among the drums — which was right — and none of them went to Ferreirastown, which was very wrong, as the speeches they were making on May Day should have shown them. And that mistake cost us all a great deal of heartbreak.

They knew it

Nor were the Socialists unaware that things were not as they should be. The anonymous writer of the article in 1921 had this to say:

It is for us to see that the day shall not be allowed to lose its character as a hostile demonstration by the oppressed masses against their exploiters — a day of hatred and contempt for their snobbery, flummery and thieving — a day of alarm for them. They sit easy still because the Native proletariat is still a stranger to the May Day spirit. Two years ago, while we were spouting on the Union Ground, a little band of black demonstrators at Vrededorp were batoned out of countenance by the police, while an aeroplane hovered over their heads. Last year a Native attempting to march in the procession in Johannesburg was kicked and chased down a side street by the bystanders.

Colour does not seem to arouse such antipathy in the Cape, but in Johannesburg there is something notable in last Monday's achievement when a handful of Native workers voluntarily claimed to form fours under the ISL banner and marched with the rest of us, while "the people stood beholding" without a murmur. Let their example be followed wholesale next year; let the labourers in their hundreds of thousands turn out and "process" with their white fellow-workers next May Day.

. . . When May Day thus becomes truly proletarian, the sparks will begin to fly, for it would be the most painful wound that we could deal to them. And until we deal some such wound we have still to win our spurs as the South African branch of the Communist International.

After the bitter year 1922 and the bitter years that followed, the message of May Day began to strike home. The African workers began to organise. Solidarity became the key word.

In 1928, African workers showed their power on the Rand with a great May Day march of thousands — among them a small number of Whites and Coloureds. Their celebration dwarfed the Labour Party's little lily-white demonstration. From that time on — with big ups and downs — there were big united demonstrations of the people of all races right through the years until the Nationalists came to power.

Biggest of them all

And then on May Day 1951, there was the biggest May Day demonstration of all — the nation-wide protest strike against the Nationalist laws, which was most effective on the Rand, bringing industry to a standstill. Many lives were lost on the night of May Day when the police drove through the streets of African townships firing sten-guns. The people replied on June 26th of the same year with a Day of Mourning.

Since then June 26th has become a day of great importance — which is a good thing. But May Day has become an all-but-forgotten day marked only by the routine May Day features in *New Age*. And that is a bad thing.

New Age 1 May 1958.

162 "The Youngest and Proudest Cardholder"

Time for a Socialist Party?

All of those who have participated in the discussion on whether or not we should have one single all-in Congress seem to agree that in principle it would be a good thing for people of the different national groups to work together in one body. The point of disagreement is simply whether or not we are able in practice to mobilise more people into the anti-Nationalist struggle through our present form of organisation than we would through one all-in Congress.

I wonder if we may not be posing the question the wrong way.

The Congresses grew up to meet a particular political need. The ANC was formed because the Africans are hit in a particular way by our politcal system and have felt the need to unite as Africans to further the legitimate interests of Africans. The Indian Congress was formed similarly because Indians felt a need to unite to fight for their own cause.

In the face of their common oppression, and as a result of their advanced political understanding, the African, Indian and other Congresses have, in comparatively recent times, formed themselves into a firm alliance with a common programme — but that is because each of the Congresses realises that its own interests are best served by a united fight for the interests of all.

The fact that there is the Congress Alliance must not be allowed to obscure an equally important fact — that each of the Congresses continues to serve the particular needs of its own members. The leading role of the Indian Congress in the fight against Group Areas is but one example of many.

We fight racialist theories because they assert falsely that some races are superior to others. We reply that there is no difference between the capabilities of the different South African nationalities, and that all shall have the right to full equality as citizens of a single South African state.

But the fact that we are all South Africans does not mean that we can blind ourselves to the existence of different national groups with distinctive languages and cultures and subject to distinctive forms of political oppression. The experience of every other similar country proves that as long as this continues to be, so there will also continue to be separate national organisations to express the special aspirations of each national community. Merging the Congresses into one all-in body would, therefore, solve nothing. For immediately there would again, inevitably, arise new national bodies to serve the special requirements of each community.

But this does not mean that the arguments in favour of a single political organisation composed of people of all national groups are wrong.

One organisation

There is a very urgent need for a single organisation in which Africans, Indians, Coloureds and Europeans can work together, plan together, study together and organise together on the basis of full equality.

Keeping Alive Socialist Debate 163

The Congress movement has often stressed that it is not a political party. It is a united front made up of people of the most diverse philosophies, who have come together out of a common desire to fight apartheid.

But there is a need, in addition to the national organisations, for a single multi-national political party with a long-term political programme. Such a party, which would naturally be composed of Congress members, and would give unstinted support to the Congress movement, would be an immense asset to our country.

For such a party to succeed it must not scamper nervously behind the Congress movement, as does the Liberal Party, always frightened that the Congresses may do something "rash", always sniffing about for "communist influence", never sure whether it is more scared of getting too close to the Congresses than of getting too far from them.

What we need is a party based firmly on the most militant and advanced section of the population, the non-European working class. It is significant that socialism, the international philosophy of working-class parties in all countries, is publicly recognised by almost all national liberatory leaders, from Nehru, to Nasser, to Nkrumah, as the only way to bring about a swift and lasting improvement in the living conditions of the people.

Smashing apartheid will lift a very great burden from our shoulders. But it will not mean an end to our problems. Far from it. A new and greater challenge will face us — the building of a nation free from want. Both in the fight against apartheid and the planning of the future, the Congress movement needs a partner in struggle — a multi-national socialist party.

New Age 16 July 1959.

Stalin and Dictatorship

We are in favour of the withering away of the state, yet we are at the same time in favour of strengthening the dictatorship of the proletariat which represents the most powerful and mighty of all forms of state power that have hitherto existed. The supreme development of the power of the state, with the object of preparing the way for the withering away of state power — such is the Marxist formula. Is that self-contradictory? Yes it is self-contradictory. But this contradiction is a living thing and it is a complete reflection of Marxian dialectics. (Stalin, 1930)

One of the biggest self-contradictions in politics is the fact that intellectuals who are attracted towards the Communist Party not through direct participation in the working-class struggle but through theoretical conviction, are often attracted precisely by the fact that communists are in the forefront of every campaign in defence of civil liberties and for the extension of freedom. Freedom — *Liberté* — *Merdeka* — *Freiheit* — *Inkululeko* — in every language of the world communists have rallied behind that banner.

164 *"The Youngest and Proudest Cardholder"*

And yet, paradoxically, the chief characteristic distinguishing communists from Labour Parties and Social Democrats (all of whom believe that freedom, both political and economic, can be won only if capitalism is crushed and replaced by socialism) is the insistence by communists that, owing to the certainty that the desperate forces of capitalism ousted from power will resort to every means including war and violence to prevent the march to socialism, it is necessary in the period immediately after the people seize power, for the state to be ruled by a form of dictatorship — the dictatorship of the proletariat.

True, communists have stressed that this is a dictatorship different from any known in the past; one based on the interests of the majority of the people and not on those of the oppressing minority, but they have never denied that it was dictatorship nevertheless, and dictatorship is an evil involving restrictions on freedom — freedom to organise opposition parties, freedom of the press, of speech, of travel.

Progressives saw the dictatorship of the proletariat as a temporary stage which the Soviet Union had to pass through in order to achieve a society where there would be no slums and starvation, no pass laws and jails, a society where not only would dictatorship be a memory of the evil past, but even the whole machinery of state which limits liberty — the police forces and laws and parliaments — would wither away, and mankind would live as one family on a new level of existence.

Progressives have always looked confidently toward the day when the Soviet Union would find herself so secure that she could begin to relax the dictatorship. While the fear-ridden western countries retreated from the real freedoms of bourgeois democracy towards oppression and dictatorship, the socialist state was advancing from dictatorship to democracy on a new, higher, level.

The first signs of readiness for such relaxation have been apparent over the past two years or so, with the easing of restrictions on travel, the relatively uninhibited flow of scientific information, the raising of the tight security guard which surrounded the government leaders.

But the real signal for a dramatic change, after the mild hints in the published reports to the 20th Congress of the Soviet Communist Party, was Kruschev's secret statement on the cult of the individual. A trustworthy text of this statement is not yet available, but though the details are not yet certain, the overall picture is. And that picture shows clearly that progressives outside the Soviet Union — and inside it — who had believed that the men at the summit of the dictatorship were of so superhuman a calibre that they were able to reduce the evils of dictatorship to a minimum were wrong.

The very leaders — Stalin included — who had written and spoken so clearly to emphasise the dangers of individual decisions instead of democratic ones; who had emphasised that power must be firmly based on the democratic decision of the whole party and not on the caprice of individuals no matter how gifted; who had insisted on the need for utmost

Keeping Alive Socialist Debate 165

"socialist legality" in dealing with offenders — had all, according to Kruschev's report, been living a huge lie for the past twenty years.

When people asked communists to explain the adulation of Stalin, they said that it was a necessity during a particular historic period, that the tributes paid were not to him as an individual but to him as a symbol of the whole party and the first socialist state, and that Stalin himself was a modest man who hated the excesses but submitted to them because this was the will of the Party. It seems that they were wrong and that, according to the Kruschev report, Stalin had come to love and believe in the tributes as being directly addressed to himself.

And it seems that while it was believed that it was a truth that hardly needed mentioning that all important decisions were the result of the fullest possible democratic discussion with the Party, and that none was ever taken arbitrarily by Stalin himself, this was also not so. A number of decisions, it seems, were made by Stalin alone, and the inevitable resulted . . . some of them were wrong.

And, worst shock of all, it seems that a number of people — and possibly a large number of people — who supported policies in opposition to the party line were treated as traitors though their opposition was quite legitimate, or if not legitimate, did not amount to treason.

The reaction to Kruschev's revelations have differed extremely widely in different countries. In the colonial and formerly colonial countries there has been no turmoil. The huge Communist Party of Indonesia and the very active one in India have done no more than publish the official statements made in Moscow and Peking. Their leaders have welcomed the positive effects of the announcement and they appear well pleased with the situation.

At the other end of the scale, there has been an enormous impact on the very small hard-core Communist Party in the United States whose newspapers have played up their horror at the injustices revealed and have carried a number of articles in which communists write of the "heavy load of guilt" which they feel they bear; and there has been a similar impact on a far smaller scale in Britain. There Harry Pollitt suggested that the intellectuals in the Party were focusing too much attention on the reassessment of Stalin while the workers were, more correctly, chiefly concerned with the new opportunities for the expansion of the Party that were now offered.

In South Africa, for reasons somewhat similar to those in the colonial and semi-colonial countries, the harmful effects of the revelations have been limited and there seems to be enormous scope for stressing the positive aspects and their significance for our progressive movement. Though the public is eager for discussion, progressives have been slow to take the opportunity offered.

What are the positive aspects that need stressing and which can serve to assist the march to freedom?

166 "The Youngest and Proudest Cardholder"

Standing out most boldly is this. That by bringing the criticisms of the methods of the Soviet party leadership during the past twenty years mercilessly to light, Kruschev has taken the best means of ensuring that now a new era is indeed beginning. With the immense burst of discussion that has taken place throughout the Soviet Union, with the progressive movement all over the world alerted, there is little doubt that the conditions which were created for dictatorial rule will not again be able to arise.

Deliberately Kruschev has focused the world spotlight on the Communist Party so that progressives in other countries will know with confidence that the era is past when they should feel it their duty to rally under all circumstances to defend the actions of the Soviet Union against her enemies. How is it imaginable after this that anyone, on the lowest committee or the highest, will be able to set himself up as the man who makes the decisions and must be obeyed?

There are two types of questions asked about the Kruschev statement. One is "Why on earth did he make revelations like this which he knew would be seized upon by the enemies of the Soviet Union?" and the other is "How do we know that this can't happen again?" The two questions answer each other. The searing criticisms of the past which exposed the torn flesh of the Communist Party were necessary precisely to put people on their guard, to show what had happened so that they would not let it happen again.

Progressives who felt it their duty to refrain from joining in attacks on the Soviet Union under any circumstances in the past — and who feel no "guilt" at all for doing so — will now feel it their duty to voice constructive criticisms and misgivings in the future. To start off with, they are saying that there are aspects of the very announcement of the errors of the past which are not completely satisfactory. Why was it left to the capitalist press to break the news to the world? Has there yet been full self-criticism? But that is of course the subject of a separate discussion.

What stands out and cannot be sufficiently emphasised is this — that the despotism of the tsars meant absolute misery, despair and darkness for the people of Russia and her colonies; that this misery, despair and darkness have been replaced in the Soviet Union by a full life of hope; that the strength of the Soviet Union has made possible the more rapid winning of freedom by the people of China and of other countries which have suffered the yoke of imperialism — and that this transition from tsarism to socialism was possible only through the dictatorship of the proletariat.

That there are aspects of that dictatorship which led to injustice and bloodshed is clear. But just as all the mess, blood and agony are part of the birth of the human baby, so the mess, blood and agony of the Soviet people have given rise to their socialist state.

Inasmuch as their sufferings, experiences — and strength — now smooth the paths of other peoples to freedom by new routes, what an enormous debt we owe them!

Lessons From Hungary 1956

The daily press, naturally, is exaggerating and distorting the events in Hungary. But making the maximum allowance for lies and hysteria, the facts must remain hard for most progressives to take.

There has been a large-scale revolt against a people's democratic government. The fighting in the streets of Budapest has come as a shock to us and the best way to overcome the shock is to face the facts that underlie the revolt.

It cannot be explained simply in terms of US spies and provocateurs — though they have certainly played their part. It can only be explained in terms of intense dissatisfaction on the part of a section of the least politically conscious workers themselves — dissatisfaction strong enough to make them ready tools for the hard-dying Hungarian capitalist class and its foreign allies. The fact that it was necessary for the Hungarian government to call Soviet troops to its aid is clear enough testimony that a fair number of workers must have been, at best, neutral in the conflict. For every factory has its well armed, well trained workers' defence group, and had this workers' militia been united and enthusiastic, the uprising could have been smashed without foreign aid.

What is the basis for the dissatisfaction which both the Polish and Hungarian governments have admitted to exist and to be at least partly justified?

There have been terrible errors and terrible barbarities in the building of that new world. But they are not even a tiny fraction of the cruelties, suffering and inequity which are perpetrated daily and deliberately in the old order. The socialist world is painfully exposing its own crimes as a warning that they must never be allowed to happen again. But the western world can only exist by the continuation of merciless cruelties — the hangings in Cyprus, the mass shootings in Algeria are regular pages in the history of imperialism.

And in our own country we know the daily injustice of innocent people herded into jails, of mothers separated from families, of people torn from their homes and livelihoods at the whim of a cruel dictatorship. The local newspapers which are so oblivious to the evils which stem from racialism have a hopeless task in trying to turn the African peoples against the people's democracies with hypocritical cant about the absence of civil liberties in Hungary.

On the contrary, it is precisely because it is so self-evident that it is the Soviet Union and the people's democracies who are the allies of every people struggling for freedom that has made many progressives reluctant to see the faults in these countries — or where we have, have explained them away, or brushed them aside as unimportant.

But they were not unimportant. Hungary proves that. And Poznan proved it. And the Berlin strike proved it, but most of us weren't ready to see it.

168 "The Youngest and Proudest Cardholder"

I lived and worked in one of the most advanced of the people's democracies for two years during the "Stalin" period and I'll put down my impressions now — belatedly — in the hope that they will assist in understanding what is happening.

It was the period when Tito was being described — by me as well — as a US agent and fascist; when the security stranglehold was at its strongest, and heavy sacrifices were being demanded of the people. I worked in an international organisation with a large number of other young people from all over the western world and we all developed a cynicism towards the things about us that was a nagging worry to every one of us. One had the choice of being cynical or being bitterly critical — and it didn't enter our heads to be bitterly critical. The reason for this is another question — it certainly was not cowardice, for among us were Spaniards and Germans and resistance fighters who had fought for and been prepared to die for liberty.

Almost each day we sat and discussed the grotesque examples of red tape, inefficiency and buck-passing which marked the work of almost every civil servant and minor official we had dealings with. In the evenings we very often sat by candlelight for hours while the city's power plant rested — and wondered how it could be that years after the war one of Europe's greatest, wealthiest cities should suffer the humiliation of a black-out for lack of generating plant.

We watched the production statistics soar and were happy at the clear proof that socialist planning was so effective. But it was a standard topic of discussion that apart from basic essentials — which were cheap — everything was incredibly expensive or unobtainable. And every time one of us made a trip to the west he was loaded with requests: bring back some razor blades, a decent tin-opener, a pot scourer, and for the married couples the ever-urgent — don't forget to bring contraceptives.

How could we make light of the censorship? No western publications could be obtained and there were even times when you couldn't get the *Daily Worker*. Or the steady monotony of the films. I remember at a fairly trivial French film which had drawn big crowds for weeks (*Fan Fan la Tulipe*), getting into a conversation with the man next to me who was wearing a Communist Party badge on the reasons for the film's popularity. "There's nothing about peace in it!", he said. "Our films — peace, peace, peace. It makes you sick!"

Worst of all, perhaps, something that we couldn't explain away or be cynical about — the fact that the Soviet delegates in our organisation were privileged people, expected to be respected and to have the best of things — and let's face it — looked down on everyone else! (How noticeable it was, and what a constant topic of discussion, that the Chinese were always modest and unassuming and lived together with the other delegates, refusing to accept any privileges.)

Taken in all, they were small things and big things. Things which had good reason and things which had no good reason, and probably mainly things that fell somewhere between the two extremes. But even when there were things which were obviously bad, instead of recognising them as such, I blamed my own middle-class background as the reason for the fault-finding. Others did the same.

All these big things and little things explained the phenomenon that we in that city discussed so often. The fact that while there was, on the one hand, a big body of politically conscious, enthusiastic and vigorous people backing the regime, there was an alarmingly large number of ordinary citizens who were against it. Tell the taxi-driver you're going to England and he shakes you with his "Ah, it's better there". Speak to the judge and he'll complain of pressure in political cases. Speak to the nurse and she'll tell you her father was a surgeon — her grandfather was a surgeon — but she couldn't register at the medical school because she wasn't of a working-class background. "Theatre nursing is the closest they would let me get." Speak to the architecture student and he'll tell you he doesn't like sitting up late studying all that damned Marxism instead of designing.

The election results showed that 97 per cent voted for the government. Our standard wry joke was "I met the whole opposition this morning." What is misleading, and what made it so difficult to conceive of a revolt, is that even these people were fully aware of the achievements of the socialist regime. I met hundreds of people who were vehemently anti-government.

But I never met a single one who wanted to return to the days of capitalism.

They wanted to keep the social security and freedom from the fear of unemployment which socialism had brought; the health facilities, the new opportunities for children. But they didn't recognise the need for the bad things which had come with the good.

Mainly they were probably wrong. It was probably absolutely necessary to sacrifice living standards to the development of heavy industry and defence; it was certainly necessary to impose limitations on freedom to prevent counter-revolution.

But in some degree they were undoubtedly right — the sacrifices called for were too great, the limitations on freedom out of all proportion to the need. This has now been boldly stated by the governments of Hungary and Poland.

And the governments of the Soviet Union and the people's democracies are pledged to bring about the necessary changes — without in any way sacrificing the achievements of socialism.

A new future dawns for the world. The bitter lessons of the past have been learned — and we of other countries are the gainers, for our transition to the new age will be all the simpler.

New Age 1 November 1956

Part Four:
The National Question

The two periods of debate on the national question, in 1954 and 1958/59, generated a substantial body of writing, most of which could not be included here. The contributions of Kenny Jordaan of the Unity Movement, and Thomas Ngwenya of the ANC to the symposium on the national question organised by the Forum/South Africa Club, as well as the articles by those who participated in the year-long debate published in *Marxism Today* in 1958 and 1959 are available in the Forman Papers lodged at the Mayibuye Centre at UWC. A number of articles by I.I. Potekhin, the Russian scholar who several articles on African nationalism, can also be found there. Some of Potekhin's letters have been freely edited because of the poor quality of translation from Russian to English. This is in keeping with the generally liberal approach adopted by the editors in order to ensure readability and to overcome constraints of space and economy. Serious scholars should consult the originals at UWC for the complete record.

11. The Debate Fuelled

Don't Spread Malan's Lie!

The ruling classes in our country know that it is in their interests to keep the people confused about the meaning of certain words. The philosophy of our rulers is based on many falsehoods, and they have been very clever in managing to get the whole country echoing one of the most important of these lies. The most important word the South African rulers use to spread their poisonous philosophy is "race". They say there are different races and some races are born inferior to others. They talk of a "Bantu race" and a "White race". Everybody except the supporters of apartheid knows that scientifically this is sheer rubbish.

But the rulers have an enormous power to spread their false ideas. They control the newspapers, the schools, most of the churches, the radio. Everywhere you hear this word "race". Even we, the people against whom the whole idea behind this false word "race" is a powerful weapon of the destruction of liberty — we ourselves start using this word. By doing so we assist in spreading the philosophy which keeps us in slavery.

That is obviously something we should stop doing — and quickly. For if, when we discuss our liberation, we use a meaningless word, our whole discussion is in danger of becoming meaningless. When we call for "an end to race discrimination" or for "racial harmony" we are not using the best words. And because of this we make it possible for people who look deep into the meaning of what we say to become confused. And for those who do not look deeply we make it difficult to obtain a clear understanding of the truth.

The youth festival committees have as a slogan, "For Racial Harmony". That's very nice, and we wanted to write this editorial explaining what a good idea it is. That's where the trouble began. If these different groups coming together at the festival aren't "races", then it's not racial harmony that's coming out of the festival. Don't think we're quibbling and that everyone knows what they mean when they talk about racial harmony. The fact is that this incorrect term obscures the meaning of the festival.

If the different groups aren't races, what are they? And if you think of them that way, your ideas flow easily into the right direction. No one is likely to think of developing their "racial" culture or their "racial" heritage. But all of us are drawn by the thought of developing our national cultures, of building on our national heritage. All of us have a healthy national pride.

The festivals are a wonderful opportunity for young South Africans of all national groups to come together in friendship and equality; to make known to others their own national cultures, and to see something of the national cultures of their fellows.

The Debate Fuelled 173

This spirit of healthy nationalism is a progressive force. It is a people's nationalism, proud of its own people's achievements, but respectful of the rights of other nationalities and eager to benefit from the best aspects of the cultures of others. It is completely different from the rich man's nationalism, which seeks to oppress the peoples of other nationalities for profit — the nationalism of the apartheiders.

Use of the correct terms helps us to get a better insight into what should come out of these festivals. Youth will have the opportunity of seeing something of the great cultural wealth of the African people. They should be given the opportunity of understanding how the oppressors have sought to destroy African culture and even the African languages. The festivals will make it clear for the participants what terrible attacks are being launched against the national cultures of the people of our country.

It is clear, then, that the festivals will go further than an amorphous idea of "harmony". They will show how important it is that different national groups should have the opportunity to study and speak their own tongue, write their own literature, develop their cultural heritages. More, they will make sections of the youth who are unconscious of the deliberate assault on the cultures of our peoples aware of, and indignant at, this crime. The youth must leave the festival determined to abolish national oppression. If they do not, the festivals will not have succeeded.

For some people there is a taint of suspicion about the word "nationalism". They associate it with the narrow-minded, greedy rapaciousness of modern-day Afrikaner nationalism. But that is not people's nationalism. That is the nationalism of the narrow-minded, greedy, rapacious capitalist class.

Why is it progressive to foster a spirit of people's nationalism? What is it that should be fostered?

The most important thing we must encourage is a thriving national culture. Our Zulu poets must sing sagas of liberation in their mother tongue — the people must rock with laughter at Sotho satires on the Nats. Let our very folk dances exemplify a kick in the pants for Malan and our music the drumbeats of freedom.

The great exaltation which fills a person's body when one knows one is fighting for freedom, must not be confined to the relatively small section of our people who are able to read the news of liberation in *Advance*. Great flowering national cultures must carry the ideas of freedom into every kraal, hessian shanty and *pondokkie* (hut) in terms the people can understand.

The need has been recognised by the Cape African National Congress, who, while calling on every African to read and support *Advance*, point with regret at the absence of a liberation paper in the African language.

Advance will make a start.

Advance is written in English because that is the language that can be understood by elements of all national groups. But what a great day it will be when *Advance* appears also in African language editions!

174 *The National Question*

This is up to our readers. It is only *Advance* which could possibly carry out such an undertaking at present. And if the people want it enough to be prepared to make it possible, it will be done. Meanwhile, we remind readers that if they wish to express their views through our columns and are unable to do so adequately in English, they may write in their own language and we will ensure translation.

It is necessary for us to pay more attention to this factor of so great importance to the future development of the liberatory movement. We must study and understand fully the forces of progressive nationalism and utilise them in the struggle for freedom. And obviously we must begin by taking care not to spread the false "race" ideas by careless use of words. From this issue *Advance* will make a start by paying particular care to avoiding the terminology of the oppressors. Our readers are asked to keep a sharp watch and to write us their criticisms every time we slip.

But, of course, there is still far more to it than that. It would be simple if all that was required was to change the word "racial" to "national". We have to grasp the whole vitally important difference between the concepts.

Would you believe it? In spite of the fact that every one of us talks of a "national liberatory struggle", of "nationalism" of "nation" and of "national group", if a number of us were to come together in public today to say what exactly we understand by the term "national group" there would probably be as many opinions as people.

The urgent problem that is spotlighted is this. Our national liberatory movement will stumble and falter unless we have a clear understanding of the national question. It is an urgent political task to open the widest discussion. The columns of our newspaper will play an important part in this.

Advance 1 April 1954.

"Neither Duty nor Task of Editorial"
by Dr Y.M. Dadoo.

I read your editorial headed "Don't Spread Malan's Lie!" in the 1 April issue with interest but not without some measure of misgiving.

Whether the word "race" should be used or not used is not a matter of such supreme import as to warrant an *Advance* editorial. Theoretically, the use of terms such as "racial harmony" may be meaningless and inexcusable. But to cavil at the use of such terms in a long *Advance* editorial is to "strain at a gnat." These terms, in the context particularly of South African conditions, have a definite meaning and a connotation understood by all. For example, the term "national harmony" would not be as readily and clearly understood by the people as "racial harmony".

Be that as it may. I seriously consider that it is not the business of *Advance* editorials to indulge in such matters of theoretical controversy. The important business of *Advance* editorials should be to deal with and give guidance to the readers on vital questions which affect the people, such as the Western Areas Removal Scheme or the amendment to the Suppression of Communism Act. Guidance which would help in mobilising the masses of people in the day-to-day struggle against apartheid tyranny and fascist reaction of the Malan government.

If one has to indulge in theoretical controversy about whether "race" is a myth or reality it should be done as separate articles so that the readers may be given an opportunity for a full and free discussion.

But it is my firm belief that this is neither the duty nor task of an *Advance* editorial.

Advance 8 April 1954.

The Fog Under Which We Tend To Work
(A reply to a letter from Joe Matthews)

I think you rather overestimate the impact of our editorial. As a matter of fact before I got your letter, I had the impression that nobody read the things at all.

I agree with you fully on the importance of this question of having a correct approach to the question of nationalism and of the importance it can be in our work. There are a large number of problems that have not yet been tackled in this field at all. For example, the very definition of the term "national group" is clear, I think, and that, according to the classical definition, there are no nations at all in South Africa. South Africa itself might be a nation. But if we take as a definition of a national group (though I haven't seen such a definition and I have been looking for one) . . . that a national group is a potential nation, then there are a whole number of questions to be solved as to which South African groups are the national groups. Here I think that you would be able to give some very firm opinions. How would you stratify the different African peoples into national groups? It would necessarily have to go along language lines, but then would some of the languages justify having people grouped as more than one national group speaking the same language and so on. The whole issue is very fogged by red herrings of tribalism and so on. But I would very much appreciate your opinions on a rough stratification.

What are the different national groups? Specifically among non-Europeans. I think one could say very clearly the Afrikaners are one national group, the Jews probably fall as a national group, we could even define the English as a national group. But I have still difficulty deciding how the Coloured people would fall under any definition . . . it is essential that we get clarity while we can, from discussion. I hope to write some more on this matter too . . . (and) on the relationship between the class struggle and the national struggle and also to do something on the void that seems

176   The National Question

to have fallen once we stop using the word "race", "race discrimination" and so on. I think that we should adopt the American term for race attitudes — namely, chauvinism.

I am most intrigued by your report of the interest in the editorials on the need for leaders in the struggle. The editorials speak for themselves and I don't think it necessary for me to add any gloss to them. The statement stands, there can be no successful army without leaders. It is so self-evident, so much almost a pious platitude that it is most interesting that people should consider that there is something new in it. Once again there is demonstrated the fog under which we tend to work.

Discussion on South Africa's National Question

The editorial opening discussion on the national question aroused, as it was intended to, a considerable amount of controversy. Comments have ranged from the opinion that the objection to the use of "race" instead of "national group" was "left sectarian" to the view that the editorial "knocked the bottom out of the policies of the reactionaries".

Whatever its merits or demerits, the editorial succeeded in showing that a study of the nature of our national groups has been astonishingly neglected. One direct result of the editorial will be an open discussion of the problem by speakers with different viewpoints at a Cape Town discussion group next month.

What a nation is

Since the discussion of the analysis of South Africa's different national groups began, I have looked through a wide range of material for previous articles on this branch of theory. I have not been able to find any real down-to-earth analysis of what are our national groups and how they should be defined . . .

Let us begin from the ground that has been charted. The term "nation" has been very clearly defined by political scientists. A nation is a stable community of people who have lived together in the same territory from generation to generation, speak the same language, have an internal economic bond welding the community into a whole, and a common "psychology" manifesting itself in the common culture.

The nation is not based on race. Every nation existing is composed of a mixture of races. Nor is it tribal. Most — maybe all — nations resulted from the coming together of different tribes into one nation. On the other hand, there is no reason why a community of people, tribal in origin, could not become a nation.

What can be seen from the definition? This: that South Africa is not a nation. It is a multi-national state consisting of a number of nationalities.

Why it matters

Why worry about what a nation is, anyway? The reason these particular working-class political scientists paid such close attention to the definition of a nation was because the states in which they were waging the struggle for freedom were multi-national (Austro-Hungary and Tsarist Russia). Dominant nations were keeping other nations in subservience and exploiting them.

Because of their careful study and understanding of the nature of the communities involved, the working-class parties were able to put forward the correct political demand — the right to self-determination; the right of nations to secede from the multi-national state and create their own national state if they wished. As a result, when the workers took power in the Soviet Union this right became embodied in the constitution of the country.

The evolution of this policy — the lengthy and bitter arguments — looked at in cold print today, may seem to be academic theorising, straining after gnats. But it was nothing of the sort. It arose out of the urgent needs of the moment — the revolutionary national feeling of the oppressed people and the need to put forward a correct policy to gain the confidence of the people and direct the struggle towards the winning of freedom.

The foremost writer on this topic sharply criticised those who put forward views which showed "an underestimation of the internal strength of the national movement and a lack of understanding of the profoundly popular and profoundly revolutionary nature of the national movement."

There are theoreticians in South Africa who could well ponder the fact that the error criticised gave rise to the false notion that the national movement is only "a question of competition between the bourgeoisies of various nationalities."

Because of this same profoundly popular, profoundly revolutionary national feeling in South Africa we must set about, without delay, in taking the foundation which has been laid and building on it principles to guide our own demands on the national question.

Not nations but nationalities

In their discussion of the problem, the leading writers refer in passing to communities which do not fall strictly within the definition of a nation as "national groups" or "nationalities". It is the definition of this term "national group" and the evolution of a detailed national policy which will result from an analysis of those groups and their demands which is one of our most important tasks in South Africa.

What is a national group or nationality?

In an informal discussion of the editorial, someone who has given much thought to the problem put forward the tentative definition of a national group as a community "which aspires to nationhood."

Clearly this is the correct beginning to work from, for it is this "aspiration", this national consciousness which is the very life-blood of our national movement.

It is necessary, though, to take the definition further. A national group is a community which has some, but not all, of the qualities of a nation. It is a potential nation which is striving to be a nation.

A fundamental factor to the striving for nationhood is common language, fundamental in turn for the commonly held culture. Whatever may be the desires of the bourgeoisie of the national group, it is their language and their culture which the common people cherish so greatly. The defence of the national language when it is under attack, and the demand for full recognition of their language, has always been an important demand of the people.

The demand for full status for the African languages in every sphere is an essential part of any policy of national liberation.

Secondly, every national group has the desire for a homeland, the territory which it may feel to be its own. (Such territory is, of course, essential before there can be economic cohesion.)

A definition proposed

Here is a proposed definition, then: a national group (nationality) is a stable community which has existed for a long time, speaks the same language, has a common psychology manifesting itself in a common culture, and which, lacking its own territory and economic cohesion, aspires towards them.

The two characteristics of nationhood which a community may lack and still be a national group are territory and economic cohesion. But every national group aspires to acquire these. The implications are obvious. Their unpopularity with those who refuse to perceive a national liberatory struggle because they think that it "blurs" the concept of class struggle make the arguments no less valid (and this validity must be proved or disproved in further discussion.)

But the class struggle must not be blurred

Through everything, before there can be complete understanding, must shine clearly and unmistakably the fact that basic to everything is not the national struggle but the class struggle. The oppression of the people of South Africa and the whole framework of colour bar laws is the result not of "racialism", but of capitalism. Laws designed to ensure a cheap labour supply to the capitalists are capitalist laws. The laws designed to divide the workers of different nationalities into hostile groups are capitalist laws.

Understanding of the nature of capitalism is essential to an effective national liberatory struggle. The national liberatory struggle must strike at the very roots of capitalism. And it is essential to take to the people the fact that the entire system of national oppression is created by the capitalist class in their own interests; that the enemy is not the white worker but the whole capitalist class, and that in a crisis sections of the white workers may be won as allies against the common enemy.

But clearly it is lunacy to argue that because national oppression is a facet of class oppression, one should fight "only on the class front" and ignore and discourage a national struggle.

We must get over this weird idea that all national liberatory movements are "bourgeois-national." They are not. Under working-class leadership they become "profoundly popular, profoundly revolutionary." Such was, and is, the case in China.

I agree in full with the Eastern Province Youth Leaguer (Joe Matthews) who wrote:

> Progressives have been suspicious of Nationalism and tended to regard even the use of the expression by anyone as a mark of reaction. This gave a chance to reactionaries to pose as "nationalists" to get support from quarters which normally would not support reactionary ideas. Through your editorial and, I hope, others still to come, you have knocked the bottom out of the reactionary policies of these people.

> When nationalism is taken in hand by the working class, then reactionary nationalism is more easily distinguishable. By putting forward clearly and boldly People's Nationalism, it is possible for the people to see the opposite in its true light. No longer are reactionaries enabled to hide under the blanket term "nationalism." They must now come out either for people's nationalism or reactionary nationalism.

> They must be taught always to take up a class position with regard to every question, including nationalism. They must ask "which nationalism? What class does it serve?"

> The history of the Soviet Union and now of China shows that progressives must not and cannot be national nihilists. On the contrary, the system of People's Democracy is the one in which national cultures and languages flourish and reach full bloom as a prelude to the fusion of all cultures into one world culture, which can only happen when the whole world is Socialist.

Advance 22 April 1954.

A Symposium on The National Question

In May 1954, the Forum Club in Cape Town staged a symposium on the national question at which the speakers were Lionel Forman, K.A. Jordaan, Thomas Ngwenya and Jack Simons. Their contributions were later published and in a Foreword the organisers (E. Marney and I.O. Horvitch) explained the purpose of the symposium as being

> "to encourage and develop a unity of ideas in the movement, especially on the National Question, by encouraging thorough dis-

180 *The National Question*

cussion and even polemics, on a national scale. The numerous avowed and unavowed differences between tendencies and factions on this, as on other questions, do not preclude such a discussion. On the contrary, they make such a discussion imperative for the health of the movement. If we cannot achieve a unity of ideas, we must achieve, at least, a clear demarcation of the differences.

Our movement suffers not only from sectionalism (racialism), but is also ridden by a crippling sectarianism which puts the interests of sects above the interests of the movement, and is the main obstacle in the way of vigorous discussion and the achievement of theoretical clarity. In the absence of discussion, sectarianism thrives and the best interests of the whole movement are sacrificed.

It may not be too much to hope that this joint effort on the ideological plane may initiate a general onslaught on sectarianism in all fields of activity in the democratic movement: political, civic, youth, peasant and worker struggles; education; culture; etc. etc. But we are confident that it is a step in the right direction — a step towards the closing of the ranks in the democratic camp . . . It seems to us that failure to adopt a serious attitude to such discussion can arise only from extreme backwardness, hardened sectarianism or political infantilism. Clarity of ideas is the essential condition for giving the people confidence in the liberatory movement; for winning mass support in the struggle for emancipation, and for giving the struggle proper guidance (conversely, the experience of the masses through struggle will exercise proper correctives upon theory) . . .

Nationalisms in South Africa
by Lionel Forman

When we talk of the "National Question", we sometimes incorrectly pose the problem as being one of the choice between two different viewpoints. On the one hand, you can see the struggle for liberation as being essentially a class struggle, with the proletariat of all national groups fighting the capitalists of all national groups. Or, on the other hand, you can have all the people of the oppressed nationality, whatever their class, pitted against the dominant national group as a whole.

I don't think there will be anyone here who will not agree that for South Africa neither approach is by itself completely correct — that the correct path to liberation is by means of joining together into one unity the many forces opposed to the South African ruling class, of welding together into one the struggle against capitalism and the struggle for national liberation.

It may be most fruitful to begin with the things on which we have definite agreement, and to move on to the things which are still doubtful

The Debate Fuelled   181

— not because we disagree, but because we have never got round really to thrashing them out.

We all agree that basic to everything in South Africa is the capitalist system. The primary laws of the country are designed to assist the capitalist class in exploiting the workers. Capitalist exploitation is basic and it is important that we always remember that. It is sometimes said that it is the "racialist policies" of the government which are basic. That is incorrect. For proper understanding it is necessary to go behind the racialist policies to the economic system underlying them.

But at the same time, we will all agree on the second point. That distorting the class struggle in South Africa is the double yoke of oppression. The vast majority of Africans face oppression not only as proletarians, the value of whose labour is stolen in profits, but also they suffer national oppression. Their language rights are not equal. Schools are not provided for them. They are confined to particular jobs. And the development of a petit-bourgeoisie and a bourgeoisie is hampered and restricted. Nationality cuts across class in that there are things the humblest white can do which the richest African can't do.

National oppression is designed to serve the ruling class in two ways. First, it is a means of ensuring cheap labour and limiting competition. Second, national oppression serves the capitalist class — for by bribing white workers, and by spreading the race lie, they obscure the class struggle and even win white workers as allies.

But, as is the case with everything the capitalist class touches, national oppression in turn creates the conditions for the overthrow of capitalism. In capitalist states which are not multi-national, the ruling class relies on the intellectuals and the petit-bourgeoisie as allies against the people.

In South Africa, as a class of intellectuals of the oppressed nationalities grows larger, and as a petit-bourgeoisie comes into being, it finds itself implacably opposed to the government for it is frustrated and not bribed. Together with the proletariat, these groups are strong opponents of the government. But the intellectuals and the petit-bourgeoisie do not see the class oppressor so clearly — they see mainly national oppression.

So you have a proletariat aware both of class and national oppression, and intellectuals, petit-bourgeoisie and peasants concerned with national oppression. (For to the peasant, it is always the oppressing national group which is seen coming to take his land or his cattle or his money.)

Now comes the problem of the best way to ensure that these anti-government forces combine most effectively to fight and defeat the entire economic system on which oppression is based — not only to defeat national oppression but to defeat also class oppression.

So far we've dealt with things we've got to be in agreement with before we can really understand each other to argue any further. But it is the next stage that we have to begin feeling our way a little.

During the war there was a substantial body of opinion which argued like this: The national liberatory movement is led by the bourgeoisie and

182 The National Question

petit-bourgeoisie. They are fighting for a bourgeois democratic revolution which we must support. When there has been such a revolution, it will then be possible to talk in terms of a class struggle and the achievement of socialism.

Developments since the war have gone a long way to show the falsity of this approach. To a great extent, the direction of the national liberatory struggle has been wrested from the hands of the bourgeoisie and more conservative elements, and leaders who understand the need for struggle against both national oppression and its imperialist economic roots have come to the fore.

The process is far from complete. But the basis certainly exists for the national liberatory movement to be truly a people's movement — one which will not allow a mere transfer from national oppression to economic oppression, as is the case in Nehru's India, but will push forward to people's democracy, as in China.

For the most advanced elements to retain the support of the national liberatory struggle, it is necessary for them to be, in fact, advanced. They must know before the events the direction in which matters are tending. They must be able to anticipate trends and popular demands, so that they may be completely identified with them, influence them and speed them on. This is only possible when the advanced elements pay particular attention to scientific theory.

If we read some of the Chinese theoretical writings, we find again and again the great care with which the leaders set about marking out and defining the different groups. There are essays on "What is the Proletariat?", "What is the middle peasantry, what is the poor peasantry, what are the landed gentry?", and so forth. The reason is clear. Given similar conditions, the poor peasantry in one part of China have much the same demands, will react in much the same way, all over China, so that, once one really understood the problems and demands of poor peasantry, and once one knew how to identify which groups were part of that class, one had considerable assistance in one's analysis of likely developments.

In the same way it is essential for us to understand what is the nature of the oppressed nationalities in South Africa. One possible answer is that there is no need for such an analysis — that there is no national question, only a proletarian question. Now this is an attractive formulation, but the fact is that there exist strong liberatory organisations based on national lines. And these organisations are not artificial but are based on strong national feeling among the people.

How far is this really a national feeling? Certainly the resentment of the ordinary African takes the form expressed by "This country belongs to the Africans and the white man has stolen it." But this feeling is not itself really a national feeling unless it has a far more complex basis. A struggle for national liberation requires, if the words have any meaning, that an oppressed nationality or national group is doing the struggling.

And if the people struggling are indeed nations, then an important part of our policy must be the demand that these nations have the right to self-determination.

If they are not nations, and if they are national groups aspiring to be nations, then in turn they have the right for the conditions to be created by which they may become nations with the right to self-determination.

This means that it will become part of working-class policy to guarantee to those nationalities which have not their own territory that they will be given territory which they will be able to administer autonomously, in which their own language will be one of the official languages and in which their national cultures may flourish.

We know what a nation is. It is a stable community who have lived together for a long time in the same territory, speak the same language, have an internal economic bond and a common psychology and culture.

Which of South Africa's peoples are nations? I would not like to say. Possibly there are several communities in South Africa which are full-fledged nations. But I think the majority of communities which have a common language and psychology in South Africa are not full nations, but national groups. That is, I think they are aspirant nations, lacking their own territory and economic cohesion, but aspiring to achieve these.

What I am particularly interested in is to hear views on which of South Africa's many communities are nations and which are national groups, for I think if we knew this, we would go further towards a national policy. I hope Mr Ngwenya will give his views on the Xhosa people as a nation, and that members of the audience will contribute on the knotty question of the Coloured people. Some people have tended to be a little shy of opening the whole discussion because they think it reactionary to talk, say, of giving Zululand to the Zulu people.

Superficially it seems to run right across the grain. The whole of South Africa and all its cities belong to all people, and Durban is as much a city of the Zulu people as it is of anyone else. Superficially, guaranteeing a people their own territory makes superficial thinkers jump because they are so correctly conditioned to fight every idea that seems to divide the people. It looks like apartheid. But of course the guarantee of national autonomy in a people's democracy bears not the slightest resemblance to apartheid. Though the citizens will have their own national territory where their language and culture reigns supreme, they will be free to go and to live where they please, and where they are a substantial group outside their territory, there too they will have language and other rights.

But in their own national lands they will have every opportunity of developing the wealth of the country to their own benefit and for the benefit of all. Such is, for example, the case in the national republics of the Soviet Union, which were backward and starving before the revolution, but now have flourishing national industries and universities while students are able also to study at Moscow University or at those of the other republics if they wish.

184 The National Question

The encouragement of people's nationalism is a great progressive force. For the ability to do this, we must know more about the demands of our different national groups, and the desires which, though not yet expressed, will ring the strongest chords among the people.

Nationalisms in South Africa
by Dr. H.J. Simons

Every political question ought to be examined in the light of the theoretical principles relevant to the problem, and the specific and historical conditions applying at the time and place under consideration.

The "national problem" which we are here discussing is, first, what are the "nations" or "national groups" in South Africa? Second, what is the correct attitude towards them? — correct, that is to say, for South Africans who wish to replace the existing system of exploitation by a free and harmonious multi- racial society.

Our theory provides us with a definition of "nation" that can be applied anywhere. It is an aggregate or community of persons having a number of specific characteristics in common: language, territory, economy, traditions, and psychology. Some students would include another attribute: the desire, realised or unfulfilled, for self-government.

Leaving aside for the moment the question as to which groups in South Africa fall within the scope of our definition, let us examine the standards by which we are to measure the values of nationalism as a political force.

We can do no better for this purpose than look at the comparable experience of other countries where the related issues have come under scientific scrutiny by persons looking for a guide to the reconstruction of society on a rational basis.

Multi-national states of Europe

One important source of experience comes from the controversies over the multi-national empires of Austria-Hungary and Tsarist Russia, which had spread outward, absorbing border regions and their inhabitants and subjecting them to alien rule. The policy of the dominant classes in each empire was to hold it together by force, resisting separatist movements and repressing the language and culture of the minority groups.

The middle-class liberals and working-class social democrats who struggled for the liberation of the oppressed nationalities developed two opposing viewpoints: the concepts of "cultural autonomy", and of "national self-determination." The Austrian and Russian social democrats who urged the former policy wanted equal recognition for the Slavs, Magyars, Czechs, Poles and other "national" minorities, which were, however, to remain within the framework of the multi-national society. Each "nation" would have its own representatives in the central legislature (a form of "communal" representation), and its language would be given equal status with any other in schools and official circles. It would manage its own affairs as far as possible.

These claims of the "cultural autonomy" school were really implied also in the "right of self-determination"; but the adherents of this policy went much further in that they wished to secure to the nation the legal and political right to secede from the imperial state and establish itself in a separate territory as an independent state.

Although the theory emphasised the discretionary nature of this right, and the possibility of the nation preferring to remain within the empire (which it would do as a result of free choice only if the advantages of remaining in the empire clearly outweighed those of secession) the struggle for the recognition of the right inevitably carried in itself a threat of dissolution. The ruling class therefore resisted the claim. In the upshot, it was established by means of mass support, insurrection and war, out of which emerged the national states of eastern and central Europe.

Colonial national movements

Before considering the lessons to be drawn from the European experience, we might turn our attention to another type of nationalism which developed during the course of this century in Asia and Africa under the domination of European imperialist states.

The conditions shaping the national movements in Asia and Africa differed from those operating in Europe in the following respects:

(a) the imperialist state and the colony were situated in different continents; consequently conquest and domination were carried out by relatively small numbers of emigrants from Europe who became the ruling class in the colonies;

(b) the colonial peoples differed from the imperialists not only in culture but also in physical type, and the physical differences rather than the cultural became the basis for discrimination;

(c) cultures in the colonies were tribal and feudal, but in any event pre-industrial, and the effect of imperial conquest was to undermine and reshape the traditional culture in the process of exploiting resources by modern techniques;

(d) contact between the imperialist representatives and the upper social classes of the colonial peoples was slight and formal, in contrast to the intimacy of the relationships between the upper classes of the dominant and minority nationalities in the multi-national states of Europe.

Nationalism in the colonies bears the imprint of these characteristics. It attaches less importance to the recognition of language and culture than to the achievement of equal and democratic rights; it works for the elimination of the gap in education, technical skill and living standards between the people of the colony and the inhabitants of more advanced countries; and it demands, not a separate territory for the national group, but self-government and the right to secede from the empire. These features result

186 The National Question

from the special geographical, cultural and ethnic (i.e. racial) factors involved in the type of exploitation found in overseas colonies.

We may conclude that the Europeans will not become a permanent community in the colonies as members of multi-national societies, though we should not rule out the possibility of the colonies becoming full and autonomous partners with European states in a socialist commonwealth.

In South Africa

The special features of South African nationalisms arise from the combination of an imperialism and its dependent colony in a single political and geographical region. The large, permanently established European population attempts to dominate the rest of the population in typical colonial fashion, while the various national groups have interacted and fused in a manner closely resembling the integration that takes place in multi-national societies such as developed in Europe.

Because of the colour bar on the one hand and the high degree of interaction between the national groups on the other, the oppressed nationalities do not raise the demands characteristic of national movements in European history or in the colonies. They do not demand "cultural autonomy" or "self-determination" or "secession". In fact, these concepts are regarded with doubt and even hostility, because they resemble outwardly the "ideology" of the racialists who use them to mask and justify race oppression.

The African, Indian and Coloured people are not deceived by the Nationalist appeals to "respect and preserve their way of life" to "develop along their own lines" or "build a separate Bantustan" (this last proposal being varied in the case of the Indians with the insolent demand that they return to "their" country). The oppressed nationalities recognise in these formulae of apartheid a thinly-veiled attempt to perpetuate non-European backwardness and inferiority for the purpose of an exploitative economy.

It is the racialist in the European ruling class who stresses the "peculiar" features of "Bantu" culture, urges the African to "respect the ways of his forefathers", forces him through the Bantu Education Act into a separate education system, revives the traditional rule of tribal chiefs under the Bantu Authorities Act, and instructs him that his "national" home is in the reserves, not in the "European town and cities."

We all know that similar efforts are now being made to transform the Coloured people into a "nation" by such means as the Group Areas Act, Population Registration Act, Mixed Marriages Act, a Coloured Affairs Department and the rest of the segregation paraphernalia. Our hatred of apartheid and the other varieties of racialism should not blind us to the advantages of a genuine, healthy and dynamic nationalism. It is necessary, however, that we examine carefully and even suspiciously any theory, no matter how well-intentioned, that savours, even if only superficially, of the Nationalist formula "development along own lines." That certainly is not what the movement for national liberation wants in any shape or form.

The demand for equality

The national liberation movement demands equality. And that demand is not the same as the programme of "cultural autonomy" or "secession." Equality does not imply a withdrawal from or expulsion of the European population. It contemplates a common society with Europeans on a completely equal basis. Equality means, in the first place, equality in law; i.e. the removal of all statutory and public forms of racial discrimination; in short, of the colour bar. This kind of equality is implicit in the theory of the "liberal" state based on private ownership of the means of production, free competition and parliamentary democracy.

Legal equality does not itself ensure social equality. The latter can come about only through the elimination of the taproot of inequality, namely private property. To achieve actual equality, the people will have to introduce social ownership of the productive section of the economy.

The national liberation movements in South Africa limit their demands to the first kind of equality and must therefore be described as a form of inter-class nationalism which embraces both an exploiting and an exploited class. This kind of nationalism is progressive as long as it opposes discrimination and oppressive policies, but the exploiting element is always a source of potential support for class discrimination, i.e. inequality caused by private ownership of the instruments of production.

A recent case of the emergence of the exploiting element in colonial nationalism comes from the Gold Coast, where the Prime Minister, Dr. Nkrumah, associated his government and party with the attack upon socialism. India and Indonesia provide other similar examples.

Prediction is always tempting, if dangerous. Yielding to temptation, I should say that the influence of the exploiting element in the South African national liberation movement is likely to decline because of the effects of the colour bar, which is designed to stifle the growth of social classes above working-class level in the African, Indian and Coloured communities. While the "middle class" grows very slowly or even declines, the number of urban workers grows rapidly because of the rise of industry. We may therefore expect to find that the national movements acquire a definite working-class character.

More or fewer "nations"?

Workers, like other people want to use and develop their language and preserve their customs. They therefore resent and resist restrictions being placed on their "national" culture. I think it is right to say, however, that workers are less involved emotionally in their "national" culture than such persons as teachers, ministers of religion, journalists and writers, traders and professional people. The latter associate almost exclusively with their own people, also in business, and have a strong material, as well as intellectual, interest in cultivating pride in the national language and tradition. Workers, on the other hand, mix at places of employment with members of other national groups, and tend to develop an "international"

188 The National Question

outlook based on common class interests. For these reasons, a national movement led by workers is less likely than one led by exploiting elements to exaggerate the importance of purely "national" issues.

Personal experience leads me to believe that African working men and women of the kind active in the ANC do not want to divide their people into "nations" according to language: Xhosa, Zulu, Tswana, Sotho, Pedi, Venda and so on. They put the emphasis on the common factor: they are all "Africans", victims of the colour bar, and linked in a common struggle. They view with suspicion efforts to encourage a "tribal" outlook and condemn them as a "divide and rule" device.

I think they are right. Africans are engaged in a gigantic task of nation-building under great difficulties. Their whole attention is concentrated on mastering the new environment of which they have become part, and of adapting their traditional life pattern to these new circumstances. There is much in the old tribal culture that is a handicap and burden. Their only hope lies in forging ahead to build a wider society embracing all Africans of all tribal origins.

It is the racialist who stresses the differences between people, who wants to "preserve" chieftainship, "Native law", and "Bantu tradition." Does he do it in order to help the African, or to save his own privileges and power?

Objectives

To conclude, I should say that the African, Coloured and Indian people are not trying to drive the Europeans out of the country, or to break away from a common society and form a separate, independent state, or to divide the population along racial lines into distinct "cultural communities." On the contrary, their struggle is aimed at the creation of a common South African society guaranteeing equality of right and opportunities to all sections and races.

In this struggle, the working class is likely to become the dominant and leading factor, and its policy will centre around the common interests of all workers, regardless of race. It would be wrong to disturb or deflect this development by stressing tribal, racial or cultural differences. On the contrary, the stress should be placed wherever possible on the values and interests common to all persons in the national liberation movements.

This international outlook is quite consistent with the demand for the full and equal recognition of the languages used by the different sections of the people.

Lionel Forman's response to remarks made by Professor Simons during the discussion period.
I must express surprise at the interpretation Dr. Simons has put on what I said. It is particularly difficult because no matter how badly I may have expressed myself, I feel sure that he knows that the right to national self-determination does not imply that one advocates that the people of Zululand be confined to a pastoral life and "perhaps take up fishing".

The Debate Fuelled   189

Nor does it imply that one is not in favour of the obvious end aim — one single, united South African nation. I would go further; national self-determination makes possible not only one South African nation, it lays the basis for an eventual single world culture. But the only correct path towards a single South African nation is through the creation of conditions by which the different national cultures in South Africa may first flower, and then merge.

Nor does the development of the backward areas imply that there will not be one fully integrated South African economic system. Of course there must be.

In the different areas where a particular national group has a majority, it should have the right to schools, theatres, newspapers, local authorities conducting business in their own language, while, of course, the rights of all other groups are fully protected. Far from meaning that this will keep backward areas backward, it will be accompanied by the development of great industries. The example of countries where this is happening is probably known to many of the people here.

Equally absurd is the suggestion that the right to national self-determination implies that people will be urged to move or remain within any particular territory. All that there is is the creation of conditions under which people may, if they wish, avail themselves of the opportunity to be part of their own distinctive national culture.

It has been argued that the African people don't want to study in African languages. While it is perfectly true that the present economic set-up makes it essential for Africans to have the opportunity to learn in English — because text-books are in English, because the economy of the country is conducted in English — it is hard to see how it can be argued that when these conditions are changed by a people's government, national groups should not have the right to study in their own language . . .

12. The Debate Resumed

Correspondence between Lionel Forman and Dr I.I. Potekhin of the Institute of Ethnography, Academy of Sciences of the USSR, Moscow.

Forman to Potekhin, 18 January 1958

I have been shown extracts from the *Formation of Common Nationalities of the S.A. Bantu* by I.I. Potekhin, issued by the Department of Ethnological Studies, which is at present being translated into English by someone here. We intend to issue this excellent work in mimeographed form very shortly and are certain that it will have a profound effect.

I was, needless to say, delighted to see that my own articles in *Advance* and the Forum Club discussion on the national question received mention. I am in full agreement with the book's thesis. and hope at a later stage to send on to I Potekhin additional data which was not available to him.

I would be even more pleased if he could find time to let me have his fuller comments on the points of view as expressed on the one hand by Dr Simons and on the other by myself, at the Africa Club discussion. I have since completed a somewhat fuller discussion article on the issue, but the prevalent majority approach is that of Dr Simons, namely, that in view of the fact that the primary political issue here is unity of all the oppressed — i.e., of all non-whites, irrespective of national differences — it is incorrect even to discuss at this stage the national question.

I.I. Potekhin says in his book that discussion of the national question regrettably ceased as a result of the banning of *Advance*. That was not the reason. The discussion ceased because it was felt to be harmful. I have been continuing work on the problem for publication when the decision is reversed, and I may say that Potekhin's book is all the more welcome in that it will inevitably lead to the re-opening of the discussion, and, not only that, but will get it off on a magnificent foundation.

I wonder if you would let me know if the following books referred to by Potekhin are available in English:

    (i) *South Africa After the Second World War* by E.P. Yastrebava (1952);
    (ii) *S.A. Gold in the Sharpening of Anglo-American Contradictions*
       by Z.S. Katzellenbaum (1954);
    (iii) *People of Africa* (Part of a series) (1954).

Could you possibly arrange to send me these books if they exist in English? Otherwise could you let me have them in the Russian edition and I will arrange translation . . .

Also, if there is any other work — articles, etc. — on the national question in South Africa available, we would be grateful, as well, as for anything in English about South Africa generally. I am at present at work on a history of the Communist Party of South Africa and its interrelationship with the national liberatory movement . . .

As direct correspondence between my country and yours often disappears en route I am sending this via London . . .

Reply from Potekhin, 17 March 1958

I have received your kind letter, which has given much pleasure to me. For more than a quarter of a century I have devoted myself to African studies, and many books and articles are already issued by me, some of them even in *Umsebenzi*. I know personally many leaders of the national liberation movement in SA. But in recent years my liaisons with SA have been interrupted, so a letter from far Africa South was really a happiness for me.

I was glad to learn that my book [reached] SA and could serve there to progress. This book is a result of my investigation in South African problems for more than 20 years . . . In last 2-3 years, I have [somewhat] removed my attention from these studies, having transmitted them to my grown-up pupils. I am writing now a book on Ghana's (Gold Coast) history, so I have visited Ghana last year for a long journey. But I still pay much attention to the struggle of progressive forces in SA and particularly the trial, in which you participate as "condemned No. 83". Maybe after publishing the book on Ghana, I'll return to SA. I have already some interesting scientific plans. With a great impatience, do I wait for account on the last population census.

All our works on Africa are published in Russian. *Peoples of Africa* now is in translation, but the English edition will be ready not earlier than in summer 1959. I send you now the Russian one. Katzellenbaum's book is out of print but I hope to send it to you as soon as I get it. Yastrebova's book has got old, you'll find nothing worth attention in it . . .

I can't agree with Dr Simons' point of view, that a study of national composition of population will prevent the success of uniting forces in the struggle for national freedom and democracy. Quite on the contrary, knowledge of the problem will safeguard of mistakes. To carry out a right policy, one must know what occurs in life. It is rather a strange position — to shut oneself's own eyes on facts. It is an ostrich-like policy. As more fully and exactly will be taken into consideration facts of the real life, so tighter will be unity in the struggle. Should you give me some occasion (for instance, by publishing a note on this question in your journal) and if you would leave for me some place in your journal, I would be sure to enter in a discussion. My fingers are already itching to do it.

I greet wholeheartedly your intention to write a book about the history of the Communist Party. It's high time to do it. I have already much thought about it. I have many interesting materials of the twenties and thirties, but almost nothing for the war and post-war years. You have all of them, so you have all the possibilities to do it well. I shall wait anxiously for your

192 The National Question

book. Once I was very near to the South African Communist Party and knew it's work in detail.

Your journal is well known here and widely used, too . . . Your country is very far from ours, contacts are poor, information comes badly. And surely anything you will send will be of great interest . . .

The Development of Nations in South Africa
by Lionel Forman

"South Africa belongs to all who live in it, black and white", the Freedom Charter declares. "Our country will never be prosperous or free until all our people live in brotherhood, enjoying equal rights and opportunities."

Only when this has been achieved will it be possible for a South African nation to develop. And before it does, the likelihood is that a number of different nations will come into being in our country, and that they will flower and prosper before they merge into one.

A single African nation in South Africa is likely to develop before a single South African nation does. And similarly it seems likely that Zulu, Basotho and other nations will develop before they merge into a single African nation in South Africa.

The Africans will constitute the main element in the future South African nation and we therefore begin with a study of the origins of African nationalism. They are comparatively recent. The development of a single African political consciousness in South Africa only really begins in the 1880s. Until the nineteenth century, the economic basis did not exist for the amalgamation of the numerous African tribes into states. They were cattle-grazers and small-scale farmers, and as they required large areas of pasture and lived at subsistence level, the tendency was towards dispersal rather than concentration of population. Even when, with the accumulation of wealth, a ruling class and a state developed, it was capable of exercising its authority only over a limited area, and when conflicts of interest arose it was powerless to prevent dissident tribal groups within the tribe from moving off to pastures new.

As new techniques were acquired, making possible a greater division of labour and the development of a standing army, groups of African tribes would have developed towards a statehood and unification just as people did in Europe, and this is clearly demonstrated early in the nineteenth century by the Zulus from the time of Tshaka, and the Basotho from that of Moshoeshoe.

Nevertheless, it is not impossible that, taking the long view, British imperialism hastened the development of a single African nation rather than retarded it. The huge inflow of capital which came with the discovery of diamonds in 1870, and of gold sixteen years later, transformed South Africa from a collection of primitive pastoral and agricultural communities into a single economic unit, and smashed the tribal system and sped up the process of unification of the Africans.

The Debate Resumed 193

Long before the industrial revolution wrought by the discovery of diamonds and the imperialist intervention in South Africa, the voluntary amalgamation of all the black people to make a stand against the white advance had been a dream of the most far-sighted African leaders and the nightmare of all the Europeans. But it had remained a dream. Far from there being unity of the African tribes, a handful of Europeans were able to exploit inter-tribal conflicts so skilfully that in every decisive campaign by far the main burden of fighting, on the European side, was borne by Africans.

At the diamond fields, men were transformed from Zulu, Xhosa or Basotho tribesmen into African workers. Members of a myriad of separate tribes came for the first time, to see themselves as a single brotherhood united by their common economic interest. Theirs was not a working-class consciousness, but an African working-class consciousness, for they were subject to political disabilities on the ground of race, which, by giving the lowliest white worker the status of boss over all black men, almost completely obscured any common interest between white and black workers.

Though handicapped by the absence of a common language — the *lingua franca* was Dutch — the black workers were not slow in evolving the weapon of workers' unity. There was an African strike at Kimberley in 1882, before there is any record of a strike by European workers in South Africa. At the same time, a tiny African petite-bourgeoisie, composed of mission assistants, priests, teachers and clerks, was coming into existence in the Eastern Cape, and in the early 1880s the first bodies cutting across tribal barriers, the first African bodies, came into being. Most important of these were mutual benefit societies at Kimberley (embryo trade unions), the African Educational Association (composed of teachers and priests around the mission stations of the Eastern Cape) and the general political organisation, *Imbumba Yama Afrika*.

The *Imbumba* was the counterpart of the Afrikaner Bond (which incidentally coined the phrase "Africa for the Africans", meaning by that Afrikaners) and it may be described as the first non-European national organisation — the direct forerunner of the African National Congress. Like the Afrikaner Bond, it came into being as the result of the heightened national oppression which followed the decision of the British government, in 1874, to establish complete control over Southern Africa.

From the formation of *Imbumba* onwards, the drive towards the unity of all Africans continued steadily. By the time of Union there were political organisations uniting men, not as members of tribes but as Africans (though the word "African" was not yet used) in each of the provinces, and with Union their merger into the South African Native National Congress was a natural development, the description "Congress" probably coming from the Indian Congress, via the Natal Indian Congress.

With Congress came the conscious assertion of a single African nationhood. The tribes had long been described as nations. Now the word "nation" came into common use both as a description of the individual

194 The National Question

tribes and for the African people as a whole. Strictly speaking, the use of the word "nation" is inaccurate in both cases. Socialists define a "nation" in clear terms. If a community does not share a common language, territory, economy and culture, it is not a nation.

The everyday use of the word, however, is at variance with the scientific usage. Progressives use definitions as tools, not as straitjackets, and it would be pedantic to make any issue about the everyday use of the word — specially when we are not always quite sure what the correct word is. But when it comes to serious theoretical analysis, the situation is quite different. As Potekhin says: "It is by no means an argument about words. To give a definition of a 'nation' is of vital importance for the peoples. A nation is not an imaginary or mystic concept — it is a very real phenomenon, and as such needs an exact definition, without which it is impossible to understand the national question which plays such an important part in the life of the peoples of the present time" (*Marxism Today,* October 1958, p. 308).

Are there any nations in South Africa?

It has long been recognised that it is possible to have a nation which does not have it's own state. South Africa is an example of a state which has no nation. A glance at the definition is sufficient to show that there is not a South African nation. The South African people have a variety of languages and cultures. For the same reason the Africans are not a nation.

What of the Zulus, Xhosa, Basotho, Tswana, Swazi and Tsonga? What of the Afrikaners, English, Coloureds and Indians? Are they nations in South Africa? No South Africans can vie with Verwoerd's Nationalists in the fervour with which they express the conviction not only that they are a nation, but that they are *the* nation.

But are they? They have a common language and culture, certainly, but can it really be said that they have a common territory? They inhabit the same territory, South Africa, in common with all other South Africans, black, white and brown, all inextricably mixed throughout the country. But there is no substantial territorial area where the Afrikaner is in the majority.

"Common territory" must mean a territory on one's own, because basic to the national question is that of self-determination and the right of secession. There is no part of South Africa which the Afrikaners could, by mere reason of their numbers, claim for the exercise of the right of secession. In this respect their position can be compared with that of the Jews in Russia, who, Stalin remarked in his argument showing that they do not constitute a nation, "are spread all over Russia and do not constitute a majority in a single Gubernia".

A further esssential to nationhood is a common economy, "in a word, a single national market" (Potekhin, *Marxism Today,* October 1958 p. 309). Just as is the position with regard to territory, so it is with the common economy whose existence is dependent on that of the common territory. South Africa has a single national market — the Afrikaners have not. Nor (again like the Russian Jews) have they a normal class structure, which is a factor to be considered in determining nationhood.

The ruling class has created a completely distorted class structure among the Africans. The great majority of them are peasant migrant labourers and proletarians with only a tiny petit-bourgeoisie and an infinitesimal bourgeoisie. The complementary effect has been the distortion of the class structure of the Europeans. The white workers are essentially supervisors of African labour; there is an exceptionally big stratum of professional men and salaried officials. The Afrikaners are employed throughout government service, manning the enormous repressive apparatus, and with a working class well bribed and entirely petit-bourgeois in outlook.

For analogous reasons to the Afrikaners, the English, the Coloureds and Indians fail to qualify as nations.

When freedom is won, the Afrikaners and other national groups, if they so desire, will, no doubt, obtain the opportunity to develop into nations, being given the essential territorial basis for such development, as has happened in the USSR and China.

The African "pre-nations"

The African communities are in a different position. Let us consider the Zulus. There is no doubt that they have a common territory in Natal, in a substantial portion of which they are an overwhelming majority of the population. Similarly they have a common language and culture. In one respect only have they not yet attained nationhood, and that is with regard to the development of a single Zulu market. The government has strangled Zulu economic development because it is in the interests of the ruling class that the Zulus be kept at the level of unskilled labourers. There is no doubt, however, that this stifling of the Zulu nation will not endure, and that the Zulus are on the threshold of true nationhood.

The Russian term for this type of community is *narodnost*. The closest English translation is "nationality", and as that has a different connotation in ordinary speech, I would suggest that we use the word "pre-nation". Other "pre-nations" in a position similar to the Zulus are the Basotho, the Xhosas, the Swazis, the Tswana, etc.

Self-determination

The position of the pre-nations is also different from that of the Afrikaners and the English — who have no territory of their own — when it comes to a consideration of the right to self-determination. Progressives might, in certain circumstances, accord to a pre-nation the right to self-determination. In fact, that is already our policy with regard to Basutoland where we recognise the democratic right of the Basotho to decide for themselves how best they can march towards nationhood.

196 The National Question

Although in Europe the demand for self-determination in some form was a characteristic feature of the national struggle, this is not the case in South Africa.

What is the reason for this? In the first place, the national oppression has quite a different basis from that of Europe before the First World War. The national oppression here has not the primary purpose of keeping the bourgeoisie of the oppressed people out of the market place, as it did in Europe. The oppressive laws here have the purpose, first and foremost, of driving the African workers to the factories and farms. The restrictions on the non-European bourgeoisie, crushing as they are, are quite secondary to the legal enslavement of the African workers, through the Pass Laws, the Master and Servant Acts, the industrial Colour Bar Acts, the complete ban on strikes and the Suppression of Communism Act.

Further, the repression is not that of a dominant nation in one territory oppressing another in a different or adjacent territory. It is more that of a small minority, spread throughout a single country, oppressing a big majority also spread out.

Whereas in Tsarist Russia the Finns, Armenians, Georgians and the dozens of other peoples were separated, were oppressed in different ways and to different degrees, the Africans are in close contact and suffer identical oppression.

Thirdly, the demand for self-determination is one which comes in the first place from the petit-bourgeoisie and in particular the traders, and this class is still infinitesimally small.

The demand of the people, therefore, is not for secession and self-determination in their own areas, but of full equality throughout the whole country. This is only a reflection of what we have already seen — that there are still no nations in South Africa.

The absence of a demand for self-determination does not mean that one should have no policy on the question. A quotation from Stalin is very apposite:

> When in 1912 we Russian Marxists were drawing up the first draft of our national programme, no serious movement for national independence existed in any of the border regions of the Russian Empire. Nevertheless we deemed it necessary to include in our programme the point on the right of nations to self-determination, i.e. the right of every nationality to secede and exist as an independent state. Why did we do this ?

> Because we based ourselves not only on what then existed, but also on what was developing in the general system of international relations; that is, we took into account not only the present but also the future.

> We knew that if any nationality were to demand secession we would fight to ensure the right to secede for every such nationality.

The Debate Resumed 197

At the same time, it is necessary to clear up a common misconception — that because they fight for the right of nations to self-determination, socialists favour the exercise of that right.

A large state enjoys obvious advantages over the small one and the world tendency is towards merger rather than to splitting. Normally, no progressive would support any splitting up. He would oppose it. But the essence of socialism is that it is truly democratic. A nation has the democratic right even to follow a wrong path, though socialists point the correct one. By analogy, most people will agree that Mr and Mrs Smith should be allowed to have a divorce if they want one. That does not mean that they think that Mr and Mrs Smith should be divorced.

We should not ignore the existence of "pre-nations" and the likelihood that there will develop, when democracy is won, a brotherhood of different South African nations before a single South African nation emerges.

On the contrary, we should consider whether we are succeeding adequately today in identifying ourselves with the specific progressive national aspirations and ideas of the "pre-nations", just as we have completely identified ourselves with the demand that all share in common for the ending of apartheid and the achievement of democracy. The dearest possessions of the "pre-nations" are their language, their culture and traditions.

It is obvious that to really get to the hearts and minds of the people, particularly the rural masses, it is necessary to develop to the full a presentation of our message which has its roots deep in the popular culture.

It is necessary to produce socialist literature in the language of the people — not merely in translation but in the original idiom. Because English is the most widely understood language, it is natural that it should be so widely used for conferences and countrywide newspapers. But this is no excuse for neglecting the majority of the population who have not been fortunate enough to obtain sufficient education to read or to follow an argument in English. In this respect, we could learn from Indian socialists who also use English as the international tongue, but at the same time produce extensive literature in the vernacular languages.

If there is any neglect of these people, it is still a hangover from the old days when there was a feeling that the intellectuals were the only important people in Congress, and when, in turning their backs on tribalism, the intellectuals tended to turn their backs also on their language and culture. The need to remedy this situation is already widely recognised. The effect of the deeply moving and inspiring African political songs and music which have been created in recent years is evidence enough of the importance of this type of development. Now what are required are plays and poems and dances of liberation which will inspire and teach people who know no English, and which will give them that added consciousness of dignity which pride in a national culture instils.

198   The National Question

Further Correspondence between Dr I.I. Potekhin and Lionel Forman ·

This exchange was facilitated through a friend and fellow member of the South African Communist Party in London, Vella Pillay. The section is introduced by a letter from Pillay to Forman, dated 1 May 1959.

I am enclosing a letter which Potekhin has written . . . dated 27 April 1959 . . . I was pleased to see your article in *Marxism Today*; it has been a basis for discussions we have had among mutually interested friends here. We found it extremely useful and in certain respects pathbreaking. There are one or two problems arising from your article which I have asked one or two chaps to put down in writing and send you in the near future. It would appear that your concept of "pre-nations" is extremely interesting and certainly new, but that, in so far as it could be applied to South Africa, the impact of industrialisation and the rapid rate of African urbanisation is not given its due place to the possible fashioning out of a South African nation in the immediate future without other or small nation groups emerging first. But on this we hope to write to you more lengthily in the future.

Some of the confusions in the *Marxism Today* controversy on Potekhin's article appear to arise from the impression that is given that national liberation must await the development of nation groups. I am afraid your article does not tackle this explicitly, but it would be useful if you would consider this in the future. There is a view, which I think must be taken into account, that existing frontiers between African territories, though of strong colonial origin, are nevertheless of long-standing and that these territories have accordingly imparted a certain element of oneness to the people within the confines of such frontiers. This may and will certainly influence the course of African nationalism and the future structure of African liberated states . . .

Letter from Potekhin to Forman, 27 April 1959

It is a genuine pleasure for me to read your letters. Firstly, I have no other contacts with the Union of South Africa (though I have exchanged letters and books with Patrick Duncan, and in December last year, I met him at the Accra Conference).

Secondly, you and [I] are interested in the same problems and, finally, we are of the same points of view concerning these problems. I was particularly pleased at having received from you *Chapters in the History of the March to Freedom* and *The Development of Nations in South Africa*.

Your book is wonderful. There is much new to me in it, and for many other people the book will be a discovery. I'll do my best to publish it somewhere . . . I congratulate you on your first success and wish you from the bottom of my heart further success in your hard path. I hope you will give us pleasure of a new book in the nearest future.

I have read *The Development of Nations in South Africa* with even more interest. I have found no divergence of your viewpoint with my works on the subject. However, I haven't understood the meaning of the following sentence: "Nor (again like the Russian Jews) have they (Afrikaners) a normal class structure, a factor which, as Stalin shows, is to be considered in determining nationhood".

What is "a normal class structure"? It is quite understandable with respect to the Africans, but the class structure of the Afrikaners is quite "normal" — it is the class structure of a bourgeois society.

Evidently, you are right, that "a single African nation in South Africa is likely to develop before a single South African nation does." This is a very sound idea.

If you don't mind, I shall try and publish this article of yours in one of our journals. But I would like you to write a brief history of the discussion on the subject as an introductory part of the article. Now, if the article is to be published, a new question arises: by what name you would sign it — Lionel Forman or some other name? Is it possible for you to publish an article in the Soviet press under your own name? Won't a pseudonym do better? I believe you already have the article by B.R. Mann in *Marxism Today* titled "On African Nations" where he severely criticizes my article. But his criticism is no more than typical revisionism. [Ed. note: B.R. Mann is a woman — Potekhin's error was not corrected]

The proposition by V.I. Lenin that "Nations are an inevitable product and an inevitable form of the bourgeois era of social development", have belonged to the arsenal of Marxist theory for a long time. As far as I know, no Marxist tried to dispute this proposition. Proceeding from this thesis by Lenin, Stalin wrote: "there were not and could not be nations in the pre-capitalist period", "nation is not simply an historical category, but an historical category of a certain era, the era of rising capitalism."

B.R. Mann has the opposite point of view: "Nations existed from the dawn of history", "Capitalism does not create the nations, on the contrary, it presupposes their existence." (pp. 92, 93)

Hence the divergence in all other questions. Fighting against my viewpoint, he acts like a typical revisionist. He ought to have argued not with me but with Lenin and Stalin, because their propositions are the basis of my conception. But in that case it would have been clear to everyone that he comes out against Lenin, that he subjects Lenin's view of nation to a revision. He pretends to hit Potekhin even cites Lenin, but actually he hits Lenin. That is the whole point. It is in such devices that the danger of revisionism is concealed.

I intend to answer him on the pages of *Marxism Today*.

200 *The National Question*

Forman's Reply to Potekhin,16 May 1959

. . .Thank you for your letter. The things you say about my little pamphlet
are, of course, far too kind. Its only merit is that it is a beginning of a
task that must be done for the only serious work in existence in English
at present is Roux's book (*Time Longer Than Rope*) which is very bad. I
am at present at work on an outline people's history which will deal with
the early African tribal society, its impact on the earlier Bushman (Batwa)
and Khoi-Khoin inhabitants of South Africa, and, in turn, the impact of
white colonists on African tribal society, leading to the emergence of the
national movement, and finally (the main part of the work) the development
of the national movement and its interrelationship with the working-class
movement, led by its vanguard organisation.

As you can imagine, I am already half-buried under hundreds of pages
of manuscript, and what with my full-time occupation as an advocate,
coupled with my work on *New Age*, I sometimes almost despair of getting
the thing finished. I have been fortunate that Cape Town University has
registered my subject (under the title "History of African Political Organisations") as the work for a Ph.D. degree in History . . . though I must
say that I don't think that I will be given a doctorate for the thesis I finally
produce! I hope to complete the draft of the first portion — from the tribal
system to the early stirrings of nationalism in the Cape in the 1880s under
the first impact of British imperialism — by the end of July and I would
be most grateful if you would permit me to send you a copy of the
manuscript for your criticisms.

With regard to the article on the *Development of Nations in South
Africa*, your query about what is meant by the statement that the Afrikaners
do not have "a normal class structure" is very much to the point. Class
structure varies from society to society and from time to time and it is
almost meaningless to talk of a "normal" structure. But what I had in mind
was the situation described in my next paragraph — the fact that among
the Afrikaners there is a far greater preponderance of professional people,
white-collar workers, skilled workers and administrators of the state machinery — and that a large proportion of the Afrikaner workers are little
more than the supervisors of African labour, so that the Afrikaner class
structure is not one which is typical of a bourgeois society. Because the
African is the unskilled and semi-skilled labourer, this stratum is relatively
small among the Afrikaners.

I may be wrong in taking this into account as a factor bearing upon
Afrikaner nationhood — but nevertheless, I am inclined to think that it is
a factor.

As you may have seen by now, the article was printed in the British
journal in which your original contribution appeared. Thank you for your
thoughtfulness in suggesting a pseudonym be used if the material is reproduced in the Soviet Union, but there is still no law here which makes it
illegal to write for overseas journals and I believe that it is good policy to

The Debate Resumed 201

assert one's remaining rights with the utmost vigour! I enclose the brief introductory material you request.

The same applies to the Congress of Orientalists. My passport has been seized by the government and there is no possibility whatsoever that it will be given back to me to permit me to attend such a conference . . . Nevertheless I should be delighted to receive an invitation . . . I shall apply for my passport to attend and publicise the fact when it is refused, for every passport refusal is further public evidence of the despotism of our government and causes uneasiness even among the allies of the Nationalist government.

Incidentally, I was puzzled at first about the suggestion that I may be invited to a meeting of Orientalists, because I have no specialised knowledge of the East at all, and I only realised afterwards that African studies are probably a subsidiary of your Oriental studies. Really, I must say that it is time that the scholars of the USSR ceased to think of Africa merely as a big peninsula hanging down at the bottom of Asia. Africanists of the World Unite, and rename the meeting as the Congress of Orientalists and Africanists!

Patrick Duncan wrote an article on his meeting with you in his journal *Contact*. I suppose he sent you a copy. (I will check with him and have it sent to you if he did not do so). As you no doubt discovered, Mr Duncan is a man dedicated to the mission of saving South Africa (and Africa generally) from "Russian Communist imperialism". He saw the Accra conference in nightmare terms of a battle between the "Communists" represented by a "Moscow-Cairo axis" and the "anti-Communists" of the rest of Africa led by Nkrumah and Padmore and considered the final resolutions on non-violent struggle to be "a great victory over the Communists". On local issues he has declared that the Communists are a greater danger to South Africa that the Verwoerd Nationalists, and although the Liberal Party (of which he is national organiser) is committed to a policy of co-operation with the liberatory movement, Duncan is one of the small group which hampers such co-operation.

I resume this letter ten days after I began it (26 May 1959). You asked for some notes on the background to the discussion on the national question as an introduction to readers if my article should be published, and I intended putting aside your letter for half-an-hour while I prepared a summary in a few paragraphs to send off with the letter.

But I began to be fascinated by the material and found a great deal which has not been published before, and as you see, my few paragraphs grew into 25 pages and my half-an-hour into ten days, and my "background to the article" has become, in my view, a far more valuable contribution than the article itself [see Chapter 4]. For this you are directly responsible.

To avoid further delay, I am sending it off more or less in its first draft, although I am aware that it must have many weaknesses — for example, it needs a fuller exposition of the policies of the Congress and the ICU,

202   *The Debate Resumed*

and also a more adequate presentation of the economic and political developments in South Africa over the period covered.

During these ten days also some good discussion has been aroused by the appearance of my original article here, and the tendency (which is mentioned on page 25 of the article attached) to discourage the raising of the national question is very clearly now on the way out. For this, again, you are partly responsible ! One comrade (Fred Carneson) has been aroused into writing a fierce reply. (He is a fellow-worker on *New Age* and although you may not realise it from the tone of his article we are very warm friends!) I asked him to send you a copy of his article (which has also gone to the British periodical) and I am enclosing the reply I have sent them . . .

On the Formation of Nations in South Africa
by John McGrath [pseudonym for Fred Carneson]

Lionel Forman, in his article on the "Development of Nations in South Africa" in the April issue of *Marxism Today*, arrives at some novel — and, in my opinion, quite erroneous — conclusions, chief among them being his statement that there are no nations in South Africa.

According to him, none of the peoples of South Africa can be considered nations either (a) because they do not predominate numerically in a compact territorial area, and therefore do not have the right to self-determination; or (b) there is no single national market which they can call their own; or (c) they do not have a normal class structure.

Discussing whether or not the Afrikaner people constitute a nation, Forman says: "'Common territory' must mean a territory of one's own, because basic to the national question is that of self-determination and the right of secession."

Stalin's well-known definition setting out the four essential characteristics of a nation is evidently insufficient for Forman. He adds a fifth, that of the right to self-determination and secession. In doing so, he merely succeeds in confusing the issues.

The question of a nation's political rights is one thing; the question as to whether a given people constitute a nation is quite another. The two categories, though interrelated, should never be confused. The right of self-determination, the right to secession, is basic to a solution of the national problem; it is certainly not basic to the definition of a nation.

Forman quotes Stalin on the Jews in Russia in support of his contention that the Afrikaners do not constitute a nation because they are dispersed among other peoples. The comparison is not a valid one, and is a good example of his failure to apply a correct historical approach.

In the first instance, the Jews were far more widely scattered — and the different groups more isolated — in Russia than are the Afrikaners in South Africa. The Jews were at no stage capable of acting together "whether in time of peace or in time of war" (Stalin, *Marxism and the*

National and Colonial Question, p. 12). They were widely dispersed among a politically dominant, powerful people, far more advanced than they were (in the national sense).

Most important of all, the Jews were scattered over a huge territory, not only extremely backward economically but sadly lacking in internal means of communication.

The Afrikaners

The position is quite different with the Afrikaners. They have shown their ability to act together in war, as British imperialism found to its cost during the Anglo-Boer wars. Right now (to the detriment of other peoples, it is true) they are showing no mean ability to act together in time of peace. They are by no means a numerically insignificant minority scattered among politically more dominant and advanced peoples. They are an extremely powerful minority, even in the numerical sense, and well-organised politically, culturally and economically. They are more, not less, developed as a nation, than any other people in South Africa.

Most important of all, they live within the well-established boundaries of a comparatively highly developed capitalist state, well served with modern means of communication, making contact between the "dispersed" groups an easy and speedy matter. (The remarkable absence of dialect in modern Afrikaans is one indication of how close this contact has been).

It is precisely these significant differences between the position of the Jews in Russia and that of the Afrikaners in South Africa which should have engaged the attention of Forman, and not the superficial similarity of dispersal on which he places such great store.

But, comparisons apart, there still remains the question whether it is theoretically possible for a people to constitute a nation where they do not have a territory or a common economic life of "their own", but share a common territory and a common economic life with others. Stalin throws some light on this in a passage where he says: "But the persons constituting a nation do not always live in one compact mass; they are frequently divided into groups, and are interspersed among foreign national organisms. It is capitalism which drives them into other regions and cities in search of a livelihood" (Stalin, *Marxism and the National and Colonial Question*, p. 28).

It seems, therefore, that there is at least a theoretical possibility that the existence of a shared economic life, and a shared common territory, are not insuperable barriers to the formation of different nations within the bounds of a multi-national state. The same argument applies to the question of a national market, which is bound up with that of territory.

When dealing with abnormality in class structure, Forman not only again draws a false analogy between the Jews and the Afrikaners, but is also guilty of giving a completely distorted picture of the white worker. It is simply not true to say that white workers are "essentially supervisors of African labour", nor is it true to say that they are entirely petit-bourgeois in outlook.

Had Forman attempted to prove his bald assertion, the falsity of his position would have been manifest. He could only have done so by completely ignoring large and essential categories: steel workers, building workers, railway workers, transport workers, clerical workers, post office workers, distributive workers — the list is endless.

Even a cursory glance at the voters' rolls of any of the urban constituencies would have shown him that the overwhelming majority of white workers are by no means "essentially supervisors of African labour", but workers in their own right. His assertion that white workers are "entirely petit-bourgeois in outlook" is another misconception. The white worker may be pampered and petted, protected and privileged, completely under the political influence of "his" bourgeoisie, but he is by no means petit-bourgeois in his general outlook. And what applies to the white worker in general applies to the Afrikaner worker.

Class structure

The Afrikaners have a normal, bourgeois class structure. Unlike the Jews in Russia, there is a "large and stable stratum" associated with the soil; there is a developed and fast-growing bourgeoisie, an equally fast-growing middle class, and a clearly defined working class. The growth of capitalism in South Africa has made these class differences more and more distinct, not blurred them, as anyone who has taken the trouble to study the history of the Afrikaner people would soon realise.

In the peculiar conditions prevailing here, distortion of class structure is inevitable and is to be expected among all South African peoples, but it is by no means as distorted among the Afrikaners as Forman would have us believe.

In any case, an abnormal class structure is not necessarily proof that a people is not a nation. Distortions can and do arise at given stages of a nation's history, depending on other factors. The Russian people remain a nation to this day, in spite of the fact that their present class structure is certainly "abnormal" compared with that of a "normal", "bourgeois" nation — they haven't any bourgeoisie at all!

Now let us leave theory for a moment and look at Afrikaner people as such.

They are a people who, over a long period, have developed a distinctive language of their own; a distinctive culture which finds expression in many ways, including literature, and distinctive national characteristics. They live within the confines of a single territory and are closely bound together by a single economic life, even if shared with others.

In the same way as Americans, they do not regard themselves, nor can they be regarded, as "Europeans". They call themselves "whites" (in contrast to the English South African, who still calls himself a "European"). Indeed their very name, the one they have given themselves, means

"African". In their struggle to maintain their rights, these African people have fought two wars against British imperialism, successfully resisted all attempts (whether by Dutch or British) to destroy their language, and equally successfully resisted assimilation with other peoples.

For the past sixty years at least, their development has taken place under conditions of rising capitalism (i.e., under the very conditions which give rise to the birth of nations). Today, in a modern, independent bourgeois state, they supply the bulk of the armed forces (the standing army and the police force), staff the civil service and, through the medium of a powerful national political organisation, impose "their" will (which is the will of their landowners and bourgeoisie) on the rest of the South African peoples.

As Forman, quoting Potekhin, says: "a nation is not an imaginary or mystical concept — it is a very real phenomenon". The very real — if peculiar — phenomenon of the Afrikaner nation cannot be wished out of existence by describing them as a national group, whose right to self-determination, to political secession, Forman, by implication, rejects.

Self-determination

It is when dealing with the right to self-determination that Forman paints a very peculiar picture indeed. It is precisely on this issue that his contention that there are no nations in South Africa leads him into the realms of speculation, where the harsh realities of the present-day national struggles almost cease to exist.

"When freedom is won," says Forman, "the Afrikaners and other national groups, if they so desire, will, no doubt, obtain the opportunity to develop into nations, being given the essential territorial basis for such development, as has happened in the USSR and China."

No doubt. But being given the opportunity to develop into a nation is one thing, and the right to self-determination, the most important element of which is the right to secession, is another. And who is to give them this "right", the right to develop into nations? The other people of South Africa? Yet the other peoples, according to Forman, are only pre-nations whose own right to self-determination depends entirely on "progressives" who "might, in certain circumstances" accord them that right.

Where there are no nations, there is no right to self-determination, to political secession, except in the dim and distant future, when the "national groups" or the "pre-nations" have developed into nations. For the present, and until nations have developed, there is only the right to regional autonomy for national groups and nothing definite at all for the pre-nations.

That is where Forman's arguments lead us, and they come uncomfortably close to a denial of the right to self-determination. They open the door to opportunism, for dominant nations, as in South Africa, are ever ready with the cry: "You are not yet ready. Wait a little while longer."

The recognition of the right to self-determination, to secession must be unconditional even if, as Lenin said, "the chance of secession being possible and 'feasible' before the introduction of socialism is only one in

206 The National Question

a thousand" (quoted by Stalin, *Marxism and the National and Colonial Question* p. 198). The recognition of the right to secession does not, of course, mean the same thing as support for any particular demand for secession.

Forman, as I said earlier, deserts reality for speculation when dealing with the right to self-determination. He discusses it in the abstract, as if we already had a single socialist, soviet state in South Africa. He forgets that the struggle has not yet been won, and that the course of the struggle might take a very different path to that he has mapped out.

Reality makes nonsense of his assertion that "although in Europe the demand for self-determination in some form was a characteristic feature of the national struggle, this is not the case in South Africa." The question of the right to self-determination, in one form or another, is ever present in South African politics, and therefore cannot be ignored.

The Afrikaner has raised it time and time again vis-à-vis British imperialism, and even today the demand for a republic figures prominently in the Nationalist Party programme. It arises in relation to the Protectorates and South-West Africa. More important still, the Afrikaner bourgeoisie is raising the issue (although distorted) in an increasingly sharp form internally vis-à-vis the African peoples in particular.

The arch-apostles and theorists of apartheid have been moving steadily from the concept of "horizontal" apartheid to that of "vertical" apartheid, i.e., the creation of separate territorial areas. This concept finds concrete expression in the controversial Promotion of Bantu Self-Government Bill now before the Union Parliament, whereby the Nationalists seek to create a fantastic edifice of "autonomous" tribal regions (with, however, no real rights) for the African peoples.

Some Afrikaner bourgeois theorists have gone even further (and by so doing have inadvertently exposed the reactionary, oppressive and fraudulent nature of the Nationalist Government's policy). For example, a certain Professor Coetzeen recently proposed the creation of *separate and entirely independent states*, even if this meant, as he put it, "a considerable displacement of the white population".

So we see that the Afrikaner bourgeoisie, in their desperation, are themselves pushing the question of self-determination very much on to the agenda, as it were, and thereby make it a matter for practical (as opposed to speculative) politics.

The oppressed non-white peoples, on the other hand, strenuously oppose the policy of apartheid, of separation, whether horizontal or vertical. Their counter-demand is for a single, multi-national state, in which full democracy for all will guarantee the rights of the different nationalities.

The most significant factor in the national liberatory struggle in South Africa, the factor which distinguishes it from previous similar movements in Europe and, indeed, from similar movements in the rest of Africa today, is the fact that here it is the working class and revolutionary intelligentsia among the oppressed peoples which is taking the lead in the struggle.

The revolutionary working class tends naturally towards unity, internationalism; the bourgeoisie tends, just as naturally, towards disunity, national exclusiveness.

The demand for a single, fully democratic, multi-national state is therefore not merely a negative "absence of a demand for self-determination". It is, above all, a positive demand which has a specific working-class revolutionary content.

One further point remains on the issue of self-determination, for it will be asked: how is the Afrikaner, at present dispersed among other nationalities, to exercise the right to secession in the absence of a separate territory? What part of South Africa would we give him? Are we not being impracticable when we say his right to self-determination must be recognised when no opportunity exists for him to secede?

No, we are not being impracticable. If the Afrikaner, either on his own or together with others, were to demand the right to secession, the opportunity for him to do so would have to be provided in the shape of a separate territory. To force him to remain within the same state as the others, against his will, would not only violate his right to secede but leave the national problem unsolved.

How it would be done, and what separate territory would be provided, is not a question which we need answer now. For, as Lenin said, dealing with this very question of "practicability", "it is a matter that will be determined by a thousand factors, which cannot be foreseen." It might never arise, for the course of history is not yet run.

The important thing is not when, where or how, or whether the Afrikaner will ever demand secession, or even whether it is desirable. The fear the Afrikaners have of being "swamped" in a multi-national, fully democratic state is one on which the Afrikaner bourgeoisie is constantly playing. To recognise the right of the Afrikaner to self-determination now will go a long way towards dispelling those fears. It would assist in weaning the workers, and other sections away from "their" bourgeoisie, and make it easier to persuade them to move in the opposite direction — towards a truly democratic, multi-national South African state.

What form such a state would take, whether it would be a federation of states or a collection of autonomous regions, or something else again, is really a matter for speculation, and I am quite willing to leave that aspect to Mr Forman.

Space does not permit me to deal with the question as to whether any of the African peoples can be considered nations. That would require far more detailed treatment than is possible here. Suffice it to say that the question is far more complicated than Forman realises. Among other things, one would have to examine very carefully the effect which the impact of capitalism has made on the different peoples. It cannot be answered by juggling with formulae. Potekhin says, for instance, that several of the African peoples in South Africa (e.g., the Zulus and Xhosas) had already reached the "narodnost" stage at the beginning of the present

208 The National Question

century. Almost sixty years of intensive political, social and economic development have taken place since then, and it might very well be that some of these African peoples have already reached the stage where they may be considered as nations.

Forman's Response to McGrath (Carneson) and Other Critics

It was not as a mental exercise that the Bolsheviks went to such great pains, in 1913, to state clearly what it was that they meant by the term "nation". They did so because there was an urgent practical need to define clearly the type of community for which communists would advance the slogan of self-determination.

This required an analysis of the specific characteristics which make a community so tightly knit and economically integrated that it is capable of leading a separate political existence.

Stalin's definition, involving common territory, language, culture and economy, as expounded by Potekhin in the article which began this controversy (*Marxism Today* October 1958), has been tested in practice through the years, and found to serve its purpose so well that it has been accepted universally by communists as the starting point of all discussions on the question.

Stalin declares "there is no nation which at one and the same time speaks several languages" (*Marxism and the National and Colonial Question*). I would be the last to suggest that Stalin's words must be treated as gospel, but I certainly do suggest that Comrade J.T. Adams should lay some sort of theoretical foundation before he in effect declares blithely that this definition is obviously wrong: "Quite clearly a nation exists in South Africa — not Afrikaans, not English — but South African, composed of people who use Afrikaans and English languages and cultures" (*Marxism Today* July 1959, p. 3).

Comrade Adams appears to equate the terms "State" and "Nation", as, for example, where he talks of Switzerland, the Soviet Union, India and even the Boer Republics as nations, and seems, from his concluding paragraph, to argue that a single national market (meaning in the context a single state market) is all that is required for nationhood. He may well have something valuable to add to Marxist theory, and I do not question that, according to his own definition, there is a South African nation. But before we can examine Comrade Adams' contribution, he must tell us in what way his definition is better than the one at present used by Marxists. Until he does so, it is futile to continue the discussion because we will be, in effect, arguing in different languages.

John McGrath, like Comrade Adams, takes issue with me for claiming, in Comrade McGrath's paraphrase, that a nation "must have a territory and a common economic life which they can call 'their own'". It seems to me simple logic that a community which, because it nowhere has a piece of territory in which it constitutes a majority of the population and which is therefore physically incapable of seceding from anywhere, cannot be a nation. This does not add anything to Stalin's definition as Comrade Mcgrath claims — it is implicit in the "common territory" in that definition.

I agree with most of the things Comrade McGrath says about the white Afrikaners, and endorse that they are vastly different in most respects from the Jews of Tsarist Russia. All I say is that they are not a nation. Incidentally, almost the whole of Comrade McGrath's first description of the Afrikaners, from their "ability to act together in war", right up to their "modern means of communication" applies equally to a large and efficient army of occupation. Such an army would also not be a nation.

Nor is it necessary for Comrade McGrath to devote pages to proving the obvious facts that many nations are widely dispersed and share their territory with others. All such nations have somewhere, some territory "of their own", meaning by that a territory where they constitute the majority of the population.

I am fully in agreement with him about the leading role of the African working class in the national movement and his attempt to make an argument about this is artificial.

Comrade McGrath makes the very emphatic demand for the right of the Afrikaners (meaning white Afrikaners) to secede. To accord them the right to develop into a nation, capable of secession, is not enough, he says. But the whole point is that you can't secede without a bit of territory to secede with you. And surely the rights of the Afrikaners are not so much greater than the rights of other South Africans that we can force a non-Afrikaner majority of any part of our country to secede with the Afrikaner, or to move somewhere else — for that is the only way that we could at present guarantee the white Afrikaner the right to secede.

Comrade McGrath is a clear-thinking man, for whose views I have a great deal of respect, so I can only assume that he was over-tired when he thought up the idea that the Afrikaner nationalist policy of driving the Africans into labour reservoir "bantustans" bears any sort of relationship to self-determination. And I am utterly aghast at his statement that the new apartheid bill is a "concrete expression" of a move "from the concept of 'horizontal' apartheid to that of 'vertical' apartheid". The claim by the Nationalists that they are only trying to change the position from the unjust one in which the whites are at the top and the blacks at the bottom in South Africa, to one in which whites and blacks live equally side by side in separate territories has been exposed by the Congresses, by *New Age*, by Comrade McGrath himself, and by almost everyone else outside the Nationalist ranks as a complete fraud. The Bill does not, in fact, change the situation of horizontal apartheid, with whites at the top and blacks at the bottom, in one society, by one iota.

It is necessary, however, to add an important qualification to my remarks about the Afrikaner nation. My article and the replies of Comrades Adams

210　The National Question

and McGrath considered the Afrikaners in the lily-white image painted by Afrikaner nationalists. But if there is in fact an Afrikaner nation, it does not consist of the one-and-a-half million Afrikaners who can claim white identity cards, but of about two million people. Once one breaks through the Nationalist smokescreen, one sees that the Afrikaans-speaking Coloureds are part of the same national community as their whiter brothers — common language, economy, culture and all. Except for political and social discrimination, there is nothing at all to distinguish the very substantial proportion of Afrikanerdom which, though technically Coloured, passes for white from that proportion which is too dark or too proud to pass.

And what is so ironic is that the Coloureds are one of "Afrikanerdom's greatest national assets". With them, Afrikanerdom has a territory where it is in the majority, with a few good-sized towns; and it has a much better-balanced class structure.

Although the present leaders of white Afrikanerdom would choke at the idea, it is very possible that under conditions of freedom the single white and Coloured Afrikaner nation will be one of the first to consolidate itself, and that its Afrikaner language and culture will blossom as never before.

At the same time, it must be noted that the position is by no means static. The political discrimination against the Coloureds is creating something akin to a Coloured national consciousness, separated from that of the white Afrikaner, and comparable with that of the Negro of the USA. The South African Coloured People's Organisation is thought of as a national organisation like those of its African and Indian allies in the Congress Alliance. But an optimistic estimate of the time required for winning freedom would preclude the development of a separate Coloured nation born of "race" oppression.

Comrade McGrath is right when he stresses that the demand for a single, fully democratic, multi-national state is not merely a negative absence of a demand for self-determination but a positive demand. The African National Congress has, since about 1947, had, as part of its standing policy, the demand for self-determination, and it can properly be said that the oppressed national groups in South Africa have made it clear that the way they wish to determine their own destinies is within the framework of a united South African state.

But the big question is whether it is realistic for us to think, as Comrade Adams does, that the people's democratic South Africa will be a ready-made, single, fused nation; or whether, as I believe, the correct Marxist perspective is to recognise the fact that South Africa is by no means a single nation at present, cannot become a single nation until democracy has been won, and will not, even with a people's democratic government, become a nation overnight.

If the latter view is correct, then the words of Stalin, in his report to the 6th Congress of the CPSU in 1930, are apposite for South Africa:

It may seem strange that we, who are in favour of the fusion of national cultures in the future into one common culture (both in form and content), with a single, common language, are in favour of the blossoming of national cultures at the present time, in the period of the dictatorship of the proletariat. But there is nothing strange in this. The national cultures must be permitted to develop and expand and to reveal all their potential qualities, in order to create the conditions necessary for their fusion into a single, common culture with a single, common language. The blossoming of cultures national in form and socialist in content under a proletarian dictatorship in one country, with the object of their fusion into a single, common socialist (both in form and content) culture, with a single, common language, when the proletariat is victorious throughout the world and socialism becomes an everyday matter — such is the dialectical nature of the Leninist presentation of the question of national culture.

Under conditions of democracy the national communities which inhabit South Africa will flower into nations, and it is through this brotherhood of equal South African nations, united in a single state, that a South African nation will one day come into being.

Potekhin's Response to McGrath

Responding to McGrath's (Carneson's) contribution to Marxism Today, *Potekhin wrote to Carneson and copied the letter to Forman. Extracts are reproduced below:*

I have received your letter and the article — the answer to Lionel Forman. I am very glad that my article in *Marxism Today* has sponsored a vivid discussion which will help us to understand much of the national problem. The question of the formation of nations in modern Africa is a difficult one. The main danger in its solution is dogmatism and flatness of thought. African nations are formed in quite new conditions, in conditions of struggle of two social systems and the collapse of colonialism.

There are no grounds to doubt in the scientific trustworthiness of the statements by Lenin and Stalin about a nation, but they must be applied with a creative spirit. . . It seems to me you and Lionel Forman are making too hurried and categorical conclusions.

It is a pity that my book is not translated into English and is thus unavailable to you. Here I cite some of my conclusions:

There is now a process going on in the Union of South Africa of the formation of national entities — Bantu and Anglo-Afrikaners.

There are no prerequisites yet for the formation of a sole nation, absorbing Bantu, Coloureds and Anglo-Afrikaners . . .

There are enough pre-conditions for a merger of Bantu *narodnosts* (national groups) of the Union and Protectorates into a single nation: they inhabit a common territory which is firmly united economically; they speak languages that are so close that they may be regarded as dialects of one

212 The National Question

language; they have a common ground of culture; they feel themselves to be an entity. But there is not yet a single Bantu nation; there is no common literary language, each *narodnost* has one of its own . . .

There are also some conditions for forming a specific nation of Zulu (including Swazi) and Xhosa. There is a common territory, a common language, still with some dialectical differences, and a common culture. But there is no such nation as yet.

South African Bantu have not yet formed their nations. We may state only the existence of requisites, potential possibilities and the beginning of the process of their formation. Their outlines are not yet clear, and it would be incorrect to attempt to give a definitive solution of the question now. The question of national delimitation will be solved by the peoples themselves, when they are free of imperialist domination. The main task of all Bantu *narodnosts* now is to join their efforts in a united national front, and together with the progressive forces of Anglo-Afrikaners, Indians and Coloureds to achieve the destruction of the regime of race discrimination, to conquer political rights, equal with the European part of the population.

I say that now the process of formation of Anglo-Afrikaner nation is going on. You somehow forget the Englishmen, speaking only of Afrikaners. But how to deal with the Englishmen, they are also a constituent population of the Union of South Africa. There cannot be two nations — Afrikaner and English. The existence of two languages means nothing. There may be a bilingual nation. The important thing is that people belonging to the given nations could understand each other . . .

One cannot mix a common territory and a common economic life. In every multi-national state, capitalist or socialist, there is a common market, a common economical life of all nations of this state . . . The USSR has a common economy, a common economic life of all the peoples of its population, developing in common. But simultaneously each union republic has its economic base, its internal economic ties, its national market. The common economic life of the peoples of the USSR is an organic entity, including in it an economic life of each republic. Economic community of a nation is not an autarchy. It signifies nothing else but an economic mutual dependence of areas peopled by this people. This does not exclude some economic ties of one national territory with other national territories.

In the Union of South Africa there is a common capitalist economy, a common market for all the peoples of its population. My book has a special chapter titled "Economic Community". I cite a summary: "An analysis of the economic life of the Union of South Africa from the point of view of the formation of a Bantu economic entity leads us to two conclusions: i) each ethnic territory of the Bantu is a sum of more or less firmly economically tied areas; ii) all ethnic territories are in a firm economic connection and together form a united bourgeois economic complex."

With a territorial community the matter is not like this. The Ukrainians, Georgians and other peoples of the USSR participate in a common economic life, but all of them have a national territory of their own. Each nation must have its territory. People may also live there who are not included in this nation, but the nation must constitute the majority of the population, else the territory cannot be regarded as its national territory. I read your article again and again in an attempt to understand your definition of the national territory of the Afrikaner nation. I found nothing. One may conclude that you mean all the territory of the Union of South Africa as a national territory of the Afrikaners. In this case you state as impossible national self-determination of the Zulu, Xhosa, etc. A national self-determination is impossible without a separation from a multi-national state of some of its part and the creation in this part of a national state. Lionel Forman is quite right on this question. You are wrong. If your conception of a territorial community is adopted, we must give up the slogan of national self-determination of the Bantu peoples and take on a programme of national cultural autonomy, so brilliantly criticised by Stalin, and with which you agree.

These two questions — national territory and the programme on the national problem — are connected. You have to choose — whether you support the slogan of national self-determination (and you do), and then you have to agree with Forman, or you adopt the programme of national cultural autonomy . . .

Some words about self-determination. You are quite right that the "question of the right to self-determination . . . is ever present in South African politics, and therefore cannot be ignored." But I could not understand what exact context you mean by this question.

First of all one theoretical question. One cannot agree with your statement: "Where there are no nations, there is no right for self-determination, to political secession." If we accept this statement, the majority of African peoples have to give up their right to self-determination, because their nations are not yet formed. Every people, despite its level of development, despite whether it has formed a nation or not, has a right to determine its destiny, that means a right to self-determination. And then, the formation of nations is a slow process and nobody can tell precisely when it is over.

The statement of Forman's — that for the Bantu this process is not yet finished, that the Bantu are in a "pre-nation" position, has nothing in common with the task of self-determination. You write: "The oppressed non-white peoples . . . oppose the policy of apartheid, of separation, whether horizontal or vertical. Their counter-demand is for a single, multi-national state." I agree with this demand. It is the only correct solution of the national problem But what is the multi-national state? Is the co-existence in it of many nations possible, each of them having its specific national territory, and some degree of national (not cultural, but territorial) autonomy? Surely, yes. Then the slogan "multi-national state" does not contradict the slogan of national self-determination. But I have understood you thus: a multi-national state is a state where you find a mixed position of people with different cultures, psychology, languages etc.

214   *The National Question*

living together. In the Union of South Africa it is impossible, because the Zulu, Xhosa and others have their national territories, they want to develop their languages and have a literature in their languages. A multi-national state in South Africa is possible only as a state where each people has some degree of autonomy within its national territory. Some part of this people may also live in a mixed position in the territories of other peoples. And maybe in future they will merge into one nation; i.e. Forman's formula will be right.

The main weaknesses of your position are these:

1. You accept a possibility of a nation existing without a territory of its own, or of many nations on the same territory;

2. You mean all the territory of the Union of South Africa to be a national territory of Afrikaners, while the Bantu people are denied the right to have their own national territory where they could do without the interference of Afrikaners;

3. The centre of your speculations are Afrikaners, and not the Bantu who constitute three-quarters of the total population. When trying to understand the national problem in South Africa, one must base it on the interest of the national development of the Bantu peoples, having in sight a full and complete safeguarding of the rights of Afrikaners and Englishmen as national minorities.

I have pointed out only some of the questions raised in your discussion with Forman, and left many other disputable problems out. I want to stop with the words of the start — let us discuss, but never hurry with final determinations. We need more flexible opinions. The question is difficult, politically sharp, and therefore demands carefulness.

Letter from Forman to Potekhin, 31 August 1959

The only comment I would like to make is to query the view about the coming into being of a single Anglo-Afrikaner white nation and the statement "the existence of two languages means nothing. There may be a bilingual nation. The important thing is that people belonging to the given nation could understand each other." It seems to me that when we talk of a common language as a basic requisite of nationhood, we mean more than simply that the people should be able to understand one another. The language must be cherished in common, it must be a binding force.

Whether or not a whole people can ever really be bilingual and share two languages with equal facility and regard I don't know, but I do know that in South Africa there is certainly no such situation. The official statistic that close on 70 per cent of white South Africans are bilingual means no more than 70 per cent of the whites claim to be able to understand the other language, and understanding is in most cases at a fairly elementary level. As an advocate I am required to have sufficient Afrikaans to be able to conduct a court case in the language, and I am therefore probably more bilingual than most — but like the overwhelming majority of English-speaking people, I have to struggle to formulate ideas in that language and I only use Afrikaans when I have to, and since my schooldays I have not dreamed of reading an Afrikaans novel or poem or attending an Afrikaans play. This, I repeat, is the position with the great majority of English-speaking South Africans. One factor, of course, is that the heavy hand of Afrikaner nationalism ensures that almost all Afrikaner culture is either racialist, anti-scientific, church-dominated, obscurantist muck, or else, as an escape, the translation into Afrikaans of the cheapest, most sensational and sex- and sadism-ridden American "literature."

The rise to power of Afrikaner nationalism has not increased bilingualism. The Englishman is now forced to get a working knowledge of the language, but goes no further than that, but on the other hand, the Afrikaner, who was previously forced to get a working knowledge of English, and who can now manage with the barest minimum of that language, is less bilingual than he used to be.

No. While the Afrikaners will cherish their language, and will see it flower when freedom comes to South Africa, I can see no possible reason to believe that English-speaking Europeans will merge with them linguistically. There is no incentive, for remember that when freedom comes, English will almost certainly be the country's working language for some time, and Afrikaans . . . (hated by Africans as the language of the police) will very rapidly dwindle in importance.

The whole situation here seems to me to negate the idea of an Anglo-Afrikaner bilingual nation and to demonstrate the correctness of the statement by Stalin, "there is no nation which at one and the same time speaks several languages." (*Marxism and the National and Colonial Question*, p. 6)

Reply from Potekhin to Forman, 7 October 1959

You object to my statement that the process of the formation of the Anglo-Afrikaner nation is now in progress, on the ground that there could be no bilingual nation. From the theoretical standpoint, you are wrong: there could be such nations. As far as the concrete case — that of the formation of the Anglo-Afrikaner nation — it's for you to know the best, though I, for my part, don't see any other prospect of national development. Perhaps you are right concerning the "single South African nation". But on the base of what language? Did you think about it? . . .

Part 5:
A Trumpet From The Housetops

On the morning of Monday, 19 October 1959, the last morning of Lionel Forman's life, he wrote a 13-page letter to his wife from the hospital before his open-heart operation. Extracts from the letter are reproduced, as are a few of the tributes that poured in. The speech that Jack Simons made at the Memorial Meeting held for Lionel on 25 October is included.

13. "A Shining Sword"

Extracts from the letter Lionel Forman wrote to his wife, Sadie, early on the morning of 19 October 1959, shortly before his heart operation was to begin.

If this doesn't come off, you're not to mourn for me. I'm going in without the slightest fear of death and, if I die, it will not hurt me at all, except in the thought that it will hurt you . . .

I want the children not to be taken to any funeral service, nor should you go to one. And if there is any meeting of friends, what I want said there clearly and unequivocally is:

All his adult life he tried to be a good communist. All his life he strove to be a good communist . . . Now I am legally as safe as houses, I want it trumpeted from the housetops, Lionel Forman believed in communism for South Africa with a burning passion till the day he died, and in all his adult years that passion never once diminished.

All my love my darling loves. All my love to all . . .

Some bits may be found useful in my history notes, but I'm afraid I couldn't get it into form, still . . . some usefulness may come of it . . .

No, I'm sorry, I can't fight this confounded drug. I didn't want it, because I am as calm as can be but they insisted.

Tell the treason court we'll achieve freedom in the lifetime of Karl, Frank and Sara — and you Sadie — whether they like it or not.

Forward to the total abolition of the colour bar — forward to communism in South Africa . . .

Once again . . . don't mourn, and don't let the children mourn. Tell them they must have love for their fellowmen, they must exorcise all race prejudice and understand why it is abominable and they must try to understand why it is that justice can only be won for all men and the full free personality allowed to flower under communism; and that the one way they can pay a small tribute to their old dad is by at least looking at the marxist works and seeing if they appeal to them . . .

If anything is written, they must say he tried to be a good communist. Often he failed but he tried and his life was to bring — no, it isn't the dope that's gettin me, but they've come for me. All my love my loves.

Lionel.

Tributes to a Comrade

From Jack Simons at Lionel Forman's memorial meeting, 25 October 1959.

Brothers, Sisters! We have come together to mourn Lionel's death, but we rejoice in his life. His life was like a shining sword pointed at the heart of injustice and oppression. Many here will live much longer than it was given to Lionel to do, but all of us would be glad if our lives could show as much achieved as he had accomplished. The tributes that have poured in from men and women of different races, political beliefs and organisations, throughout the country, testify to the grand scale of his achievements.

We think here of the qualities of courage and devotion that were needed to overcome the physical handicaps under which he laboured. Few of us, living ordinary, untrammelled lives would find them easy to endure. He not only bore them with fortitude, but carried out important and exacting work in spite of his weakness and suffering. He found the strength for his efforts in his communism. For, as his last message proudly declared: he died as he had lived — a communist.

His message proclaimed a faith not only in the struggle against injustice and reaction, but in the positive vision of a future for all mankind, based on a society in which men would eliminate injustice and rivalries between races, colours and creeds. His vision was that of a society in which class privileges would be unknown, in which the threat of war would cease to harass men's minds, consume their resources and breed suspicion and hatred.

Lionel was not only a communist, he was also a devoted South African. He felt deeply an urge to apply his principles to our own situation, and work out in terms of his basic philosophies an answer to the problems that have up to now held back our people from achieving the good and harmonious society to which all here assembled aspire. He thought of a South Africa that would be free of racial strife, and in which the hearts and minds of our people would join together in a common enterprise for the good of all.

I want to tell you something about these ideas, for they are going to capture the imagination of many South Africans in time to come. As you have been told, Lionel was working on a book before he died. It was to have been his major work. He had not got very far, but he did enough to enable him to see the outlines of the landscape on which he was engaged.

It was to have been a book about the origin and growth of the liberation movement in our country with special emphasis on African political movements. He hoped to penetrate into our traditions and history in order to trace the origins of the divisions among our people, throw light on obscure trends in the past, and by so doing bring clarity where now is much confusion and dissension.

He began with the period when Africans started on the long road from tribalism to a modern industrialised society. He set out to discover the growth of modern ideas of democracy in the African population, the men who gave expression to those ideas, who founded the first African newspapers and formed the first political organisations. What was the content of the ideas and beliefs that guided their actions?

As he worked over his material, he became more and more convinced that a great deal of strength lay in the Africans' tribal past, and that it constituted even today a rich source of inspiration from which present and future generations would draw comfort and guidance for their work in building a new society. He held the view that the main tribal divisions — the Xhosa, Zulu, Sotho, Tswana, Venda, Tsonga — would yet develop into separate nations, each with its own traditions, language and culture. Therefore, he contended, the liberation movement would gain enormously if it were to recognise this traditional origin of the African people, and inculcate in them loyalty towards, and pride in, their language, literature and customs.

Lionel was not, however, a tribalist or nationalist. His belief in the value of the tribal past strengthened his vision of a single, united and free South Africa embracing black, brown and white peoples in a great fraternity. He was an internationalist who believed that unity would come out of diversity. He believed in the brotherhood of man, that ideal which the best of the human race has embraced throughout the ages. To him it was not only an ideal, but a political weapon of the greatest importance for resisting and defeating reaction.

We are not likely to underestimate the strength of reaction. The presence of members of the Special Branch on this solemn occasion symbolises its character. It is typical of the strategy that the government has consistently employed. But the presence of the police and the kind of repression used to intimidate people are not the most serious threats that the progressive movement has to endure. A greater danger comes from the attempt to impose on us an acceptance of the official doctrine — against which Lionel contended with all his power — that South Africans belong to different human species and are eternally doomed to live apart and in fear of one another.

All of us, men and women of different colour groups here assembled, and representing in our varieties the many hundreds of thousands of people outside who belong to distinct communities — we have to recognise that the great danger to our peoples and to our country comes from the efforts of the state to divide us, to condition us to the notion that black, brown and white must not meet in halls, mix in our homes, associate on an equal plane as free people. Lionel delivered his main blows against this evil repudiation of the eternal truth that all men are brothers. He sought to resist it by demonstrating that out of diversity come unity.

He has left enough to make us realise the contribution he would have given if he had been able to live the full span. He had gone beyond the stage of merely reproducing general principles and proclaiming universal truths. He was trying to apply his principles to the specific conditions of our society. In doing this, he gave the principles new forms and contents. The work that he has done puts us greatly in his debt. He has defined problems, but their solution will have to be achieved by those who follow him. There could be no greater tribute to him and his cause than that the younger generation should take up the work where he left off and pursue it with the same vigour, enthusiasm and optimism that he displayed.

"A Shining Sword" 221

From the Treason Court in Pretoria, 20 October 1959

We are deeply shocked to hear of Lionel's death and our thoughts this morning are with you and the children.

Our deep feelings of sorrow are not easy to express, for we knew Lionel for almost half our lives and shared the pleasure of working in the movement with him where he stood as a giant above us.

Although Lionel was only 31 when he died, his contribution was so enormous that good people all over South Africa knew and respected him for what he was — a devoted communist — and we shall always remember him as a good friend who died at his post.

Please accept our warm feelings for you and rest assured that you do not mourn alone — a fact that should give you much comfort.

Our best wishes to the children who we hope are well.

Yours comradely,

signed: Leon Levy and A.M. Kathrada.

From the underground South African Communist Party, 28 October 1959

We want to convey to you, and through you to those who knew him as one of us, our deep regret and sense of loss at the death of Comrade Lionel. He gave his brilliant gifts unsparingly and to the utmost for the liberation of man and the noble cause of communism. His courage, revolutionary ardour and devotion will not be forgotten by the people whose cause he served. His memory will live as a continuous inspiration to us all.

From Chief Luthuli, President of the African National Congress

On behalf of African people I express to you deepest sympathy on passing of your husband. His loss will be deeply felt by his family and all freedom-loving people. His courageous stand in the freedom struggle will always inspire us.

From *Fighting Talk* (December 1959). Tribute written by Ruth First

Before we knew that Lionel Forman would undergo that open-heart operation, *Fighting Talk* had asked him for an article for this issue on "Current Soviet Writing on Africa". Four days before he died Lionel wrote from his hospital bed to say: "Sorry I can't do the article this month but it involves looking up references I can't get at . . . I hope to tackle it in time for the January issue".

The piece will not appear.

Lionel's death cut short his work on a thesis on the history of African political organisations, a study of the national question in South Africa, weekly articles in *New Age* analysing world trends, countless other writing and study projects, and prodigious and unceasing political activity though most of his youth and all his adult life were dogged by serious ill health.

Lionel was a man of versatile talent and great vigour of pen. From him flowed sober analysis, earnest argument based on his socialist principles,

222 A Trumpet from the Housetops

the results of his historical research, and also satire and sarcastic humour written in breezy and biting style . . .

Lionel will be missed not only as a writer, the field in which he made his greatest mark in the last years of his short life, but as a political figure in the South African Liberation Movement, as a fellow fighter, as one of the 156 men and women of all races arrested in the treason swoop of December 1956, as a comrade who held tenaciously to his convictions.

His friends knew him as a man of lively and alert mind, serious and taciturn at times, at others puckish and amusing, always considerate, gentle and undemanding.

Lionel lived the greater part of his life knowing that his heart condition could prove fatal at any time, yet he refused to be considered an invalid or to spare himself. In the last few years he was devoured by an anxiety to complete as many as possible of his research and writing projects in the shortest possible time. He lived and worked under great odds, yet with determination, enthusiasm and an impressive courage, and the freedom movement and South Africa are the poorer for his death.

From Douglas Maquina friend and fellow-activist. *Douglas Maqina earned a living selling* Advance *and its successor papers. On behalf of himself and other comrades, Douglas sent Sadie a written tribute in Sehosa which is translated below*:

> Lionel Forman is as big as Table Mountain. He was big because of his deeds. His deeds made him prosper and his work was so hard on his body. He looked small and short when he stood before the court and defended the freedom fighters. That is where he became big and tall as Table Mountain.

> Mr. Forman's conduct was that of a man with love, kindness and sympathy and a beautiful understanding of the law. He succeeded when he defended the oppressed in the court under apartheid, the capitalist police state in South Africa.

> After he left us, we made a song for Forman to encourage the freedom fighters with this hero. The village cried with tears and hunger on the day we were left by Lionel Forman. Sleeping down underground are the bones of an African. The bones of an African are white underground. Mayibuye. In our lifetime we want freedom.

The text of the song is below:

> Lionel Forman yindode encinane enkundleni mkhulu njenge ntabas yetafile
> Mhla sashywa ngu Forman
> Walile Umzi akwatyiwa mhla sahuzwa ngu Forman
> Amhlophe phantsi ko mahlaba amathambo om Afrika
> Isahleli entliziyweni umsebenzi ka Forman
> Amhlophe phantsi ko mahlaba amathambo om Afrika

Lionel Forman is a small man but in court he is as big as Table
Mountain
When Forman passed away
All homes were unhappy when Forman passed away
The white bones of an African are underground where he used to
stand
The spirit of Forman still remains in our hearts and so does his
good work
The bones of an African are underground where he used to stand)
His spirit will live in those who come after and continue.

Index

Abantu-Batho, xxvi, 55, 57, 58, 69
Abdullah, Sheikh, 150
Abdurahman, Dr, 34, 37, 41, 43, 44
Abrahams, Lionel, xiv
Adams, J.T., 208
Advance, xviii, xxi, xxii, xxiii, xxviii, xxxii, 88, 119, 143, 146, 152, 153, 173, 174, 175, 179, 190, 222
Africa South Journal, xxi
African Communist, xxix
African Educational Association, 193
African languages, recognition of, 178, 188, 189, 197
African National Congress (ANC), xi, xiii, xix, xx, xiv, xvi, xxxii, 1, 25, 30, 35, 37-42, 54, 55, 57, 63, 66, 67, 69, 75, 79, 80, 83, 90, 93, 94, 101, 104, 114, 152, 153, 157, 162, 171, 173, 188, 193, 210, 221; and the Communist Party, xxii, 72-89
African People's Organisation (APO), 1, 32-5, 40, 41, 43, 63, 69, 90
African population, 50, 52, 55, 56, 58, 60, 61, 69, 186, 188, 196
Africander League (Coloured), 30
Afrikaner Bond, 30, 193
Afrikaner population, xxv, 30, 36, 48, 61, 73, 84, 173, 175, 194, 195, 199, 203, 207, 209, 214; class structure of, 200, 210
Aidit, D.N., 73
Alexander, Ray, 159
Algeria, 167
Ali, Mohammed, 150
All-African Convention (AAC), 81
Allen, James S., 137
Am Metal company, 148
Am Smelting and Refining company, 148
Amalgamated Society of Carpenters and Joiners, 27, 159
Amalgamated Society of Engineers, 53

Amarasingam, S.P., 151
Andrews, W.H. (Bill), xi, xii, xviii, 45, 46, 47, 48, 50, 51, 59, 60, 72, 75, 77, 78, 159, 160
Anti-Fascist League, 81
anti-war campaigning, 51
Anti-War Manifesto of Second International, 45
apartheid, xiii, xix, xx, xxxi, 95, 100, 102, 103, 105, 113, 115, 163, 183, 206, 213; and churches, 115
Aramco company, 152
Arenstein, Jacqueline, xxvi
Arnold, G., 72
Asmal, Bob, 111
Asvat, Zainap, 107
Attlee, Clement, 140, 144
Austro-Hungarian Empire, 184
Autshumao, Chief, 4, 8-9, 25

Bambata, Chief, 33-4, 36
Bantu Authorities Act, 186
Bantu Education Act, 186
bantustans, 186, 209
Barnard, Christiaan, xiv
Barry, Jacob Dirk, 2
Basotho peoples, 2, 192, 193, 194
Basutoland, 195
Batson, Professor, 128
Beach, Hicks, 21
Bernstein, Hilda, xxviii
Bevan, Aneurin, 145
Beyleveld, Piet, xiii, 97, 113
Blackwell, Justice, 117
Bloomberg, Charles, xvii
Boer peoples, 11, 12, 14, 16, 18, 19, 29, 36
Bokala, Isaac, 113
Botha, Louis, 36, 41
Botha, Gideon, 47
boycott of mine concession stores, 64
Branding Act, 24

Index 225

British imperialism, 14-20, 203, 205
Brockway, Fenner, xxiii
Broederbond, 116
Brown, Forrester, 47, 68
Brownlee, J., 18, 22
bucket strike, 66-9
Bukharin, N., 78
Bunting, Brian, xviii, xxii, xxiv
Bunting, R., xxvi, 72, 78
Bunting, Sonia, xxii
Bunting, S.P., xi, xii, 45, 46, 47, 48, 49, 50, 52, 53, 54, 55, 56, 57, 58, 59, 62, 63, 66, 69, 70, 72, 78, 76, 81
Busa, Julius, 104
Bushman peoples, 200

Calata, J.C., xxiv, 113
Callinicos, Luli, xxiv
Caltex company, 148
Cape Socialist, 42, 43
capitalism, 181; creation of, 26
Carneson, Fred, xxii, xxx, 105, 113, 126, 129, 202; Forman's response to, 208-14
Catlin, George, 134
Centlivres, Justice, 115, 117
Cetiwiye, A., 69
Cetwayo, Chief, 2
Ceylon, 151
Chamile, Andries, 111
Champion, A.W.G., xxvi
Chapman, T., 72
China, xxx, 145, 158, 166, 168, 179, 182, 195, 205
Chinese labour, import of, 27, 36
Chora, Chief, 7, 8
Christian Express, 24
Clarion, xxii, 95
Clark, A., 51
Clark, C., 134
Clark, J.A., 47
Clark, P.L.C., 51
class structure: among Africans, 195; among Afrikaners, 204
class struggle, 178, 180, 181; relation to national struggle, 176
Clementin, Jean, 148
Coetzeen, Professor, 206
Cole, G.D.H., 155
Collins, Richard, Lt-Col., 16
colonial national movements, 185-6
colonialism, 2-24
colour bar, xi, 29, 38, 42, 50, 59, 60, 61, 66, 76, 84, 86, 124, 178, 186, 188, 196; resistance to, 53
Coloured Affairs Department, 186
Coloured population, xxx, 18, 19, 29, 30,

43, 44, 48, 62, 65, 73, 77, 90, 104, 109, 126, 160, 175, 183, 186, 188, 194, 195, 210, 212
Commercial Advertiser, xxii
communism, xv, 201, 218, 219, 221
Communist Manifesto, 49, 65
Communist Party, xxvi, 48, 90
Communist Party: of Great Britain, 119; of Indonesia, 73, 165; of South Africa, xi, xv, xviii, xix, xxiv, xxvi, xxix, xxxii, 1, 121, 126, 132, 155, 159, 163, 168, 191, 192, 198, 221 (aims of, 156-7; and the ANC, 72-89); of Soviet Union, 210; of US, 165
compound system, 53
Congress Alliance, xiii, xviii, xxiii, 90-8, 210
Congress of Democrats, xiii, 90, 96
Constitutional Socialist League, 72
Coordinating Secretariat (COSEC), xvii
Cope, R.K., 46, 159
Craig, General, 14
Crawford, Archie, 63, 68
Creswell, Colonel, xi, 45, 47, 51, 58, 72
cultural autonomy school, 185, 187
Cyprus, 167

Dadoo, Dr Y.M., xix, 90, 95, 117, 174
Daily Worker, 168
Damons, Stella, 109, 113
Dawood, Asa, 104, 113
de Buys, Coenraad, 12, 13
de Chambre, Guy, 148
democratic movements, 180
den Bakker, J., 72
Development of Nations in South Africa, 198, 200
diamonds, discovery of, 20, 25, 27, 29, 30, 192
dilution of labour, 61-2
Dimitrov, G., 120
Dingane, King, 25
Dingane's Day, xxv, 79
Dinizulu, Chief, 33
Disarmament Act, 21, 22, 24
Disarmament Law, 22
disenfranchisement of Africans, 31, 32
Donges, T.E., 131
Dryburgh, D.L., 72
du Bois, W.E.B., 75
Du Pisanie, Sergeant, 101
Dube, John L., 39
Dulles, J.F., 140, 143, 144, 145, 146
Duncan, Patrick, 198, 201
Dundas, General, 15
Durban Indian Workers' Union, 63

226 *Index*

Durban Social Democratic Party, 51
Dutch East India company, 3, 6, 17
Dutch language, use of, 193
Dutch Reformed Church, 115
Dutt, R.C., 40
Dwane, James, 32
Dwanya, Daniel, 32

Eden, Anthony, 140
Egypt, 141
English language, use of, 197
English peoples, 212
equality, in law, 187

Fascism, 84, 128; fight against, 81
Feetham, Richard, 106
Festenstein, H., 127
Fighting Talk, xxiv, xxxi, 108, 156, 221
Fingo peoples, 21, 22, 23, 24
First World War, and socialist movement,
    45-71
First, Ruth, xiii, xvi, xvii, xxii, xxvi, xxvii,
    xxxi, 109, 123, 221
Ford, Henry, 136
Forman, Frank, xv, xvii, 218
Forman, Karl, xv, xvii, 101, 218
Forman, Lionel, xi-xxxiii, 99, 123-131,
    132, 156, 179, 188; correspondence
    with I.I. Potekhin, 190-202
Forman, Sadie, xii, xiv, xv, xxxi, 101, 218,
    222
Forman, Sara, xv, 218
Forman, Sarah nee Shribnick, xv
Forum Club, xix
France, 141, 145, 146, 147, 148, 149, 155
Fredericks, M.J., 34
Freedom Charter, 1, 96, 97, 98, 158, 192
Freedom, 82, 83, 86
Frere, Bartle, 21
Friedman, Bernard, 128

Gandhi, Mohandas Karamchand, 33, 34
Garment Workers Union, xxiii
Garvey, Marcus, 78
Geldblum, R., 72
Germany, 65, 68
Ghana, 158, 191
Ghetto Act, 90
Gogosoa, Chief, 7
gold, discovery of, 29, 35, 192
Goldman, A., 72
Gonnema, Chief, 9
Goodrich Rubber company, 148
Graham, Colonel, 16
Great Trek, 7
Grendon, Robert, 55

Griffiths, Col., 22
Gros, Robert, 136
Group Areas Act, 186
Guardian, xxi, xxii, 91, 92, 94, 130
Guatemala, 143
Gumeda, J.T., 77

Harmel, Michael, xi, xxii, xxiv, xxvi,
    xxvii, xxviii, 128
Harrison, Wilfred, 42
Hashomer Hatzair (HH), xvi
Heaton Nicholls, G., 106
Hertzog Bills, 81, 83
Hill, Fr Francis, 54
Hintsa, Chief, 17, 20
Ho Chi Minh, 139, 147
Hodgson, Jack, 100
Hofmeyer, Jan, 122
Holland, 3, 205
Horvitch, I.O., 109, 179
Huddleston, Fr Trevor, 107, 113, 117
Hungary, lessons of, xxviii, 167-70

illiteracy, 88
Imbumba Yama Afrika organisation,
    xxix, 1, 30, 193
Imvo Zabantsundu, xxix, 30, 31, 32, 41, 79
indentured system, 53
India, 149, 150, 151, 158, 165, 182, 187,
    208
Indian Congress, xxvi, 1, 32-5, 41, 90, 162,
    193
Indian labour, import of, 27, 32, 33
Indian population, 73, 90, 186, 188, 194,
    212
Indonesia, 151, 158, 187
Industrial and Commercial Workers'
    Union (ICU), xxvi, 50, 75, 77, 78, 79,
    80, 201
Industrial Workers of Africa, 62-6, 68, 69,
    70, 75
Industrial Workers of the World (IWW),
    65
intermarriage, 61
International, 1, 47, 48, 49, 50, 51, 52, 54,
    55, 56, 58, 59, 60, 61, 62, 63, 64, 66, 68,
    75, 80, 159, 160
International Socialist League (ISL), 1,
    42, 48-54, 72, 74, 75, 160, 161; and
    national liberatory struggle, 57-62
International Telephone and Telegraph
    company, 148
International Union of Students (IUS),
    xvii
Iran, 142
Iraq, 141, 152

Isigidimi, 31
Israel, 152

Jabavu, John Tengo, 30, 31, 32, 41
Jabisa, brother of Ndlambe, 14
Jaffe, Basil, 125, 126
Jaffe, Hosea, xxvi, 125
Janssen, Leendert, 4
Jarret-Kerr, Father, 107
Jewish peoples, xv, 175; in Russia, 194, 195, 199, 203, 204
Jewish Socialist Society, 72
Johannesburg District Trades Council, 159
Jones, David Ivon, xi, xii, 45, 47, 48, 49, 50, 52, 54, 57, 59, 61, 62, 63, 75, 78
Jordaan, K.A., xix, xxvi, 171, 179
Joseph, Helen, xiii, 97, 99, 113
Joseph, Paul, 113

Kadalie, Clement, 50, 79
Kahn, Sam, 156, 157
Kaplan, Naomi, 127, 128
Kashmir, 151
Kathrada, A.M., xiii, xxxii, 221
Katzellenbaum, Z.S., 190, 191
Kenya, 152
Kenya Africa Union, 153
Kenyatta, Jomo, 153
Khamy, Chief, 7
Khoi Khoin peoples, xxv, 4, 5, 6, 7, 10, 13, 14, 15-16, 18, 25, 200
Kikuyu peoples, 142, 153
Korea, 144, 146, 148, 149
Kotane, Moses, xiii, xxvi, 77, 79, 80, 82, 84
Kraai, H., 69
Kreli, Chief, 21
Kruschev, N., 164, 165, 166
Kuper, Judge, 111

La Guma, Alex, xxii, 109, 113
La Guma, James, xxvi, 78
Labotsabeni, Queen, 39
Labour Party of South Africa, xi, xii, 42, 44, 46, 47, 48, 49, 51, 58, 60, 65, 72, 74, 76, 77, 79, 96, 106, 121, 154, 155, 158, 159, 161, 164
Land Act, 27, 41, 54, 55
land: dispossession of, 2-24; right to buy, 86; seizure of, 25; tenure of, individual, 26
language, bilinguality in South Africa, 214
Laufer, Eric, 124
Lawson, H., 18
Lee, H., 72
Lenin, V.I., xvi, xxvii, 120, 199, 205, 207

Lessing, Peter, 146
Letanka, D.S., 69
Letsie, Chief, 22, 40
Levinson, N.B., 43
Levy, Leon, 221
Liberal Party, 96, 106, 163, 201
Liberation, xxviii, xxix
Lollan, Stanley, 109
Lucas, F.A.W., 106
Luthuli, Albert, xiii, xiv, xxiv, 96, 105, 117, 221

Maake, V., 111
Maama, Chief, 39
MacArthur, General, 144, 146
MacCrone, Professor, 117
Madeley, W.B., 46
Maharaj, S.R., xxvi
Makana, 25
Makgatho, S.M., 37, 39
Makgothi, Henry, 112
Makiwane, Elijah, 30, 32
Makiwane, Tennyson, xxiv
Malan, D.F., xix, 175
Mandela, Nelson, xiii, xxxi
Mangena, A., 39, 40
Mann, B.R., 199
Mann, Tom, 43, 159, 160
Maqomo, Chief, 19
Maquina, Douglas, 222
Marks, J.B., xxvi, 77
Marney, E., 179
Marshall Plan, 148
Marshall, George, 133
Marxism, xi, xv, xvi, 46, 61, 74, 78, 87, 163, 210
Marxism Today, xix, xxx, 171, 194, 198, 199, 202, 208, 211
Marxism-Leninism, xxx, 73, 74, 86, 87
Mason, George, 47
Massina, Luke, 70
Master and Servant Acts, 15, 196
Matomela, Florence, 112
Matthews, Joe, xix, xxiv, 175, 179
Matthews, Z.K., xxiv
Mau-Mau secret society, 153
May Day, 158-62; 1917, 59; 1918, 65; 1921, 47; 1950, 93; 1952, 94; 1958, xxiv
Maynier, Landdrost, 12, 13, 14, 18
Mazur, Paul, 136
Mbelle, Horatio, 59, 160
Mbeki, Govan, xxii
McFie, Chief Magistrate, 66, 67, 68
McLeod, Hettie, 128, 129
Meer, Fatima, xxiv
Mines Native Recruiting Corporation, 68

228   Index

Mini, William, 110
Mixed Marriages Act, 186
Mkize, Bertha, 110
Mofutsunyana, Edwin, 77, 82
Mohammed, Bakshi Ghulam, 151
Molefi, Joe, 111
Molema, Chief, 39
Molteno, J.C., 20, 21
Moolla, Mosie, 111
Mopeli, comrade, 122
Moroka, Dr, 90, 91, 93, 94, 95
Morrison, Herbert, 140
Moselekatze, 25
Moshoeshoe, 21, 25, 39
Motala, Dr, 109
Mpome, Brown, 92
Mposa, Joseph, 104, 105
Mqotha, T., 108
Msane, Herbert, 56
Msane, Saul, 41, 54, 55, 59
Mtini, John, 104
music, xix, 173
Mvabaza, L.J., 69

Naicker, M.P., xxii, xxvi, xxx, 105
narodnost community, 195, 207, 211
Nasser, Gamal Abdel, 163
Natal Indian Congress, 193
Natal Native Congress, 37
nation: definition of, xxix, 194; formation of, xx, 199, 202, 212
Nation, 133
national liberatory movements, 25-44, 178, 182, 187
national minorities, in Austro-Hungarian empire, 184
national question in South Africa, xix, xxx, 72-89, 176-80
National Union of South African Students (NUSAS), xvi, xvii, 131
nationalism, xxx, 173, 175, 179, 180, 184-9, 192
Nationalist Party, 30, 44, 48, 61, 76, 79, 96, 103, 106, 121, 124, 125, 128, 129, 194, 201, 206
nationalities, in relation to nations, 177
Native Administration Bill, 59
Native Affairs Commission, 37
Native Affairs Department, 67, 70, 94
Native Convention, 37
Native Education Association, 30
Native Electoral Association, 30
Nazimuddin, Khwaja, 149, 150
Nazism, 82, 116, 123, 135, 138, 142
Ndlambe, Chief, 12-13, 14, 15, 16, 17, 18
Needham, A., 43

Nehru, Jawaharlal, 149, 150, 154, 163
New Age, xxi, xxii, xxiii, xxiv, xxv, xxvi, xxxi, xxxiii, 42, 95, 100, 109, 113, 115, 119, 161, 163, 169, 200, 202, 209, 221
New Statesman, 133
Ngojo, J.D., 69
Ngotyana, Greenwood, 103
Ngoyi, Lilian, 109
Ngqika, Chief, 14, 17, 18
Ngugunyenko, David, 101, 102
Ngwenya, Thomas, xix, 171, 179, 183
Nixon, Richard, 150
Njali, Wilfred, 63
Nkalipe, Simon, 111
Nkosi Sikelele, 67
Nkosi, Johannes, 77, 79
Nkosi, Lawrence, 111
Nkrumah, Kwame, 154, 163, 187, 201
Nokwe, Duma, xiii
Non-European Unity Movement, xvi, xix, xxvi
Noon, Arthur, 43
nuclear weapons, 149
Nzula, Albert, 77

October Revolution, 59, 64, 75, 123
Osingkima, Chief, 7

Padmore, George, 201
Pakistan, 149, 150
Pan-African Conference, 75
Pass Act, 24
pass laws, 22-4, 34, 102, 103, 196; campaign against, 35, 53, 64, 79, 87, 90, 95
pass-burning, 79, 80
Patel, Archie, 109, 110
Paton, Alan, 106, 117
Peace Preservation Act, 21
Pelem, James, 32
Pelem, Meshach, 39
people's democracy, 179
People's World, xxii
Perlo, Victor, 138
petit-bourgeoisie, 181, 182, 193, 195, 196, 203
Philip, Dr, 19
Phooko, B.G., 58
Pillay, Vella, xxix, 198
Pincus, E.M., 72
Pinnock, Don, xxi, xxii
Plaatje, Sol, 35, 39
Plant, R., 37
Poland, 167, 169
Pollitt, Harry, 119, 165
Population Registration Act, 186

Index 229

Potekhin, I.I., xxix, 88, 171, 205, 207, 208, 211, 214, 215; correspondence with Lionel Forman, 190-202
pre-nations, xix, 195, 197, 213
Press, Ronnie, 112
Prinsloos family, 11
proletariat, 26, 181
Promotion of Bantu Self-Government Bill, 206
Proot, Nicolaas, 4, 5
PUTCO bus company, 114

Rabb, R., 73
race, philosophy of, xviii, 172
racialism, 44, 85, 180, 181
Radford, Admiral, 148
Red Army Day, 123
Resha, Robert, 113
Riotous Assemblies Act, 79
Rivonia trial, xiii
Robben Island, 8, 9
robber economy, 9-14
Rose Innes, G., 23
Rose-Innes, James, 21, 30
Roux, Eddie, xxvi, 78, 200
Rubusana, W.B., 39
Rumpff, Justice, 95
Russia, 64, 184, 196

Sachs, Albie, xxi, xxiv, xxviii
Sachs, Solly, xxiii, 99
Salomon, Jean-Jacques, 148
Sandler, Josie, 125
Sartre, Jean-Paul, 148
Saudi Arabia, 152
Schedrin, Jack, 125
Schermbrucker, Ivan, xxii
Second International, 45
Segal, Ronald, xxi
Seiso, Chief, 39
Sekukuni, Chief, 39
Selby, A.R., 106
self-determination, 185, 188, 189, 194, 195, 196, 205-8, 213
Selope, R.V., xxiv
Seme, Ka Isaka, 37, 39, 41, 67
Seperepere, comrade, 121, 122
Shahed, 151
Shall, Syd, 112
Sharp, Isaac, 100
Sibande, Gert, xiii, 109
Sigamoney, B.L.E., 63
Sigenu, Samuel, 32
Silinga, Annie, 101, 102
Silinga, Matthew, 102, 103
Simons, Jack, xix, 179, 190, 191, 217, 218

Sisulu, Walter, xiii, 93, 117, 152
sjambok, use of, 70
Skota, Mweli, 69
slavery, 3, 5, 6, 7, 8, 9, 10
slaves, emancipation of, 18
Slovo, Joe, xiii, xxvi
Smith, Col. Harry, 20
Smuts, J.C., 36, 41, 44, 52, 76, 114, 122
Snitcher, Harry, 82, 130
Social Democratic Federation (SDF), 42, 45, 72
Social Democratic Party, 45, 64
socialism, 42-4, 182, 187, 197
socialist debate in South Africa, 154-70
socialist movements, 25-44
Socialist Party, need for, 162-3
Sogoni, N., 108
Somerset, Lord Charles, xxii, 17
South Africa Act, 37
South Africa Club, xix
South African Coloured People's Organisation, 90, 96, 210
South African Congress of Trade Unions, 90
South African Industrial Federation, 45
South African Labour Party, 45
South African Native National Congress, 193
South African Trade Union Congress, 63
South African Socialist Review, xxix, 156-7, 158
South African Worker, 82
Spark, xxii, xxxi
Special Branch, 116, 117
Spengler, police Chief, 117
spoor law, 17
Sprigg, J.G., 21, 22, 29, 32
Springbok Legion, 127, 128
Squatters Act, 36
Stalin, J., xxix, 163-7, 194, 199, 202, 203, 205, 208, 210, 211, 213, 215
Strijdom, J., 105, 110, 113, 115, 117, 154
strikes, 67, 68, 69, 70, 104, 117; at Johannesburg power station, 66; 'bucket', 66-9; general, 90; of African workers, 91, 116 (at Kimberley mine, 27, 193; at Van Ryn mines, 54); of miners, 68, 80; of Saudi oil workers, 152; of white mineworkers, 75, 76; of white workers, 28, 74
Students' Socialist Party, xvi, 124-5
Stuurman, Klaas, 15, 16
Suppression of Communism Act, xvii, xviii, xxviii, xxix, 93, 95, 96, 154, 156, 175, 196
Suttner, Raymond, 20

230 *Index*

Syria, 141, 152

Tambo, Oliver, 112
taxation, 30; hut, 36; of Zulus, 33
Taylor, Dora, 26
Tembu Church, 30
Textile Workers' Union, 104
The Worker, 45
Thebedi, William, 65, 160
Thema, Selope, xxiv
Third International, 48, 72, 75, 78, 81
Thompson, Rev. D.C., 105, 115
Tile, Nehemiah, 30
Tobin, John, 43
toyi-toyi dances, xix
trade unions: of black workers, 57, 62; of
    coloured workers, 77; of white
    workers, 50, 56, 58, 60, 68, 74, 81
Train Apartheid Resistance Committee,
    xvi
Transvaal African Union, 40
Transvaal Indian Congress, 91
Transvaal Native Congress, 40
Transvaal Native Council, 57, 58
treason trial, xiii, xxiii, xxiv, 1, 99-118, 221
tribal society, 2, 197
Trotskyism, 124, 125
Tswana peoples, 3
Turok, Ben, xxi, 105, 115
Tyler, C.B., 72

Umsebenzi, 79, 81, 191
Union of Soviet Socialist Republics
    (USSR), xviii, xxii, xxx, 77, 82, 88,
    123, 133, 134, 139, 140, 144, 150,
    163-7, 177, 179, 183, 195, 199, 201,
    205, 208, 212
United Communist Party, 72
United Fruit Company, 143
United Kingdom (UK), 141, 142, 145,
    151, 155
United Nations (UN), 151
United States of America (USA), 136,
    137, 138, 139, 140, 141, 143, 144, 147,
    149, 155
United Party, 96, 121, 122, 126, 128
Unity Movement, 171

US Rubber company, 148

Vagrancy Act, 23, 24
Van der Leur, General, 14
van Jaarsveld, Adriaan, 11
van Riebeeck, Jan, 3-6, 10, 25, 42, 94
van Riebeck Day, xxv
Varsity, 125
Verges, Jacques, xvii
Vietnam, 139, 145, 146-9
von Papendorp, Sergeant, 108
vote, African qualification for, 31

Wade, Colin, 45, 53, 54, 56, 58, 61
War on War Gazette, 45, 46
War-on-War League, 45, 46, 47, 48, 50,
    52, 159, 160
Watts, Hilda, 123, 124
Wessels, P.J., 156, 157
Western Areas Removal Scheme, 175
whipping of prisoners, 95
White, Inspector-Sergeant, 130
Williams, Talbot, 63, 64, 65, 69, 160
Wilson, Charles, 139
Witwatersrand Student, 131
Wolpe, Harold, xvii
Women's League, of ANC, 112
working class, xv, 188, 193, 196, 204, 206;
    birth of, 25-9
World Student News, xvii

Xhosa peoples, 11, 12, 13, 14, 15-16, 17,
    18, 19, 20, 21, 183, 188, 193, 194, 207,
    212, 213, 220
Xuma, Alfred, 83, 86

Yastrebava, E.P., 190, 191
Young Communist International, 77
Young Communist League (YCL), xvi,
    xviii, 72, 77, 120, 132; Debating Club,
    121
youth festivals, 173
Youth League, 86, 87

Zabedi, General, 152
Zulu peoples, xix, 33, 34, 173, 183, 188,
    192, 193, 194, 195, 207, 212, 213, 220